An Accidental Icon

An Accidental Icon

How I dodged a bullet, spoke truth
to power and lived to tell the tale

NORMAN SCOTT

HODDER &
STOUGHTON

First published in Great Britain in 2022 by Hodder & Stoughton
An Hachette UK company

1

Copyright © Norman Scott 2022

The right of Norman Scott to be identified as the
Author of the Work has been asserted by him in accordance
with the Copyright, Designs and Patents Act 1988.

A CIP catalogue record for this title is available from the British Library

Hardback ISBN 978 1 529 37029 4
eBook ISBN 978 1 529 37030 0

Typeset in Celeste by
Palimpsest Book Production Limited, Falkirk, Stirlingshire

Printed and bound in Great Britain by Clays Ltd, Elcograf S.p.A.

Hodder & Stoughton policy is to use papers that are natural, renewable
and recyclable products and made from wood grown in sustainable forests.
The logging and manufacturing processes are expected to conform
to the environmental regulations of the country of origin.

Hodder & Stoughton Ltd
Carmelite House
50 Victoria Embankment
London EC4Y 0DZ

www.hodder.co.uk

Contents

For the late Leonie Marshall who, in her quiet way, instilled in me my great love of dressage; and for my dear friend, the late April Ashley, who was so much looking forward to reading this book.

PREFACE

IT'S A FROSTY autumn morning at the farm. Mist lies over the fields and there's a bite in the air as I head out to do the morning chores. There has been a dwelling here, tucked under the slopes of High Dartmoor, since the eleventh century. The current building, my home and sanctuary since 1985, is a traditional Devon longhouse, built from medieval granite blocks.

I give the horses their breakfast, open the hen-house door to let the poultry run free over the cobblestones, and start mucking out the stables. When the barrow is full, I pause to take in the beauty of the place. Across the yard in my walled garden, spiders have been busy with their lace-hooks and their webs are white with frost. My bantams are fluffing out their feathers and three white cats, my rodent operatives, sit blinking at me from their perch on the half-door, under the granite arch that leads into the house. As I tip my barrow into the muck heap, steam rises in the chilly air. The granite-lined pit was built more than six hundred years ago. It may be a humble thing, but there could be no more beautiful a repository for the numerous droppings that are an inevitable part of keeping horses. This is my real life, the life I have always wanted to lead, in deep countryside, with the company of my horses and other animals. Before I came here, my situation was very different.

My life has come to be defined by the political scandal of 1979, when Liberal politician Jeremy Thorpe was tried at the Old Bailey for conspiring to murder me. His campaign to be rid of me came to a terrifying climax on the night of Friday, 24 October 1975. A man calling himself Peter drove me up onto Exmoor, shot my Great Dane Rinka, and turned the gun on me. He pulled the trigger but the bullet had jammed. The would-be assassin tried again, but still the gun failed so he fled, leaving me alone and terrified in the darkness, with the body of my beloved dog. That incident on Exmoor was not the only attempt on my life.

I've always wanted to tell the truth about my relationship with Jeremy Thorpe: how he had taken advantage of me when I was young, naïve, and mentally unstable; how he had lied, and put me in a position where I, too, was forced to lie. The establishment closed ranks, attempting to silence and discredit me, so while I escaped being murdered, the assassination of my character was far more successful. I was vilified in the press, portrayed as a hysterical, vindictive homosexual hell-bent on ruining the career of a successful MP.

I fought to get the truth exposed, and two trials ensued from that night on Exmoor, but those who were responsible for the crime were exonerated and the press portrayed me as a lunatic. Judge Carman, in his summing up at the Old Bailey trail in 1979, described me as a sponger, a wimp and a parasite. I was none of those things. All I wanted was to see those who had tried to kill me in the dock, charged – and I am still fighting for justice, more than forty years on.

My story hit the headlines again when, in 2019, actor Ben Whishaw won his first Emmy award for his portrayal of me in the TV drama *A Very English Scandal*. He then went on to win the Golden Globe award for Best Supporting Actor, and made a moving dedication which touched me deeply: 'There's one person I really, really want to dedicate this award to and it's the man I had the privilege to portray in this show, Norman Scott, who took on the establishment with a courage and defiance that I find completely inspiring. He is a true queer hero and icon.'

To hear Ben's description felt like I had won an award. It meant a lot for someone to stand up for me in public after the years of my being dismissed or written off as mad. *A Very English Scandal* changed my life and changed many people's view of me, as well as being a wonderful inter-national success. When the drama was in development I spent many hours talking to Ben about my life. He couldn't have been a more pleasant and caring person, and I loved his performance. There are moments when he absolutely captures how I felt through those difficult times, but when the film ended, I knew there was still plenty more of my story to tell. I am glad if people find me an inspiration. I want nothing more than to help and support others, especially those within the LGBT+ community, who may be experiencing the exploitation and persecution I endured.

Now I am eighty-two. I have outlived most of the people who were involved in the conspiracy to kill me, and if the best revenge is living well, then I am certainly in the right place for that. My farmyard chores are finished and I'm ready for some tea and toast. I go in through the arched doorway, taking care not to dislodge the cats. My dogs are taking a nap in the scullery kitchen, and I step over them to put the kettle on. Dogs have always been my special friends, giving me so much support through difficult times.

The grandfather clock in the dining room strikes ten as I carry my plate and cup to the table. The sun is breaking through now, and Rex Whistler the canary, whose cage is by the window, bursts into song. This dining room is a place for companionship, for sharing tales and memories. In front of the inglenook fireplace an iron curtain rod is fixed to the ceiling, where a blanket once hung. Previous occupants would sit playing cards at the table, then gather round the fireplace and draw the blanket across for 'a warm and a tell'. These walls must have heard so many stories, through the centuries. None, perhaps, as shocking as mine.

A pile of papers lies close to my elbow, my own hand-written account from the 1970s of events leading up to the attempted murder of me. It makes painful reading now. I was desperately troubled as a young man, doped up to the limit on tranquillisers and antidepressants as I struggled to make sense of a world where I could trust no one. Where the veneer of respectability was propped up by deceit and lies.

These are very different times. The #MeToo campaign has had a huge impact, and there is also much more acceptance and understanding of the diversity of sexuality: it's time for me to tell my story from my point of view. I need to go back to the beginning, to my earliest days, but first I must clear my head and get my courage up, and the best way to do that is to be out on a horse. I head to the hall, where my riding boots are lined up, each with their own set of wooden trees. I choose a pair, and as I pull them on, I see my two tortoises close by, munching lettuce off a sheet of newspaper. Rigby and Peller, dear girls, enjoying their last meal before their winter hibernation. Tortoises have always been important to me, from right back in my childhood.

I take a bridle down from the hook, run my hand over the clean, supple leather. When I get back from today's canter over the moor, I'll be ready to make the bold leap – somewhat like the death-defying jumps I once took riding across country – of putting my life story on the page.

CHAPTER ONE

The Odd One Out

I ALWAYS FELT like an outsider in my family. Maybe it was because my mother was widowed before I was born, or because I was never close to my siblings. It could have been because I was born out of wedlock to a father I never knew. Or maybe I was just different.

My mother, Ena, was born into an Irish family and her maiden name was Lynch. There were two Lynch sisters, known as the pretty Miss Lynch and the 'other one'. My mother was the 'other one'. Her sister Josephine's good looks had such pulling power they charmed a monk into climbing over the wall of his monastery at Buckfastleigh and marrying her. My mother's first husband Albert Merritt, known as Bertie, who worked in the City of London, died of leukaemia in 1938, leaving behind five children. Edward was twelve years older than me and I never got to know him very well. Then came Gloria, who tragically died at just nineteen hours old. Next was Fleur, who was eight years older than me, then Brian and finally Ralph – pronounced 'Rafe'.

I was a war baby, born on 12 February 1940, from Oaklands Road in Bexleyheath, Kent. In the 1940s an illegitimate child brought huge social stigma, especially if you were a Catholic.

It must have been very difficult for my mother when I arrived. How she coped, I don't know, and a mystery surrounds the identity of my birth-father.

I was never told anything about him, although just after my mother's husband Bertie died, his former employer, Shaw, Savill and Albion, offered my mother a place on the maiden voyage of a brand-new liner, the *Dominion Monarch*. She set sail early in 1939 and spent some time in New Zealand and Australia, returning to England in June 1939, so it seems likely she got pregnant while she was away. My mother's faith and her strong Irish character must have stood her in good stead through this challenging time, and there was also a man waiting in the wings. Albert Josiffe had been Bertie's closest friend, and I'm sure it was a relief to my mother when they married in 1942, and I could be passed off as his son. Very soon after the wedding, I acquired a younger brother when baby John Josiffe arrived.

My earliest memories are of being in a large Silver Cross perambulator, the height of luxury for an infant in those days. By the time it had passed down the family to me it had a distinctive smell – a redolent mix of leather and baby powder. I was cared for by Nanny Hawkey, who had previously looked after my siblings. I adored her. She used to 'rose' me to sleep by stroking my face and saying, 'Rose petals. Can you feel the rose petals, Norman?' Even though I was a toddler, Nanny Hawkey seemed to delight in my sensitivity and imagination, which made me rather different from the rest of my family – a characteristic that always exasperated my mother.

In 1943, when I was three, we were evacuated. My older

brothers were sent to a farm in Norfolk, and Fleur was taken in by my Aunt Josephine. Along with my mother, Albert Josiffe and new baby John, I was relocated to Leicestershire. Just after we arrived I became ill with meningitis and was sent to Leicester Royal Infirmary. I was terrified to be left there all alone. At just three years old, I desperately needed someone to comfort me, but there was no provision in those days for parents to stay with their sick children and visiting hours were strictly enforced. My treatment was to have boiling hot poultices applied to my body every three hours – an indescribably painful experience. I still have nightmares of the white-clad nurses standing around my bed and the burning, dusty smell as they applied the poultices. I used to scream with pain, but perhaps the treatment saved my life. Or perhaps I was given antibiotics, the new wonder drugs, which first came into use in the early 1940s. At any rate, I recovered, and four months later we all returned to Oaklands Road to find our house surrounded by bomb sites.

Far from being nice to be home, the household was tense. Josiffe and my mother began to have the most awful rows, which were always about money. This had a very detrimental effect on me. With a good, caring father figure at the head of the family, I might have found stability in my developmental years and made better choices when things got difficult for me later in life, although Josiffe wasn't all bad. When a doodlebug flew over the house, he wrapped me in an oilskin and rushed downstairs with me in his arms, to shelter under the table with my siblings. The doodlebug exploded and smashed the window. Luckily, the blackout material protected us from the worst of the broken glass.

But Josiffe's kinder acts were overshadowed by his aggressive behaviour. We would sit silently at the table while he and Mummy shouted at each other, and sometimes he was very violent. Once he got hold of Mummy by her hair and threw her down the stairs. I will never forget the sound of her falling: *kerdoonk, kerdoonk, kerdoonk*. We were all appalled but didn't dare do or say anything. Josiffe had been married three times before, and with hindsight, I suspect that what attracted him to all these wives was their wealth. He had a good job as an accountant but seemed to play no part in financially supporting our family. He appropriated Mummy's car and wouldn't let her drive it, and when the money ran out, he left her for another woman and moved to Orpington, taking the car.

With Josiffe gone and my mother left with six children to raise, I had hoped Nanny Hawkey might come to babysit again. I missed her terribly. Instead, my mother's mother, who lived nearby, helped out. Granny Lynch was rather Victorian. She wore old-fashioned black bombazine dresses, which reached almost to the floor, and carried a parasol when she went out. She very much disapproved of my mother's fashionable high heels. 'Very t'ird rate, they are, Ena!' she would say, in her strong Irish accent. Cleanliness was definitely next to godliness for Granny Lynch – everything in her house was spotless and the iron cooking range was polished with Zebo blacklead and Brasso. When we stayed over, the linen on the beds was smooth and fresh, and before we went out of the door, Granny would say, 'Come here!' and spit on a handkerchief to scrub at our faces.

Grandpa Lynch was rarely to be seen. I used to ask, 'Where's

Grandpa?' and Granny would scowl and say, 'Where d'you think? Down with his bloody bees!' Poor Grandpa. He'd hide at the bottom of the garden by the beehives, as Granny didn't want his dirty boots on her clean floor.

My mother was also a stickler for tidiness and often became exasperated with us children. She could be very overbearing. At mealtimes, if any of us had our elbows on the table she would glare at us and say, 'All joints on this table will be *carved*!' Those elbows were at our sides right away. Sometimes Mummy would light a fire and the family would gather round and chat. I'd stay silent, losing myself in the drama of the flames as they flickered like dancers over the coals, before dying down to glowing embers. It was magical, like watching a theatre show. My mother would ask me what I was staring at, but I just shook my head. If I told her what wonderful things I could see I knew she would ridicule me.

We had a difficult relationship. When I was still a small child, about four or five, she began to behave very oddly towards me. I didn't understand why, and I hated it. Now, I would call it abuse. This always took place in the bathroom. Mummy, wearing a dressing-gown, would hold me in her lap, face down, so I was looking at the floor, the pattern of the blue linoleum seared into my memory. She would pull me against herself, clutching me tightly, and start moaning, a harsh, alien sound. I would think, Is she angry? In pain? I couldn't breathe and, afraid, I wanted to get down, but there was no escape. I would feel her pulling down my pants, her finger pushing roughly inside me. It hurt so much, but she wouldn't stop. I had no choice but to endure it, the pain increasing, and her moans getting louder.

I don't know why this happened but later I came to realise that my mother was a very sexual woman. Perhaps intimate relations with Josiffe ceased when the relationship began to break up, and she was looking for an outlet. Perhaps she missed the man who was my father, and when she did this to me, she was in some way bringing back the memories of him. Perhaps she was just angry, and it satisfied something in her to hurt me in this intimate way. I will never know, but those sessions in the bathroom cast a shadow of fear over my childhood. The abuse continued for several years. When my mother took a series of men as lovers, it came to an end. I could never quite forget, though. As a child, the sense of something unkind and unpleasant about to happen was always present, and through my adult life I have suffered with anxiety, low self-worth, and a compulsion to please others. It's only recently that I have come to terms with this legacy from my difficult childhood, and wondered if it might have been different if my father had been part of the family.

I often wondered about him, whoever he was. I had been given Josiffe's name, and when he joined our family I assumed he was my father. But John Josiffe, my half-brother, is nothing like me, and my sister Fleur firmly believed I was conceived on my mother's cruise. There was an apple tree in the garden at Oaklands Road, with a tree house, and Fleur would sit up there among the leaves and blossom, singing a popular Deanna Durbin song, as our neighbours came out to applaud. Sometimes she would invite me up into the tree house and speculate on who might have fathered me. 'Well, of course, you could be a purser's son . . .' she would say. I didn't know what a purser was and didn't much like the sound of it. In recent years, I have considered taking a DNA test to find out the truth about my father, and if I have relations on the other side of the world. I am deterred by the possibility that I might have been born prematurely. If Josiffe was my birth-father, I would rather not know.

Family life swept by, every week marked by going to Mass, which was an indispensable part of our upbringing. Granny Lynch especially was very devout. After Mass we would go to her immaculate house in Sidcup for Sunday lunch. There were figures of Jesus and Mary under glass domes on the chimneypiece, and paintings of the Sacred Heart on the walls, featuring the words 'I place my trust in Thee' and Jesus with his glowing heart exposed for all to see. These I found both alarming and fascinating. I had a strong sense that God was watching over me, and I took my prayers very seriously.

I found the services long and boring, but the experience was sweetened by the fact that Fleur knew a family who lived near the church and kept horses. We'd drive home joyfully from Mass in a trap pulled by a small roan mare. This early experience seems to indicate that my lifelong love for horses was innate, or perhaps the horse represented something good and safe in my difficult early life.

Our time at Oaklands Road came to an end when I was seven. The family budget had become so tight that we dreaded rent day. When the landlady came round to collect the money, she knocked on the door, then tried every window and door to gain access, while we hid in a corner pretending we were out. My mother had to find a new home and a means of earning money to feed us all. To her credit, she demonstrated a resourcefulness and an instinct for survival

I believe I have inherited. We were offered a ground-floor flat at 26 Brampton Road, a large Georgian house a mile away from our old place. The flat had been requisitioned during the war and was allocated to us because we had no means of support. My mother found a job at the telephone exchange, and, since Josiffe had taken the car, she would head off to work every day on a bicycle.

Number 26 was a beautiful house, which William Morris, the textile designer, poet and socialist activist who was a major influence in the British Arts and Crafts Movement of the late 19th century, had done up for friends of his. Mummy chose the sitting room for her bedroom and decorated it beautifully, hanging long nets over the French windows. You could get lovely things for a song in the 1940s, and she had a very good eye for interior design. My brothers and I slept in a room that was once the library, with walls that had wooden panelling and the most wonderful hand-painted wallpaper. When no one was looking, I would trace the outlines of the leaves, flowers and birds with my fingers and imagine Mr Morris drawing them and choosing the colours.

Once I started primary school, I found concentrating in class difficult, wishing I was outside instead. In 1947, *Picture Post* magazine came to the school to shoot a photo feature, and one of the photographs, entitled 'Where Youth Has Its Fling', showed a skinny little fellow in a vest, dancing around. That's me. Perhaps I was listening to one of the 1940s music-and-movement radio programmes for children. Or maybe it was just one of my 'moments', as my mother called them: a brief, happy escape from the reality of my childhood life. When she caught me having a 'moment' I would get one of her cold, hard looks of disapproval. One of my frequent fantasies was that I could fly. I'd run down to the bottom of the garden, arms held out, believing I could just take off. Sadly, I never did.

Our family finances continued to be tight, and when I was ten, I found a job at a local pet shop, which I loved. I was able to earn some pocket money and I had something to look forward to. One day, the two sisters who owned the shop gave me a tortoise. I was so excited. I carried him home, taking a shortcut through the bombed-out houses to show Mummy. My plan was to climb over the wall into our back garden and surprise her by coming into her room through the French windows. Carefully, I put the tortoise on top of the wall and climbed over, picking him up and tiptoeing over the grass to the veranda. The French windows were open so I stepped through the long white nets, holding my tortoise. For a moment I was caught in those nets but I knew my mother was there because the lights were on. 'Mummy! Mummy, look what I've got!' I called.

My mother was making a noise, groaning and crying out. Alarmed, I pushed the nets aside to see her on the bed, with a man on top of her. His thick serge trousers were scrunched down round his knees, and he was thrusting himself at her in a rough, violent way. I was very innocent about sexual matters and I thought he was trying to kill her. Terrified, I dropped my tortoise. He hit the floor and his shell cracked open. I ran for it, afraid the man might attack me, too.

A car door slammed, and I heard it driving away. I crept back into the room, but my mother wasn't there, and she didn't come to find me. I carried my poor broken tortoise to the old stables and hid him there. I was so shocked and frightened. Mummy must have known what I'd seen because she saw me as I came into the room, but she never said anything. When the ladies at the pet shop asked after the tortoise, I was afraid to tell them I had dropped and hurt him. I tried to look after him as best I could, but after a few days he died. This incident had a profound effect on me. The man's aggression had frightened me so much that when I heard boys at school talking about sex I shied away. I gave all my love and affection to animals, caring for them and enjoying their companionship, but the terrible guilt over my tortoise stayed with me.

When I failed the eleven-plus exam I went to a secondary school on Graham Road, where I found life even harder. I had always had a bit of a stammer, and when I was under pressure it would get worse. My mother insisted that I have painting lessons to cure me, and although I loved the lessons, there was no improvement in my speech. I also had a slight curvature of the spine, and at Graham Road I was made to hang by my hands for an hour at a time from the bars in the gym, which was very unpleasant.

I soon managed to get on the wrong side of my form master, Mr Bell or 'Tinker Bell', as Mummy used to call him, with a naughty glint in her eye.

'The reason you didn't pass your eleven-plus, Josiffe, is because every time I look at you you're staring out of the window!' he'd say.

'I'm not,' I assured him, on one occasion. 'I'm watching the dust particles floating round in the sun.' This was true. I found the slow, circling dance of those tiny, bright particles mesmerising but Mr Bell thought me very odd.

When Queen Elizabeth II's Coronation aired live on the television in February 1953, Mr Bell invited my family to his house to watch it. Very few households had a television set in those days and Mr Bell's was mounted in a large, varnished cabinet, with a ghastly cream Bakelite rim surrounding the tiny screen. It was very clear that Mrs Bell didn't like my mother, and I found the tension between them much more interesting than the fuzzy black-and-white images of the ceremony at Westminster Abbey. From then on, Mr Bell's behaviour towards me changed, becoming even frostier. I am pretty sure that something was going on between him and Mummy, and he must have noticed me watching his wife with her and realised I was on to him.

It was decided I might do better at St Stephen's, a Catholic secondary school, but when I arrived my reputation for being difficult had preceded me. The other children bullied me, and the nuns were horrid. My form mistress, Mother Dymphna, was especially mean. She would grab my ear and shout, 'You just don't want to learn!'

In spite of the pain, I'd gasp, 'I do want to learn. I just need it explained.'

This made her even angrier and she would shriek, 'You're an eejit!' before banishing me to stand in the corner. Once, when I muttered in defiance, 'You're a fucking old fool,' the whole classroom roared with laughter. This was very strong language for those days – unthinkable, in fact. I don't think I quite understood how shocking that particular phrase was – I'd probably picked it up from the other children in the rough-and-tumble of the playground. I didn't want to be difficult or foul-mouthed. I just didn't want to be there.

The result of my battles with Mother Dymphna was always a trip to Mr Duffy, the headmaster, who brandished a black whip-like instrument to strike me on the hands. It really hurt, my palms turning red and swollen afterwards, and once I got into such a state that I wet myself, which didn't do much for my status with the other pupils. Mr Duffy would always tell my mother what I had said to Mother Dymphna, and that didn't go down well at all. I can still remember the smell of privet hedges and the hot tarmac under my feet as I trudged home, feeling utterly miserable. On arrival, Mummy would inform me that because of my bad behaviour at school I would not be getting any supper that evening. When I protested, she would point to the welts on my hands, saying, 'Well, you wouldn't be able to hold the fork, anyway, would you?' and send me to my room.

Fortunately, when I was eleven, I found the perfect antidote to school and to my difficult family life. A local girl called Brenda had some ponies, and in return for helping to muck out the stables I had riding lessons with her. I begged Mummy for a pony of my own, but she always said no, so I secretly applied, with another friend, to the Blue Cross, an animal charity, asking for a horse. They offered us two Irish cobs called Cavan and Listowel who needed a home. My friend took Cavan, and I took possession of Listowel, without telling my mother.

Listowel lived on some allotments near Brenda's house and I paid for his keep by doing stable chores and exercising other children's ponies. A man from a nearby stables lent me a saddle. He was an odd chap, not popular with the other children. One day when I was with Listowel, he came into the stable and pressed his body close to mine, fiddling with the fastening on my trousers. I knew that wasn't right, and it certainly wasn't very nice, but nothing else happened and I loved being with Listowel. He was a beautiful horse, dock-tailed, with a shining black coat like a Fell Pony, and, a very good jumper, he was just the right size for me. He must have had a troubled past, as he was very nervous at first and used to buck me off, but once he learned to trust me we became inseparable. I absolutely adored him. Mummy was furious when she found out about Listowel, especially when he needed extra feed through the winter months. I would order it, and there'd be a row when the bill arrived, always culminating in the threat of the pony being sold. I closed my ears to it because the hours I spent with Listowel, schooling, jumping, hacking, caring for him, were by far the happiest of my childhood.

At home, I tried to get close to my mother but it was impossible to bridge the gap between my longing for warmth and understanding, and her need for a relationship with a man. Phil the telephone engineer, the man I had found her in bed with, was now a frequent visitor, sometimes joining in our family activities. He was so much younger than Mummy, only a little older than my oldest brother Edward, that I found it really strange having him around, adding to my feeling of not really belonging. One rare happy time was when I sang a solo at Midnight Mass. It was a very big thing to stay up late and participate in such an important occasion. My whole family walked to Mass and I left them to climb up into the choir stalls. When it came to my solo, 'Ave Verum Corpus', the crowded faces in the church all looked up at me and I completely lost my nerve. I have always had a fear of being in crowded places, and felt vulnerable and exposed. My voice dried up but somehow, in the end, I managed to sing. Afterwards my brother Ralph very kindly said, 'You sounded lovely, when you got brave.'

With Listowel, I always felt brave. He helped me so much, and I counted down the minutes until I could be with him. At school I was always being told off for answering back and the atmosphere at home was so unpleasant: Phil the telephone engineer became an almost a permanent fixture. He hadn't moved in full-time, as he was still living at home with his parents and I think his own mother disapproved of the relationship. I found the household too tense, and worried I would find Mummy and Phil in a passionate embrace again. I spent more and more time with Listowel, inadvertently distancing myself from Ralph and the rest of my siblings.

I decided to move Listowel further away, to a farm about five miles from home near Dartford Heath. The area is not exactly rural now, but back then it was open countryside, away from people, and the farmer and his wife were very kind to me. I used to bicycle over every day, buckets of oats for Listowel swinging from my handlebars. I built a camp from a tree that had fallen down, and a bit of old tin roof, and I'd steal a loaf of bread from home and stay overnight at the camp. My mother never came to find me, and I can't believe the farmer didn't say anything, but I loved being out in nature, with no one criticising me or getting after me. Sometimes a vixen and her cub would visit me, coming very close. I would throw pieces of bread, which they would snap up hungrily just an arm's length away, always poised to run, but I think they knew I wouldn't hurt them.

It could be bitterly cold out in the field at night, and I would wake up very early, wrapped in my coat and a blanket I'd brought from home, and see the grass all white and stiff with frost. Listowel would be dozing beside the camp, his breath steaming in the cold air and beads of ice on his whiskers. He liked to stand vigil over me while I slept, and through the night I would hear the stamp of his hoofs as he shifted from foot to foot. There was such a bond between us, a trust and an unconditional love that I hadn't experienced with people. I grew completely happy with my own company – so long as I had animals nearby. In fact, I preferred it.

This idyllic time with Listowel came to an end when I was fourteen. The man who had lent me the saddle accused me of stealing it, with a bale of his expensive clover hay. I hadn't stolen anything. Clover hay was rich and thick, the bale far too heavy for me to lift. I had ordered it, asking for it to be delivered and promising to pay later, thinking my mother would give me the money in return for me doing household chores, but she didn't. The man threatened me with the police, perhaps in revenge for my moving Listowel away from the stables, dashing his hopes of any more trouser-fiddling. Or maybe fear that I might tell someone about him fuelled his vindictive behaviour.

I gave back the saddle he had loaned me and asked my mother again for the money to pay for the hay but she refused, telling me I must pay for it myself. I'd given up working for the pet shop to have more time with Listowel and I had no way of earning any money. I shouted at Mummy that she loved her children less than her man friend, but to no avail, and things escalated. The man who had lent me the saddle insisted on a court case, and Listowel was sent back to the Blue Cross. Devastated, I never saw him again, and never knew what happened to him.

My mother came with me to the magistrates' court, looking very grand in a black astrakhan coat, and brought a friend with her – the singer Dorothy Squires, who was quite famous at that time. My mother hadn't come to back me up and instead told the magistrate, 'I'm not paying for this. I can't control him. He's just difficult.'

I don't believe I was difficult. I'd given the saddle back and I simply couldn't get the money to pay for the hay. At home, I couldn't help disliking Phil, and I think my mother was annoyed with me because I had caught her in bed with him. She knew I was aware of her relationships with men and I think that made her resent me.

That day in the courtroom I was found guilty of theft and was fined the cost of the hay, which, ironically, my mother agreed to pay. I expected to be severely told off and assumed I would have to pay back what I owed by cleaning the silver and the brass but, to my horror, I was completely wrong. Instead my mother asked that I be taken into care. I had no idea this was even an option. I couldn't believe she was saying I couldn't go home, not just to me, but in front of the strangers in the court. I was numb with shock. Just before I was taken away by Mr Stradling, a probation officer, Mummy gushed, 'Oh, he's such a difficult child. I can't do anything with him. It's beyond my capabilities.'

Dorothy Squires stood there nodding righteously and saying, 'Yes, Ena, yes.'

When my mother tried to hug me and say it was all for

the best, I dodged behind Mr Stradling. I didn't want her to touch me, or to hear the false endearments I knew she would utter for the benefit of the bystanders. Mr Stradling drove me away in his car, taking me to a remand centre 'for observation'. I looked down at the rubber mat on the car floor, fighting back my tears so it would look as if I didn't care.

The remand centre was a big old house in the village of Harrietsham, in Kent. The atmosphere was alien to me. Boys smoked and bells rang, signalling the start of the day and every lesson change. There was a pervading smell of cheap polish and overcooked cabbage, and every hour of the day was regimented. The bathroom stank of Lysol and everyone had to gargle after brushing their teeth, with a vile pink liquid called glyco-thymoline, as if they were trying to show us all how disgusting and dirty we were. It was a huge and sudden change from being at home, and the dear, gentle companionship of Listowel, especially when I got beaten up by the other boys. I felt utterly alone and in complete shock, surviving by shutting myself off. I didn't make any friends, going deep inside my head, taking myself back to the memories of the camp and Listowel. It made me sad to think of him, but it was better than focusing on the horrid rough environment around me. The staff told me off for not listening, but I got through by keeping a low profile.

I was at the remand centre for about six weeks. Christmas came, and I was told to go to the end of the drive, as I had a visitor. Off I ran, sure it would be my mother, hoping she'd relented and missed me – I hadn't seen her since the court – so it was a shattering disappointment to see Phil and my brother Brian standing on the drive. I scuffed the gravel with my feet, not looking at them. Then I said we were having lunch early at the centre and that I must go back. Phil gave me a bag of presents but I'll never know what they were, because as soon as he was out of sight I shoved it into the hedge. I didn't care about presents. I just wanted my mother to show she'd forgiven me.

A week later, I went to Maidstone to see a child psychologist and the next day, Mr Stradling (honestly, I'd have changed that name if I were he) took me out for a drive. He asked how I felt about home and school, and what my plans were for a career. I sat in silence for a long time, then explained that, while I didn't want to stay at the centre, I *really* didn't want to go back to my family. I told him about the dynamic between my mother and me, and how I'd seen Phil having sex with her and couldn't forget this. Mr Stradling seemed to understand and suggested we visit a boarding school that might have a place for me.

Finchden Manor, near Tenterden, was an Elizabethan house with beams outside and dark, panelled rooms with low ceilings. I took an instant dislike to the principal, Dr Lywood; his years in those oppressive rooms seemed to have left him with a stoop. Mr Stradling had kept telling me how wonderful Dr Lywood was but he was rather distant towards me. He kept chatting to Mr Stradling, but I could see him watching me, observing me, and that made me feel very uncomfortable.

As he and the probation officer discussed my future, one of the pupils, a boy dressed in jeans, took me on a tour of the premises. Jeans, at that time, were quite unusual and mostly seen in cowboy films. I didn't know anyone who wore them and found his attire rather odd. The historic decor of the house was defiled and neglected, and some of the living quarters were situated in rusting railway carriages. I was told the school offered a great degree of freedom to the pupils and I wouldn't have to attend lessons if I didn't want to. I met some of the staff, who wore clothes very similar to the pupils', and Dr Lywood asked me what I thought of the school.

'Ghastly,' I said.

Dr Lywood chuckled and replied, 'Ah, you will grow to like it.'

I knew I wouldn't. Everything was in disarray without any order or routine. I didn't trust it and it seemed ludicrous that I had been described as 'out of control' but was now being encouraged to join an establishment with no rules. Mr Stradling explained that I could keep a horse at the school if I liked. I was longing to have a horse again, so I pushed aside my objections and a few days later I arrived at Finchden Manor, my fees paid by the county council.

On the first night, I tried to run away but one of the teachers caught me in the grounds and brought me back. Confused and miserable, I just couldn't settle. I hated it. With no fixed timetables, I found myself walking aimlessly around. I couldn't find any classes in progress, though sometimes I'd see a pupil in a corridor attempting to get a tune from a musical instrument, or I'd stumble upon a group involved in a discussion that seemed to have neither a beginning nor an end. Some years later, the singer and gay activist Tom Robinson was a pupil at Finchden Manor, and he has said he liked the laissez-faire routine. It was a disaster for me. The lack of rules inflamed my insecurity and my sense of not belonging. The promised horse never materialised, I kept trying to run away, and after a few weeks I was sent home, on the condition that I met Mr Stradling in the Congregational Church hall for weekly reviews.

CHAPTER TWO

Horses, Horses, Horses

AN UNEASY TRUCE was established between me and my mother. She was completely preoccupied with Phil and ignored me, paying almost no attention to any of us children.

I went to Bexleyheath Boys School, the local secondary modern. Ralph and my younger brother John were already there but by now I felt I hardly knew them. Ralph excelled at sports and I wasn't sporty, so, without common interests, I drifted even further away from my siblings.

As soon as my fifteenth birthday came along, I left school. My plan was to join the Household Cavalry so I could work with horses, but I was turned down due to a foot injury from two years before. Eventually I found employment in a solicitors' practice in London, working in the post room. I still lived at home but the job got me out of the house and gave me independence from my mother.

The firm seemed to be impressed by me but I hated being cooped up, looking forward to the days when I would be sent to Somerset House. There I would search the records for one of the firm's clients, a stud farm, which meant I could browse through all the details about the horses. I didn't enjoy the commute either. It was so stuffy and predictable.

Every morning I took the train from Bexley station to Charing Cross, sitting next to rows of men in smart three-piece suits and bowler hats, all reading *The Times*. No one spoke. The only time I ever said anything was when a man got on and started spluttering. He continued to cough and sneeze and belch and the other men flinched away from him with marked movements of disgust, holding up their newspapers in front of their faces. After one particularly loud belch I said, 'Now, sir, perhaps you would favour us with a fart.'

I just couldn't help it. I think that was the thing about me. I was a shy boy, turning into a shy young man, but there were moments where I came out with exactly what I thought. Often others were thinking this, too, though they wouldn't express it, and people would either burst out laughing or look at me in absolute shock. That day, all the newspapers twitched like mad and I heard a snigger from behind the nearest copy but no one said a word.

Although I didn't warm to the work, I was very glad of it. When I started I was given a National Insurance number and my first National Insurance card. After the war, the National Insurance scheme had been expanded and now formed a major component of the new welfare state. Throughout everyone's working life, employers would pay for stamps to be added to the employee's National Insurance card – or cards, as the number of stamps increased – every week. On production of the stamped cards, I would be able to get health benefits, unemployment benefit and a pension. This sort of structure and safety net for the future made me feel secure and grown-up, motivating me to work hard. Unfortunately, in the years to come, my relationship with

National Insurance turned out to be less straightforward. In fact, this system was the beginning of my downfall.

While working for the solicitors, I was loaned a piebald horse called Sonny, keeping him in a field and stable near Bexley station. I rode him in the mornings before work, wearing my business suit, changing into a pair of gumboots that I kept at the stable to save my shoes getting dirty. I had to get up ridiculously early to spend time with Sonny but I felt so happy and alive. I knew that somehow I must find a way to spend the rest of my life working with horses. My mother was adamant that this was the wrong pursuit. She disapproved of my love of horses and told me I would never make any money, but my mind was set. After endless rows and arguments, she finally allowed me to switch jobs.

At sixteen, I started as a working pupil at a riding stables in Westerham, where I could take the British Horse Society's instructor certificate. One of our instructors was a fearsome German woman, whose philosophy was that the horse should be 'dominated'. 'The horse must lose the natural nod!' she would screech. This is a movement a horse makes as it relaxes and seeks forward for a contact with the bit, but she believed we shouldn't allow this and should restrict the horse's head and neck. I was never comfortable with that. I have always had very light hands, which for me is the key to get a horse going freely and happily. I like to get on a horse and quietly take an interactive approach: 'Now, what are we going to do? Are you going to like me? Let's trot – show me what you can do,' and so forth.

One of the good things our instructor did was to make us spend a long time riding without stirrups, keen for us to sit deep in the saddle and feel the horse's movement through our seat bones. Horses love that physical connection, when they know that the rider can feel what they are doing and goes along with it. I was lucky to have a good physique for riding, with long legs and flat calves, and whenever I was on a horse's back, I felt completely at home and, in return, the horses seemed to love me.

While I was at Westerham, I also witnessed a very different approach to horses that would influence me deeply. One morning as I was heading to the stables, I saw the most wonderful sight. A slight young woman was riding a beautiful iron-grey horse in the field. She was doing dressage exercises, helped by her father, who I later found out was Leo Harris, the chairman of the Association of British Riding Schools. I watched, spellbound. The woman was riding so quietly, with total empathy, giving almost imperceptible aids so the upward and downward transitions were totally fluid. I knew then, beyond a shadow of a doubt, that this 'dressage' was for me. Leonie, as I discovered she was called, soon became a good friend and introduced me to her wonderful horse, Oberon. Seeing Leonie and Oberon's relationship, and the way Oberon was totally tuned in to Leonie as he performed the beautiful movements, changed me for ever. Leonie was incredibly kind and helpful to me in a way that our instructors, with their philosophy of dominating the horse, were not. Her philosophy was quietly to find a way, and she proved her point when she and Oberon represented Great Britain in dressage internationally. We lost touch after Westerham, but renewed our friendship in recent years, which is a great joy to me.

Leonie's approach helped me progress and I was offered a job as an instructor at Blenheim Farm in Sussex. Blenheim Farm was a hotel as well as a riding school and I was given a room there and set to work, instructing students as well as show-jumping a big bay horse called Carriebawn. I felt relieved to be living away from my mother and full of aspirations about following in the footsteps of someone like Leonie and making a career out of my love of horses.

I also met Geraldine, my first love, at Blenheim Farm. She was about the same age as me, and worked in the kitchens, living in a cottage nearby. Her father was one of the farmhands and she was straight out of *Cider with Rosie*, red-lipped and curvaceous, with a winning smile, and had a sweet way of looking sideways through her lashes. In the quiet of the evenings, I would ride through the fruit farm's orchards, hoping to meet Geraldine as she walked home so that we could linger and chat under the trees, hidden from prying eyes. Once, when her parents were away, I spent the night with Geraldine. The cottage was very basic, a rural dwelling with no electricity, just candles. The limewashed walls were running wet, and when we got into bed the sheets were so cold they felt damp, too. That didn't bother me. It was a bucolic, blissful idyll and Geraldine was so kind and affectionate.

I was at Blenheim Farm for about six months but I was ambitious and eager to better my career and when I was offered another job through Marshall's, an employment agency for the equine community, I took it. Saying farewell to Geraldine, I moved to Cumbria as a chief instructor at a girls' school and was given on-site accommodation. I enjoyed the job but after a few months the girls started writing love letters to me, and although I wasn't interested or encouraging, I was asked to leave.

Then I took a job as an instructor for a riding academy in Cheshire where, to start with, I fitted in well. With a room near the stables and many horses to manage, I took the job seriously. In my spare time I show-jumped for my employer, Alec, who also ran the local pub and had some other businesses on the go. One day, a member of his staff, Brian, made a pass at me. He had seemed like a nice chap and we'd gone on an errand together in his car, but, when we were alone, he tried to force himself on me. I was shocked and disgusted, pushing him away. I knew nothing about sexual behaviour between men. In this twenty-first-century age of openness about sexuality, my ignorance as an eighteen-year-old seems hard to believe but this was the 1950s. There was no internet, no easy access to pornography or teenage sexting on mobile phones. Homosexuality was illegal, and a taboo subject in respectable circles. Also, nothing in my strict Catholic education had prepared me for what Brian was after. He tried hard to get me to comply with his demands, but I told him no, absolutely not, I don't want to do that. Back at work the next day, I felt very uncomfortable, and really didn't know what I should do. I assumed no one would believe me if I told them so I decided to leave.

Without a job, I had no choice but to go home. My mother was disappointed to have me under her roof again. She was enjoying having the house much more to herself because by then all my older siblings had left home. Edward was married, and so was Fleur. Ralph was a gym teacher, in the RAF, based in Cyprus, and Brian was in Aden, also with the RAF. Only my younger brother John remained at home, and he was out all day at work, which Mummy greatly approved of, making it known that she thought much more of him than she did of me.

I escaped that summer by instructing at the Holcombe Hunt Pony Club Camp at Blackpool, where I gave dressage demonstrations. I met a woman called Alison Coulton, who later went on to train Princess Anne as a three-day-event rider. Alison talked to me about the sport of eventing, with its disciplines of dressage, cross-country and show-jumping, and how it is the ultimate test of horse and rider. It was gaining in popularity in the 1950s, and I thought it might be something I would like to try. Alison was encouraging and loaned me a beautiful event horse called Marlay Password. I practised, gaining skills and confidence, and felt incredibly excited for the future. The more I learned, the more ambition I had, so I was delighted when Marshall's agency got in touch with an interesting job prospect. A three-day-event rider called the Honourable Brecht van der Vater was looking for a working pupil to take charge of his stables in return for pocket money, with specialised tuition provided. It was a step backwards to be a working pupil again, but knowing this was the world I wanted to be in, I liked the sound of it. Packing a case with my riding gear and my sponge bag, I headed off on the train to Kingham in Oxfordshire for the interview.

I was met by a lively young man who spoke with a slight lisp. He introduced himself as Brecht van der Vater but added, 'Everybody calls me Van!'

Van was more like a jaunty bantam cock than the

aristocratic gentleman I had imagined, but I was impressed when we drove up to Squirrels, the seventeenth-century Cotswold stone cottage where he lived. He asked me to tack up and ride Harbour Light, a bright bay thoroughbred ex-racer, watching me so he could assess my ability. I put Harbour Light through his paces and popped him over a few jumps. 'Why don't you stay the night? Let's see how things go,' Van said afterwards.

Delighted, I agreed, and at once began work on the yard. I was given the small bedroom above the front door at Squirrels, just down the corridor from Van's room. That night became a week, and the week became several months. I enjoyed Van's company, most of the time. We ate all our meals together. Neither of us could cook very well, so for supper we usually went over to his friend Helen's house in the nearby village of Bledington, staggering home rather the worse for wear. Van also had a housekeeper who would put together some lunch for us. She was rather a sour-faced person, who liked to cheer herself up with a nip or two of gin from the drinks cabinet. Van was careful to mark the bottle so he could keep an eye on this.

As soon as I knew I was going to carry on working for Van I gave him my National Insurance cards, assuming he would pay for my stamps. I also assumed I would receive monthly pocket-money payments as agreed, but I didn't. When I mentioned this, Van would laugh uproariously and say, 'Next week, Norman. You'll get it next week.' The money never materialised. I kept assuming and hoping it would and, in the meantime, I put my attention into the horses.

There were four horses at Squirrels. Van owned one, a

fantastic liver-chestnut mare with a white blaze called Tobruk, who was very fast and a great jumper but a temperamental ride. There was also a little bay thoroughbred called The Zephyr, who Van was eventing for someone else; Harbour Light, who I had ridden when I first arrived; an iron grey called Philomel, who belonged to Helen; and a hunter belonging to a lawyer who kept him at Squirrels. I looked after all of them with great pride. Van took stable management to the highest level, insisting that the horses were turned out to perfection, their coats shining and their hoofs oiled. I was on the yard before six o'clock every morning and didn't finish until after seven in the evening. Before breakfast I would exercise two of the horses, riding one, leading the other. After breakfast, Van and I would take the others out. For exercise, they wore rugs made from purple wool with gold binding and a monogram with a coronet. I loved this effect, and I was thrilled to be riding such wonderful horses. The rides around the Cotswold countryside were beautiful too and I got to know the neighbours, chatting to Mrs Barton and her daughter Ann, who lived at the end of the village green and had a small stud farm of thorough-bred horses.

After riding, I took the saddles and bridles to pieces and cleaned them so the leather was soft and supple as silk. I laid deep beds of the finest straw in the stables and, on Van's precise instruction, plaited the edges of the straw so that no untidy strands spilled out of the door onto the yard. If any wisps escaped, I swept them up. It was a tough regime, but I enjoyed every moment, and the old Irish gardener, John, helped with mucking out and other heavy tasks. It was John who told me, after I had been at Squirrels for couple of weeks, that the house and all the lovely antique furnishings did not belong to Van. He was just renting the property from an elderly woman. I had assumed from Van's behaviour that everything was his, but I was wrong.

I loved spending all my time with the horses, but I didn't get much tuition from Van. Occasionally he would supervise me for an hour of dressage schooling, but I had hoped for much more, as I really wanted to fulfil my ambition of becoming a top event rider. I did get some top-class instruction when I joined him for lessons from the renowned dressage instructor Molly Sivewright at her Talland Equestrian Centre in Cirencester. Years later Molly's daughter, international dressage rider and trainer Pammy Hutton, told me her mother believed I was a better rider than Van, showing much more focus. Molly said that if I had been one of her full-time students I would very likely have ended up riding for Great Britain. At the time I was young and naïve and glad to be with Van even though I should have insisted that he kept to the agreed arrangement for my time as a working pupil. I wasn't interested in money, and was so happy to be riding top-class horses that I kept letting the matter pass.

Whenever we took a break from the horses, Van liked to visit the shops in Cheltenham and Cirencester, and often took me with him. We would go to Cavendish House department store, where Van would buy jewellery and luxury goods on account. He also took some antiques on approval from a shop in the town, buying all this on credit, and there never seemed to be any problem with money. I did wonder sometimes if he might be living a bit beyond his means, but Van had a very credible air of wealth, dressing like a proper country gentleman and displaying such confidence and charm that I didn't let this worry me.

Van was great fun to be with, but sometimes his moods were changeable. When the owners thanked me for taking good care of their horses he was quick to dismiss my efforts and talk me down. I never got any praise from him for my hard work on the yard. On the other hand, when it was just the two of us, his sunny disposition came to the fore and he could be very amusing and flamboyant. Every morning our postwoman, Mrs Rainbow, would lumber through the gate with her bag, her eyes going everywhere to see what we were up to. Van's three springer spaniels would rush out and ambush her, and she'd shout at them, 'Gerroff me!' One day, just before she arrived, Van came scampering out of the house completely naked, except for a chiffon scarf tied round his dick. I was surprised to see what a hairy body he had, as he danced about the yard wafting the scarf until I ached from laughing. Then the gate creaked and in came Mrs Rainbow. I have never seen anyone move so fast as Van did, streaking back to the house while Mrs Rainbow stood there open-mouthed. I'm sure she went back and told everyone in the village.

One morning Van told me he had a friend coming to stay. That evening a black Sunbeam Rapier drove up to Squirrels. A lean, dapper figure in a homburg hat and a black coat with an astrakhan collar got out. He looked incongruous and slightly sinister in the sleepy Oxfordshire village of Kingham. His name, I learned, was Jeremy Thorpe and he was the Member of Parliament for North Devon. He had achieved a notable victory in the 1959 general election, winning the seat from his Conservative opponent.

I thought it rather strange when I discovered Jeremy Thorpe was sharing Van's bedroom, which had a single bed. I was pretty sure that Van, who could be very camp at times, might be a homosexual. I recalled him telling me that the monogram on his horses' rugs came from an aristocratic gentleman he had been involved with. I hadn't given all this much thought. All my focus was on the horses. These elite equines were the centre of my world, far more engrossing to me than any of the people I encountered. Being very shy and very aware that Jeremy Thorpe was way above me in terms of social class, I kept out of the way. That night, exhausted after my hard physical work on the yard, I forgot all about him, headed to my own room and went out like a light.

The following morning, as I was grooming Harbour Light, Jeremy Thorpe walked across the yard in his black coat and hat. He stopped by the stable door and made a pretence of being interested in the horse, though he clearly knew nothing about horses. I carried on brushing, feeling rather uncomfortable in such sophisticated company when I was clad in the brown stockman's overall I wore for yard work. I hoped he would just leave, but he kept on talking.

'I'm slightly worried, Norman. Van's an odd character. If ever you have a problem with him, I'd like you to get in touch.' He gave me his card and added, 'Don't tell Van I said this.'

Very surprised that he was even talking to me, let alone telling me I could contact him, I thanked him and took the card, although I couldn't see why there would be a problem, or why he was taking an interest in me.

Not long after Jeremy Thorpe's visit, Van went to London for several days, and while he was away Helen gave me a bright chestnut mare with two white socks called Tenby, who she was rather afraid of. She said I should keep her. Tenby had an uncooperative, sour character and Helen felt I might have more success with her. I was delighted to have my own horse and, although Tenby's character wasn't ideal, hoped I could bond with her.

One morning, just after he returned, I was eating breakfast when Van, who liked to be up early to intercept Mrs Rainbow as she came across the green to deliver the post, hurried in with some envelopes. With a gleeful look on his face, he opened the bureau where he kept his correspondence and put the envelopes inside. Then he pulled out some letters. Waving a handful, he explained, with a smug air, that these had been sent to him by some very important people. 'These are my insurance policy!' he said. 'Remember when Princess Margaret got engaged?' He brandished a postcard at me. 'This is what Jeremy Thorpe, MP, had to say about it: "What a pity. I rather hoped to marry one and seduce the other." What d'you make of that, Norman?'

Laughing, he stuffed the postcard and the letters back into the bureau. My face grew hot with embarrassment. I felt sorry for the unsuspecting people who had written the letters, especially Jeremy Thorpe, who had seemed rather kind.

I didn't dwell on Van's letters because it was none of my business and we were busy getting the horses ready for the eventing season. Every morning we would do several hours of roadwork to build their fitness: in those days, a timed roads-and-tracks gallop was part of the cross-country course at a three-day event, which was a very good test of speed and stamina.

Van and I also hunted three days a week with the Heythrop, one of the most prestigious hunts in England. We thought nothing of hacking the eight miles to a meet, hunting for most of the day and hacking home. When we hacked the twenty-five miles to Bicester for the Bicester and Warden Hill Hunt, we stayed the night with Van's friends Di Carney and Harry Tatlow (Harry's son David is currently president of the British Show Horse Association). After supper, Di took me to see her Jack Russell terrier bitch, who was snuggled up with a litter of puppies. I fell in love with one, and Di let me have her. I carried the warm handful of tiny puppy all the way home in the pocket of my riding mac when we hacked back the following day. I called her Mrs Tish, and she became my treasured companion. As I prepared the horses for one of the first three-day events, being held at Tidworth Park in Wiltshire, she was always at my side.

Just before Tidworth, I was sweeping up one afternoon when Van drove a brand-new long-wheelbase Land Rover into the yard. 'Where on earth did you get that?' I asked.

'It's ours. We'll use it to take the horses to Tidworth.' He grinned, slammed the door and walked into the house.

Some friends of Van's came with us to Tidworth, having arrived at Squirrels a few days before. Bertie St John came to stay and brought her beautiful horse Shepherd Song, who was part-owned by the Queen, and two sisters, the Cliffords, also arrived with their eventers, driving over in their old horsebox, which they slept in at night. Van made every effort to be a good host, but I could tell that with so many guests his veneer of charm was wearing thin. The housekeeper must have felt put out too, with so many people to cater for, and I noticed she paid several extra visits to the gin bottle.

On the day we left for Tidworth, everyone was up first thing, preparing their mounts. On Van's instruction, I had taken great care to turn out his horses superbly with their shining hoofs and purple rugs, but by the time we had arrived at Tidworth, Van had fallen into a 'black dog' mood. He kept snapping at me and seemed to have completely lost his sense of humour. I put this down to our early start, so I unloaded Tobruk and took off her travelling bandages. Van asked me to exercise her, as this firebrand of a mare needed at least two hours' work before she would settle down enough for the calm precision of the dressage test. He'd had a bad experience with her at Badminton where she'd ignored all his dressage aids and just carted him round the muddy arena in a huge extended trot.

I put on the cavesson and lunging rein, and Tobruk set off like a rocket as she raced in circles around me. Mrs Tish sat on the grass nearby, watching with interest. Things were going as well as could be expected when my attention was caught by a competitor's dressage test in the nearby arena. The horse was supple and balanced, and an absolute delight to watch. Unfortunately, just as I took my eyes off Tobruk, someone let their horsebox ramp down with a crash and Tobruk exploded, snatching the lunge rein right out of my hand. Luckily, she didn't notice she was loose and bucked and kicked on the spot. I dived for the end of the rein and caught it with a gasp of relief, but then I saw Van approaching, his face contorted with anger.

A horrendous row ensued. Shouting obscenities, Van yelled that I was stupid. I was dumbfounded, shocked he was making such a fuss about a minor mistake when no harm had been done. He'd often been dismissive about my work, but this was going too far so I handed Tobruk over to him and told him I was going to our caravan.

As I left, with Mrs Tish trotting at my heels, the Clifford sisters came up. When I told them how Van had reacted, they just gave me an odd look and kept quiet. By the time I had got to the caravan Van was waiting at the door. Hoping the 'black dog' had now departed, I smiled, hoping to pave the way for an amicable apology, but none was forthcoming. 'Get my bloody horse tacked up or fuck off and get out!' he shouted.

I was so hurt I picked up Mrs Tish, went straight to the station and caught a train back to Kingham, walking the one and a half miles home with my little dog trotting behind me. I always shared my thoughts with her and said, 'It'll be all right. He'll come round.' I had more or less forgiven Van. I was used to his moods – though this had been his worst outburst ever – and I was sure he would return home in his usual sunny frame of mind.

When I arrived at Squirrels, thirsty and tired, the front door seemed to be stuck and I had to push hard to get it open. When I finally stepped inside I realised that some brown envelopes had got wedged between the coconut fabric of the doormat and the bottom of the door. As I picked them up I was surprised to see that many were addressed to me. I opened them, and I couldn't believe my eyes. Each one contained an invoice, including several final demands. I went cold with shock. How could this have happened?

Shaking with nerves, I headed for the drinks cabinet. Luckily, the housekeeper's need for a regular nip meant that the lock had long ago been forced, and it was easy to open. I poured myself a gin, gulping it down, then collapsed on the floor. Eventually I pulled myself up, staring again in disbelief at the bills. After giving Tenby some hay, I finished off the rest of the gin before crawling into bed.

The rattle of the letterbox woke me in the morning and, with a feeling of dread, I went downstairs and found another bill addressed to me. Panicking, I ran across to the Bartons', clutching it. Ann was outside feeding the horses so I tried to explain what had happened, but I was so upset I could barely get the words out. Ann took me into the house and when I had calmed down a bit, I told her and her mother the whole story, including the awful things Van had said to me at Tidworth. Mrs Barton was outraged. 'Right, Norman. Go back to Squirrels. Get all your stuff and bring it over here. Clothes, saddle, bridles, everything. And put Tenby in our field.'

Relief flooded through me as I thanked her profusely.

'And bring all of those bills,' she continued, 'We'll talk to my solicitor about this.'

I hurried back to Squirrels, caught Tenby, and led her to the Bartons' field. When I returned to fetch my things, I also took the 'insurance policy' letters in Van's bureau. He had behaved so badly towards me that I feared for the people who had written the letters, especially Jeremy Thorpe, who'd been so kind when he gave me his card.

A couple of days later, when the event at Tidworth had finished, Van returned home, guessed where I'd gone and came striding across the green with his three spaniels scampering after him.

'Leave this to me,' Mrs Barton said, marching out of her front door.

Van was shouting, 'He's a lunatic! He's a horse thief!'

Mrs Barton stayed calm. 'I think something odd is going on here. What has happened is appalling.'

Eventually Van ran out of steam and went home with his tail between his legs. It wasn't long before I realised that I now had no National Insurance cards, having given them to Van when I first arrived. I really needed to get another job and earn some money, but without the cards, I wouldn't be able to. I knew I ought to confront him and ask for them back, but I just didn't dare. Every time I thought about it I imagined the outburst Van would unleash and the horrible argument that would ensue. I had lost all my trust in him, and felt completely betrayed. I couldn't bear a repeat of the awful scene at Tidworth, so I did nothing. I had no idea this would be possibly the biggest mistake of my life.

CHAPTER THREE

The Girl with the
White Cotton Gloves

ALTHOUGH VAN BACKED off from further interaction with Mrs Barton, I would often encounter him on the tracks and bridleways when I was out on Tenby. Without me, he now had to exercise all the horses himself. He would call my name as he rode towards me and, with no escape, I had to keep going and face up to him. These confrontations were very unpleasant. I always felt very threatened and tried to slip past him as quickly as I could. Luckily Tenby, who could be difficult, didn't take advantage of my nervousness and misbehave. I would ride away, shaking with fear and distress, and find myself remembering Jeremy Thorpe's words: 'Contact me if you ever have trouble with Van.' I thought about doing this, wondering whether he had really meant it, but I just couldn't. How could I bother such an important person with all this, which had nothing to do with him?

About three weeks after I left Van's the solicitor told me Helen was claiming I had stolen her mare and she wanted her returned. The solicitor advised me to hold on to Tenby, continue to school her, then sell her and keep the money in lieu of the pay I had not received while I was a working pupil. He wrote to Van, informing him of this, and eventually Tenby was sold. I didn't feel too bad about letting her go. She didn't have any enthusiasm for galloping and jumping, and I was in desperate need of money as I couldn't work without the National Insurance cards. I was still too fearful of Van to approach him about this. I was terrified of his unpredictability, and had no trust in him at all. I just wished I could forget all about him.

One day when I was helping Ann and her mother to de-warble their cattle – stripping away the tiny eggs that warble flies lay on the animals' coats – Van came striding over the green again. Mrs Barton went to head him off. They spoke briefly, then Van left. When she returned, Mrs Barton said, 'I don't think that young man will trouble us again. I've told him he must leave you alone, Norman. Now. We must decide what you are going to do next.'

The Bartons had been so good to me. Mrs Barton must have paid the solicitor's fees though she never said anything about it. But I couldn't impose on their kindness for ever. Ann Barton drove me to meet two elderly sisters, Lorna and Wyn Horsman Bailey, who were letting a flat in their country house, Foxholes. It was a crumbling Victorian building set in acres of woodland and overgrown paddocks, just a few miles from Kingham. The rent was four pounds per week, which I could afford because of the sale money from Tenby, so I moved in.

My apartment was on the ground floor with access from the garden, through the gunroom. I had a sitting room, a bedroom and a shared bathroom, and the place was filled with period furniture – rosewood tables, fine old chesterfields, and a wonderful antique brass bed – evoking the atmosphere of more prosperous times. Several other tenants lived in flats in the house. One was taken by an army family, who had recently returned from abroad, while a wealthy man and his elderly nanny lived in another. The income from the rents must have been a boon to the Horsman Bailey sisters, who were living in very reduced circumstances. There was also a terrace of cottages not far from the main house, for people whose families had once worked on the estate.

The relationship between the Horsman Bailey sisters and those families was almost feudal. In return for free milk, the occupants of the estate cottages would undertake duties in the main house. The sisters also retained their mother's lady's maid, Annie, who had been a Dame, or house mistress, at Eton, and had looked after Wyn and Lorna's brothers when they were pupils there. She had a little bedroom just off the kitchen, and in the evenings I would hear the rattle of the trolley as she wheeled the sisters' supper down the long corridor to the dining room. The trolley was always beautifully laid, with silver dishes and covers, but under those covers there would be just a few fish fingers, potatoes and peas. The Horsman Baileys were in straitened circumstances but they kept up their standards.

Wyn Horsman Bailey was a plump woman with a very deep voice, who was in charge of the farm. She taught me a lot about farming during my stay at Foxholes. 'Kelpie! Come!' she would boom, and her collie would leap into the battered old van, followed by Mrs Tish and me, ready to drive down to the cowsheds. Under Wyn's eagle eye, I learned how to milk the cows by hand. She was very eccentric: she slept on a bed outside on her balcony in all weathers, even if it was snowing. There was a leather apron she could pull over herself to keep dry. 'This is how I live, and I like it,' she told me.

Lorna's domain was the house and garden. She wore long white gloves and a large hat, and was usually found in the garden, carrying a trug as she patrolled her flowerbeds. It was she who arranged all the flowers for the house, and I am sure it was she who insisted on the elegant presentation of the food for those meagre evening meals.

Through all my time at Foxholes I felt immersed in the atmosphere of a past age. Every morning I would wake to hear the slop-slopping sound of the old tenant who mopped the tiles on the ground floor before we were up and about. And there would always be a basket of freshly baked rolls, made by Wyn and wrapped in a linen cloth waiting on the table outside my door, ready for my breakfast.

When I went through to my flat, I'd linger in the gunroom, looking at a glass case with a display of medals and commendations. It was a sort of shrine to the brothers Guy and Vivian Horsman Bailey, who had fought in the First World War. Guy had been killed. Vivian was still alive, but he rarely visited the house. There were belts, buckles and ammunition in there, too. All sorts of paraphernalia from the war. One day, I picked up a smooth, gleaming bullet and slipped it into my pocket. There were so many other things in that glass case I was sure one bullet would not be missed. As I ran my fingertips over it, it felt like a talisman, a lucky charm, kept safely in my pocket.

My new life at Foxholes helped me to feel stronger and

more resilient. I began to think again about my equestrian career. I had had such high hopes of a great future as a three-day-event rider when I started working with Van, but nothing had come of this. To get another job I would need my National Insurance cards but Van still had them. I had no inclination to approach him about it, so once again the Bartons helped. They introduced me to Christopher Parsons, who managed the William Hill Sezincote Stud, which was about ten miles from Foxholes and part of the Sezincote estate. Christopher was a real gentleman, grey-haired with a grey moustache, and offered me an apprenticeship, with pocket money, so that I could learn about bloodstock breeding. I loved caring for the beautiful thoroughbred mares and foals, and hearing Christopher talk about the bloodlines of the famous stallions who had sired them: Nimbus, Honeyway, Botticelli and Abernant. He was impressed by my enthusiasm and said I was a very quick learner.

Christopher and his wife treated me almost like a son. They loaned me a Vespa motor scooter to travel back and forth to the stud, and my pocket money was always promptly paid. As a trainee stud manager, I was kept apart from the grooms, and had breakfast and lunch with the Parsonses, then a cup of tea with them in the afternoon when the grooms brought the horses in from the fields, eventually heading back to Foxholes on the Vespa. I felt so at home and content during my time at Sezincote but my peace of mind was often disturbed when Van rode past the hedge that framed the Foxholes drive. Just as when I had met him when I was exercising Tenby, he would call out to me. I could have used those encounters to ask him to give me my

National Insurance cards but that never occurred to me. I was afraid to approach him in case of another outburst, and just wanted to be left alone to forget he ever existed.

While I was with the Bartons, their doctor had given me some Largactil tablets to help with my anxiety. Every time Van appeared, I'd think about the awful things he'd said to me, and how he had ruined all my hopes for my career as an event rider. My future felt so uncertain. The only way to reduce the anxiety I felt about this was to take more pills. In my increasingly drugged state, I began to think again about Jeremy Thorpe. Some of the letters I had taken from Van's bureau were from Mr Thorpe, and although the envelopes were addressed to Van, the letters began 'Dear Norman' (that was Van's real name, although I didn't know it at the time). They were filled with lively, affectionate expressions, and sometimes when I was doped up on Largactil, I would find myself daydreaming and wishing they had been written to me. Not in a romantic way but just because they were from someone so well respected – in those days, everyone looked up to Members of Parliament. People believed they were something very special – a cut above. I remembered how Jeremy had looked at me so kindly when he gave me his card. Though I did think about Jeremy a lot, my feelings for him were in no way sexual. So far, I had only been with girls and now I found all my solace and connection with animals – especially horses and dogs. They were the focus of my life.

One day, after I'd seen Van riding along by the hedge again, I dug out Jeremy's card and went to the boot room, where there was a telephone. I dialled the number. It rang a few times. Then there was a click on the line, indicating that someone at Foxholes had picked up an extension, so I hung up. Lorna Horsman Bailey had a habit of listening in to calls, and I didn't want her to overhear the conversation. I gave up my fantasy about Jeremy Thorpe being my friend and put all my attention into the horses at the stud until I broke my arm falling off my scooter on my twentieth birthday. I'd missed my turning, skidded and found myself sprawled on the verge with the remains of the scooter on top of me

With my arm set in plaster, I was in a fog of concussion, and for a couple of weeks the days went by in a haze of dozing and waking to be fed beef tea. At first, the concussion made me dizzy, and when I needed the bathroom the three old ladies, Wyn, Lorna and their maid Annie, took it in turns to hold me up on the way there while one or other of them made my bed.

As the dizziness lessened, a new routine of sitting in an old cane deckchair on the tennis lawn began. The sisters gave me a beekeeper's hat with a veil to keep the flies from bothering me, and late in the afternoons, one of them would come and lay a rug over my knees. They were so incredibly kind to me, as was Christopher Parsons, who visited me, bringing grapes and fruit from Mrs Parsons. 'You're much missed at the stud but you must rest and regain your strength,' he said kindly. He told me not to worry about the smashed motor scooter, though it was a write-off, because it was fully insured and the insurance company would sort everything out.

One day, as I was lounging on the lawn, I saw that a room in the Horsman Baileys' wing was being spring-cleaned. Eiderdowns and feather dusters were being shaken out in the sunshine. When Lorna brought my tea, she explained that the sisters' goddaughter, Sarah Penrose-Fitzgerald, was coming to stay. She had been very ill, and it would be good for her to have somebody of her own age, like me, to talk to. But Lorna explained that I must not question her about her recent life. That night I heard a car drive up, the distant sound of voices in the hall, then doors closing and silence. I lay awake for some time wondering about this mysterious young woman.

As I lazed on the lawn the following morning, still feeling ropy from concussion and painkillers, I fell into a reflective mood. The gracious house at Foxholes, tended faithfully by the sisters, who were growing ever older in their genteel poverty, was falling slowly into decay. I thought back over the generations who had created the beautiful estate. I visualised the sad shrine to Guy and Vivian in the gunroom and the ranks of fading photos in the hall – sepia images of the family in happier times: Wyn and Lorna as young girls with their brothers, enjoying tennis parties with the Astors from nearby Bruern Abbey. Now all this was slowly slipping away.

'Good afternoon!' A quiet voice broke into my melancholy thoughts. A tall, slender girl in her early twenties, just a little older than myself, was standing by my side with a tea tray. Long, ash-blonde hair framed her large eyes and high cheekbones, and she wore a blue cashmere dress, with flat brown shoes.

'You must be Sarah,' I said, making an effort to sit up properly.

She nodded. 'I asked if I might bring your tea. I wanted so much to meet you, and I didn't want a formal introduction.'

I watched her set down the tray and pour smoky Lapsang Souchong tea into the blue-and-white cups, adding thin wafers of lemon. I noticed she was wearing white cotton gloves, which seemed odd, but she was charming, and as we sat there in the sunshine, I felt my melancholy mood evaporate.

Over the next fortnight, Sarah and I spent more and more time together. She wouldn't emerge from her room until the afternoon, and, when she did, she would always be wearing the white cotton gloves. I was mystified by this, but Lorna and Wyn took me aside one day, and told me what had happened to her. Not long before, she had been in Africa, assisting a British diplomat. They had attended a performance of *Macbeth* by some local actors but it was an extremely hot day, and Sarah had felt as if she were going down with a migraine. She took some tablets to fend it off, but as the heat of the day increased she became disoriented, suffering from the effects of sunstroke. As Lady Macbeth took centre stage, crying, 'Out, damned spot!' and wringing her hands to cleanse them of the blood of the murdered king, Sarah jumped to her feet, her duties completely forgotten, and began repeating the lines.

"'Here's the smell of blood still . . .'" she muttered, raising her fingers to her face. "' . . . all the perfumes of Arabia will not sweeten this little hand. Oh, oh, oh.'" In her own mind, she had become Lady Macbeth. She ran off to find water to wash away the imaginary blood, collapsed and was taken back to the residence. Sarah was relieved of her duties and promptly sent back to England but her obsession with cleansing her hands remained, despite the efforts of top physicians and psychiatrists. She had come to Foxholes in the hope that a rest in the country with her godmothers might help with her problems. As we sat in the garden together one afternoon, Sarah drew off one of her gloves. Beneath it, her hand was raw and red. 'I expect you know,' she said, glancing at me shyly.

I nodded, trying to hide my shock. She was wearing those gloves to protect her sore, ravaged skin and keep it from sight. I took her poor hand in mine and held it very gently. I had my own problems. My broken arm. My fear of Van's sudden appearances and the resulting anxiety that left me panicky and unable to sleep. I seemed to be living in a strange bubble where there was no one I could really talk to and from which I could see no escape – but all of that faded into insignificance beside what this gentle girl had been through.

As the days passed we grew closer – almost like lovers, though not in a physical way. It was an emotional closeness, very intense. She would come to my room, and on one of those occasions, I showed her the letters from Van's bureau. Sarah was intrigued. Picking up one of the letters addressed to 'Norman', she looked at the signature and asked, 'Why is Jeremy Thorpe writing to you?'

'Oh, no, they're not for me,' I said. 'They're written to another Norman.'

But she was not convinced and, in the end, I gave in and agreed with her because I liked that she thought I might have a connection with someone so esteemed.

I was spending so much time with Sarah that the suspicions of the Horsman Baileys were aroused: they weren't happy we had become so close. They had been brought up in the Edwardian era and upheld the social conventions of that age and Sarah was from a wealthy family, born of good stock. I was penniless and not from the upper classes so there could be no future for us. Lorna was especially vociferous and acerbic in expressing this, and they sent Sarah back to her parents' home in Hampshire. We wrote to each other every day and sometimes we spoke on the telephone. Sarah yearned to hear me say I loved her, but I knew one of the Horsman Bailey sisters would be listening in to our calls, so I had to stunt my words and deny the deep emotions we both felt. Our conversations ended in embarrassment and tears, leaving me to struggle with a miserable feeling of isolation and powerlessness that began to consume me. My melancholy moods had started before Sarah had arrived, but when she left, I felt a new loss. Sarah was the first person in my life who I had felt a real connection with. My one true friend. Both of us were adrift in life, our bond strengthened by the kindness and lack of judgement we showed each other.

CHAPTER FOUR

Problems, Pills and Other People's Passions

MY MOOD SANK further. I began helping Wyn on the farm again, but, with my arm still in plaster, there was a limit to what I could do. The frustration of not being able to work properly added to the anxiety that mounted every time Van appeared. It had been several months since I'd moved out of Squirrels, yet I still felt afraid of him, and what he might say to me. I lay awake worrying about when he would next appear. I couldn't talk to the Horsman Baileys about Van, as they wouldn't have understood, and I found myself spiralling down into a deep trough of depression.

My dark mood led me to paint the walls of my beautiful Edwardian sitting room black and decorate it with vases of purple rhododendrons. Sitting in the darkness, I was unable to shake off a feeling of deep sadness. I became desperately worried about my future and found myself crying all the time. The Bartons' doctor, who was very sympathetic towards me, prescribed more Largactil, which helped to calm me a little but also made me rather befuddled.

I began to take long walks in the woods around Foxholes and found myself gripped by a bleak premonition that nothing would ever go right for me. I turned to drinking gin quite heavily, hoping it would numb my mind. Most nights I would buy a bottle and take it to my room, drinking until I made myself sick. Unable to tolerate the oppressive silence of the house, I would go out and wander across the fields in the dark. One evening I deliberately took more Largactil tablets than I should have done and, in my drugged-up state, the sisters couldn't communicate with me. They called my doctor, who explained to Wyn and Lorna that I had been through some exceptionally distressing rejections and betrayals, all of which had been very challenging for a twenty-year-old. I needed help and understanding.

Wyn and Lorna took this on board and, when my arm was out of plaster, encouraged me to ride their thoroughbred mare, who had been lazing in the field for years. Being back on a horse focused my mind, gave me purpose and lifted my spirits. Being outside every day in the fresh air also helped and I began to feel a little better. Although I kept taking my medication, I stopped drinking.

By the autumn, I was fit enough to go back to my work for Christopher at the stud but after my accident I was nervous about riding the scooter, especially when the roads became slippery with leaves. Instead, I started helping Tony, a local dairy farmer. Wyn and Lorna were dismayed: 'Oh, no, you mustn't. His wife has left him and he is really rather strange.' But craving fresh company, and knowing Tony needed help, I ignored them.

I felt a renewed vigour as I started at Tony's farm. I wasn't being paid, but I still had some money left over from selling Tenby and I loved learning about the cows, which I had never worked with before. Tony showed me how to look after and milk his eighty-strong herd but, though we got on well, his mood was very low. When his wife had left, she had taken their son, and as the custody hearing got nearer, Tony started drinking heavily.

I felt sorry for Tony, and guessed he was drinking to ease the pain of his marriage break-up. 'I just can't cope. I'm lonely. I'm miserable,' he told me.

Tony continued to drink heavily and soon began staying in bed all day. I really needed to be on hand first thing in the morning to do the milking for him, so I moved myself and Mrs Tish to the farmhouse. Tony gave me a room rent-free in return for the work. The Horsman Baileys were terribly disapproving but, grateful as I was for their kindness and concern, I was beginning to find their fussing over me and their old-fashioned attitudes cloying.

Tony's state of mind plummeted further and he stopped looking after himself. After I had finished with the cows I cooked meals for him and encouraged him to eat, but it was a struggle to do everything and I suggested he advertise for a housekeeper. Eventually he agreed and employed a Welsh woman. She took an immediate dislike to me, probably because we both knew she was after his money and the farmhouse. I'm sure Tony understood what she was up to, but he started sleeping with her. Soon they were staying in bed all day, while I was out in the fields doing the work, but I didn't mind. I was young and strong, and liked learning the new skills. For six months, I carried on working, becoming fond of the cows and very glad of the routine.

Tony's divorce was a nasty one. He was desperate to gain

custody of his son so when the court ruled the boy must live with his mother, Tony hit rock bottom. As soon as the decree nisi came through, he told me, 'I can't do this any longer. The milk cheques aren't enough to keep things going. The cattle will have to be sold.'

I drove the herd on foot to the market near Kingham station, heartbroken to see them going under the hammer one by one as the herd was broken up. I waited until the last cow had been sold. The housekeeper, however, had no loyalty. Realising Tony was no longer a good prospect, she left.

Since there was no more early-morning milking to be done, I moved back to Foxholes. The Horsman Baileys were thrilled to have me back, but although they were very kind, I realised the nostalgic atmosphere in their house had a profoundly negative effect on my mood. Every day I cycled to Tony's farm to do the chores, but with no cows and no income, Tony put the farm up for sale. The first prospective buyers booked a viewing immediately and I was horrified when Van appeared, marching about the farmyard, with Helen in tow.

'I want you both out of here in two weeks,' Van snapped, glaring at us.

For a moment I didn't understand how he could afford it but then I realised he must have got the money for the house from Helen. Van buying the farm made the sale even more distressing. I felt that all my effort had been in vain, and poor Tony lost everything.

Tony moved to a cottage in the village of Enstone. Almost immediately, he telephoned me, telling me he was going to kill himself. 'Nothing to live for,' he said. 'I'm putting an end to it. Easy to do. I'll just get a rope.'

I leaped on to my bicycle and pedalled the eight miles to Enstone, praying I would not be too late. I was relieved to find Tony alive but his low mood was impossible to shift so I decided to move in with him for a few days, leaving Mrs Tish at Foxholes. I had the deepest compassion for Tony. I wanted to protect and care for him, knowing that if I didn't, no one else would. But he didn't care whether I was there or not and wouldn't speak to me. He drank constantly, and his personal hygiene was non-existent. I didn't mind. I just wanted to look after him.

What I didn't expect was how much Tony's mood would affect me. Within a few days, his depression had pulled me down too. I was still taking Largactil, as well as a beautiful sea-green pill called Tuinal to help with my insomnia. I loved those 'sleepy pills': they made me feel as if I was floating away when I lay down in bed after taking them. However, Tony's black mood made me sink so low that the drugs stopped having their effect. Suddenly I was as desolate as he was. All my prospects seemed so bleak, and all the anxieties I'd had before were magnified in the dark, despairing atmosphere. Before I'd been there a week, I took all of the Largactil, all of the Tuinal, and a lot of aspirin, absolutely determined to do away with myself. This seemingly impulsive decision grew from the months of spiralling depression, and the unnerving feeling that I had lost my footing in the equine career I had been working so hard on. It was unbearably painful to think that my dreams might come to nothing.

The pills worked fast and I quickly fell into a deep sleep, coming to in a brightly lit room with a tube stuck down my throat. A doctor and a nurse were standing over me as they pumped out my stomach. I discovered later that Tony had found me unconscious and rushed me to the hospital in Chipping Norton, saving my life. Pill after pill fell clinking into the basin as the kind nurse stood by, completely non-judgemental. I felt neither relief nor disappointment to be alive, just a terrible shame at what I had done.

After the stomach pump, my throat was sore from the tube, and I was very weak – so physically unwell that I was moved to the John Radcliffe Hospital in Oxford. When my condition improved I was judged to be mentally ill, and committed to be placed in a psychiatric clinic at Ashurst – a new project set up by the Oxford Hospital Management Group. It had been built quite recently in the grounds of Littlemore, the main psychiatric hospital for Oxford. When I think about this decision, especially within the context of how mental-health treatment has changed so much since the early 1960s, I am convinced that I should never have been committed. I think the clinic possibly did more harm than good. Unfortunately, being young, impressionable and extremely naïve, I never questioned any of the doctors' decisions. Neither did I have anyone who could check those decisions were right. The Horsman Baileys thought it was the best place for me and I agreed. I felt I needed serious help, which meant accepting I was mentally unstable. With that came an addiction to the cocktail of drugs, and the mindset that I couldn't cope on my own.

I stayed at the clinic for six months, turning twenty-one there without even realising. The patients lived in two wards, one for the men and one for the women. It was quite a small place, just the two wards, a dining room, a seating area and the doctors' offices. The atmosphere was bright, light and modern, and the staff were friendly, but I was unable to stop crying. I was still in shock after my attempt to kill myself. Whenever I thought about this I was left feeling weak and shaky. I was also very alone without Mrs Tish, but I had had to leave her with the Horsman Baileys as dogs weren't allowed at the clinic. If I could have held my little dog and cuddled her, she would have helped me so much. One nurse understood this. I told her about Mrs Tish, and we had long talks about horses and dogs and what wonderful companions animals could be. Her understanding helped me as much as the therapy I was offered.

The therapy at Ashurst was revolutionary for that time. We were given medication, but there was also talking therapy. Every day we had a session with one of the doctors, and once a week there was group therapy, where we all joined together to share our stories. To begin with, I found it difficult to contribute to the group sessions. I was too ashamed of the mess I had got myself into to discuss what was happening with my life, let alone reveal the difficulties of my childhood. But I did like one of the psychiatrists, a Dr Antony Willem. He had a pleasant manner, and the first time I met him I noticed he was wearing black-and-green socks. I'd been given a new pill, Librium, also black and green, so I called them his Librium socks. After that he always wore them when we met. I felt safe with him, able to tell him about my life and what had gone wrong, and I always came away from our sessions feeling better.

While the talking therapy seemed to help, the drugs intensified all my daydreams about Jeremy Thorpe. Thinking of this esteemed member of society, who had offered to help me, gave me some escape from my wretched reality. I talked about him to the other patients, exaggerating the truth and telling them he was my friend. I fantasised about this so often that I began to feel it really was true, especially when I was confused by my medication. I also told Dr Willem that I knew Jeremy, and because everything patients said was recorded, this was written in my notes.

After a while I began to settle and became less distressed. I made friends with Brian, one of the other patients. Brian was at Ashurst to get help with the serious problems caused by his alcoholism, and he often had the shakes. Except when he was unwell, or when one of us was in therapy, we were usually together. All sorts, both grand and not-so-grand, were mixed up together in the Ashurst Clinic and we were a strange crew at our dining table. There was me and Brian, along with Eileen, a wildly funny and well-educated woman suffering from alcoholism; a European count with some kind of nervous disorder; and a girl who had anorexia called Doreen. The eating disorder anorexia, along with other mental health issues, was not talked about openly at that time, but at our table we discussed all sorts of subjects relating to our lives. Everyone was frank and open about their problems. We also talked about other social taboos, including homosexuality. Some of my fellow patients aired the opinion that the law against homosexuality was wrong, and that people should be allowed to express same-sex love if they wished. Brian was particularly passionate about the subject. When we were alone I sometimes caught him looking at me very intently. Once or twice he said, 'Norman, you are *so* beautiful!' I certainly didn't see myself as homosexual at the time – if I had any romantic thoughts they were all for Sarah Penrose-Fitzgerald. I did wonder whether Brian might be that way inclined, and I wasn't as shocked by the thought as I might have been. The clinic had opened my eyes to the extensive and varied issues so many people faced.

New patients were admitted while others were discharged, and I began to get used to my strange existence. One morning, a sophisticated woman in her early forties called Jane joined us, suffering from manic depression. From the moment she arrived, she was determined to monopolise me, which made Brian feel left out. It was an uncomfortable situation, and I didn't know how to handle Jane's dominance or Brian's sensitivity.

There was one interlude in all this tension. In the late spring, after I had been at the clinic for a few months, Sarah came to visit, arriving in her Morris Minor with a picnic hamper, and took me to Badminton Horse Trials. I'd been longing to see her, but things were uncomfortable between us. We had shared our thoughts so openly and easily before but now our conversation felt awkward and stilted. Perhaps my circumstances upset her, given her own history of psychiatric illness. I felt so sad as I watched her drive away. The visit was an anticlimax and the disappointment made me much more susceptible to the powerful character of Jane.

In the late summer, Jane announced she was bored and hatched a plan for herself, Brian and me to escape from Ashurst. Using the clinic's telephone, she arranged to rent a flat in Polstead Road, an upmarket area of Oxford, paying the deposit and the first month's rent for all of us. One morning, when no one was about, the three of us got into her car and just drove off. We were hit by such a wave of emotional release we became hysterical with laughter, possibly heightened by the fact that we were drugged to the hilt on our medication.

Although we were delighted to be out of the clinic, our stay at the flat quickly became a nightmare. Within a week, Jane had slashed her wrists and we had to take her to hospital. She told the medics in the casualty department she had broken a bottle and cut herself by accident, and they believed her, stitching her up and sending her back to the flat. That same evening, Brian got very drunk. I stayed sober, as I was taking a drug called Antabuse, which would make me very sick if I touched alcohol, and later that night I found Brian getting into my bed. He was a big, strong man and at first I was very scared of him, but he was too drunk to do more than just fondle me and try to kiss me. His breath stank of alcohol, which I found disgusting, and I pushed him off, managing to keep him at bay until he finally fell asleep.

The following morning, I woke to find him snoring next to me, and a strong smell of gas in the flat. Jane had turned on all the gas taps in the kitchen in another attempt to kill herself. The smell was dreadful and, knowing the gas must escape, I did the first thing I could think of: I picked up a heavy grandfather chair and smashed the window. As the glass crashed, the neighbours came running while I rushed downstairs to Jane, who was lying semi-conscious on the kitchen floor. I threw some water over her and she revived a little. Then I ran out to a phone box, called the clinic, and told them where we were. Dr Willem said I could return if

I wished since I was young and vulnerable and had been caught up in Jane's plan, but she and Brian were no longer welcome.

When I got back to the flat, I found Jane, recovered, packing her cases with a man in attendance, whom she introduced as her husband. 'Brian's gone,' she said. 'And I'm leaving.' She walked out of the flat, and out of my life – or so I hoped.

Alone, I found myself wondering if I had been the catalyst for all this disaster. I walked along the canal bank in the bright noon sunshine to clear my head. Why did things keep going wrong for me? What should I do? Should I go back to the clinic? Or should I try to find some other way forward?

Ahead of me, I could see someone lying on the tow path. As I approached, I realised it was Brian, sprawled out on the grass, dead drunk. When I tried to wake him, he grabbed me and tried to tip us both into the canal. As I can't swim, I felt utterly panicked. Was I about to drown? Luckily, Brian was too out of it to succeed. I half carried, half dragged him back to the flat and put him to bed. He was completely paralytic, and I thought I'd better stay, at least until he was sober. He slept on through the day, and when it got dark I went to my own bed and fell asleep too.

Once again, I woke to the sound of gas taps hissing and the horrid smell filling the room. Feeling sick, I tried to jump up, but Brian was standing over me, holding a knife. Tears were running down his face. 'Let's finish it,' he sobbed. 'What's the point of carrying on? Let's just end it.'

I was terrified. Despite his distress he seemed sober, so I talked to him gently, as if he was a frightened horse that was misbehaving, and to my relief he dropped the knife and fell weeping onto my bed. I switched off the gas taps, then came back and lay beside him, stroking his head while he cried and laughed manically until finally, as the dawn was coming up, he nodded off.

When I was sure he was asleep, I made my escape, leaving Brian what money I had, and returned to the clinic. The staff were very angry. They told me I should stay in psychiatric care but, despite what Dr Willem had said, I was not welcome at the clinic. Because I had run away, I was now deemed to be a risk to the other patients, so they said I must be moved to Littlemore, the main psychiatric hospital. I felt terribly hurt by this, as I had just been through such absolute horrors at the flat. Also, I had done my best to help Jane and Brian and keep them safe. I didn't like the idea of this other, bigger hospital, worried about what I would find there and how they would treat me.

As I was being put into the car to be driven across the grounds to Littlemore, my favourite nurse ran out to say goodbye. She waved to me, calling, 'Don't worry, Norman. You'll be all right. You'll always be all right.'

Those words meant so much to me, especially when I arrived at Littlemore. It was such a daunting place. The wards were very large, and full of people screaming and rocking back and forth. Within a week, I told the chief psychiatrist, Dr Letomondia, that I wanted to discharge myself.

He looked through my notes. 'It says here that when you arrived at Ashurst you cried for a whole month, Norman.'

I felt anxious, wondering how he could agree to let me go when I was such a wreck, but Dr Letomondia was smiling kindly. 'Perhaps that was a good thing for the other patients to see. You were releasing so much hurt and pain.'

I felt huge relief to hear to him say that. He seemed to understand that I had felt completely broken after losing my trust in Van, and my hopes of achieving success as a rider.

Then he said, 'In my opinion, there is absolutely nothing wrong with you, Norman. Nothing that life and a job to get you back on your feet won't cure. So long as you keep taking your pills, I'm happy for you to discharge yourself. But you will need someone stable and caring to support you. What about your family?'

I told him I couldn't face going back to my mother. I hadn't been in touch with her for a long time, and she didn't know I had been in the clinic. She would be so dismissive and disapproving when she found out. She wouldn't understand how fragile I was after being in the clinic and going through such hell with Jane and Brian. 'I'm just too vulnerable to see my mother,' I said.

'There must be someone.' Dr Letomondia was leafing through my notes, which had been handed over. 'What about this Thorpe person you spoke about when you were at Ashurst? The MP?' he asked. 'If you can't go back to your family, then you should go to this man Jeremy Thorpe.'

This might seem an odd suggestion now, but Dr Letomondia knew I needed support and had the same assumption as most people did in those days that a politician such as Jeremy Thorpe was a pillar of society, and, since I had no family or other friends, he would have thought it was a good option for me. When he said this I felt a sudden rush of emotion, part relief, part fear. I'd wanted to contact Jeremy Thorpe for months and now a psychiatric consultant was actually advising me to do so. Surely I must take his advice.

I agreed to contact Jeremy Thorpe, and Dr Letomondia gave me permission to discharge myself. I collected my few belongings and headed for Foxholes, and an emotional reunion with Mrs Tish. It felt very awkward to see the Horsman Baileys again. They were sweet to me and asked me to stay but I didn't want to. Kind as they were, they seemed bewildered and shocked by what had happened to me over the last months. I wanted to move on with my life and knew I couldn't go back. I told them I was going to London and explained that I was meeting an MP, who would help me get back on my feet, which greatly reassured them.

Mrs Tish and I caught the bus into Oxford so we could take the train to London. I looked out of the window as we drove into the city, clutching my little dog and gazing at the trees, their leaves golden in the autumn sunshine. The grass looked so green against the grey walls of the colleges, and there were swans floating regally on the Cherwell. Or was it the Isis? I could never work out which was which of those famous Oxford rivers. 'Cherwell? Isis? Mental crisis!' I muttered to Mrs Tish, and found myself smiling at the little haiku I had just invented. It made me smile, but did nothing to dispel my trepidation about the step I was about to take.

CHAPTER FIVE

Mr Jeremy Thorpe, MP

ON THE AFTERNOON of 8 November 1961, I arrived in London and headed straight to the Houses of Parliament. With Mrs Tish trotting beside me and my small bag of clothes in my hand, I walked down Whitehall, past Downing Street, through Parliament Square and into the Palace of Westminster. As I looked up at the vast building, I felt a sudden fear. Here I was, about to ask for a man I had met only once, and several months ago. Would he even remember me? Quaking in my shoes, I went into St Stephen's Hall – also known as the Lobby. Constituents could go there to bring issues to the attention of Members of Parliament. The policeman at the desk looked me up and down, and said, 'You can't bring your dog in, sir.'

My heart sank, but I remembered passing some big glass doors at the top of Whitehall, which formed the entrance to the Anti-Vivisection League. Surely there must be an animal-lover there who would look after Mrs Tish. I hurried back and found a kind person who was only too happy to mind my little dog.

When I returned, the policeman asked who I had come to see. 'Jeremy Thorpe,' I said.

'Is he expecting you?' the policeman asked.

'No, I don't have an appointment,' I said, wondering whether I would be turned away.

'Is he your MP?' he asked.

'No, it's a personal visit,' I replied, trying to hold my nerve.

The policeman handed me a green card to fill in with my details, so after my name, under 'nature of business', I wrote 'personal and private'. I gave the card back to the policeman and went to sit on one of the dark green leather benches near the entrance of the corridor to the House of Lords. It was a remarkable experience to be waiting there, at the core of the country's government. Groups of tourists trooped around the beautiful mosaic floor and busy secretaries clutching bundles of letters hurried to the tiny Lobby post office. I spotted former prime minister Clement Attlee making his way slowly past me. He was very old, and looked like a small sad eagle that might topple from its perch at any moment.

With a sudden feeling of exhaustion after the journey and all the drama of the previous few months, I slipped into a daze, watching as people came and went.

'Norman!' Suddenly Mr Thorpe was standing in front of me, his arms spread wide in a dramatic gesture of welcome.

Startled, I looked up at him.

'Oh – don't jump!' he exclaimed, smiling broadly. 'So, you've come! How are you, dear boy?' he asked.

I couldn't speak. It felt so surreal, that I should be there, asking this high-powered, eloquent stranger for help with my insignificant little life. He came to sit beside me and asked me if I was all right.

'Yes,' I managed, though I didn't convince even myself.

At once he stood up. 'Come with me,' he said, beckoning me to follow.

Mr Thorpe took off at a rate of knots and I followed him down interminable stairs to an interview room, where he closed the door and stood facing me. 'You look absolutely wretched. What on earth is wrong?' He was frowning in concern.

I told him about Van. About how terrible everything had been, and how unhappy I was. It was hard to get the words out. I couldn't help stammering. It seemed wrong to be talking about his friend in this way but Mr Thorpe listened. He seemed very concerned and sympathetic, his eyes fixed kindly and intently on me. I tried to make it clear that I was not being a telltale, I was just trying to make sense of the whole sorry mess of problems that had built up for me. And I had no one else to turn to. When I had finished, Mr Thorpe said, 'I'm so glad you've come to get help.'

Then I told him about the clinic. About Jane and Brian and the nightmare of their suicide attempts. Mr Thorpe looked shocked. 'This has been a dreadful, dreadful time for you.' He put his arm round me in a warm, friendly gesture. 'But you mustn't worry. I will sort things out for you. Come back at five thirty and we'll talk again.'

'Thank you so much, Mr Thorpe,' I said.

'Call me Jeremy, I insist,' he replied, smiling broadly and patting me on the back.

I felt so much lighter. Someone respected – a Member of Parliament, right in the midst of the political scene – believed me and was going to help me. Jeremy Thorpe was exceptionally and effortlessly charismatic. At thirty-two, he had already been an MP for North Devon for two years. Many of his supporters believed he had propelled the Liberals forward, putting them on the map to compete against the Conservatives. He was considered diligent and loyal, promoting local issues and championing freedom from colonial and minority rule. I had followed politics through newspapers and the wireless and was well aware of his reputation. He was showing me kindness and compassion, really seeming to care. I thought back to Dr Letomondia advising me to see him, and to the nurse's last words to me, telling me everything would work out. I felt sure they had both been right.

We went back to the Lobby, where Jeremy suggested that I collect Mrs Tish, then leave her in the care of the policeman at the door. 'I'll wait for you here,' he said.

I found myself smiling at people as I walked back up Whitehall, a new strength and energy in my step. I was almost in a state of elation. Perhaps at last my life would start on a new course.

Back at the Anti-Vivisection League, Mrs Tish leaped all over me with joy. I wasn't too sure about leaving her with the policeman at the entrance to the House of Commons. Jeremy was waiting in the Lobby.

'Now, I know it says no dogs but there is an exception,' he said, to me and the policeman at the desk, smiling with a glint of mischief in his eyes. 'King Charles spaniels are allowed in, because Charles the Second insisted that his little dogs should accompany him when he was at the Houses of Parliament, so your dog . . . What's its name?'

'Mrs Tish,' I said.

'Yes, well, I'm sure Mrs Tish can stay with this kind police officer until we get back.'

The officer nodded and took her.

I liked Jeremy very much. He emitted a positive energy that was infectious. I followed him along the corridors to the Strangers' and Peers' Gallery, from where I watched him talking to a full-faced, imposing gentleman I recognised from the newspapers as the Tory home secretary, R. A. 'Rab' Butler. At one moment Jeremy looked up, smiled at me, and waved. It was exhilarating – but almost unreal that this should be happening to me. Jeremy finished his conversation with Rab Butler and raised his arm in farewell. He swept out, beckoning me to go down and join him with his arm flung even higher in a gesture that was to become very familiar.

It was raining as we ran over the wet cobblestones of the Members' car park to Jeremy's car. Such an impressive vehicle – a Sunbeam Rapier – with running boards and a House of Commons badge on the bonnet. The interior smelt strongly of leather. A policeman held up the traffic as we left and Jeremy drove to the Lobby entrance for me to collect Mrs Tish. I felt proud to be seen with him. As I greeted the policeman, people looked at me as if I, too, were someone important. I climbed back into the Rapier with Mrs Tish, and we drove through busy streets to the Embankment.

'What's going to happen now?' I asked.

Jeremy stopped the car. He gave me a serious look. 'I have to go and see some friends in Dulwich. And then I'm taking you home to Surrey with me. I've telephoned my mother and she's expecting you. To make things simpler, I've told her you're from Colchester and are on the camera crew of the film I'm about to make in Malta. I'll be there for a few weeks but I will set you up before I go.'

My stomach dropped with shock. 'But why do I have to lie?' I asked. Lying to his mother seemed a pretty low thing to do. I couldn't understand why it was necessary and felt suddenly uncomfortable.

'It's easier than long explanations,' he said brusquely.

We drove on. What did he mean by 'make things simpler'? And why was there a need for this deception with his mother? It didn't feel right that he was asking me to pretend to be someone completely different and I really didn't want to go along with it but I didn't know what else to do.

In Dulwich, we arrived at a flat and rang the bell. A man came to the door and ushered us into a sitting room, where another man was standing at the window. He was not very tall, about thirty years old, with fair hair.

'This is Tony,' Jeremy said.

Tony was very good-looking, with a lean, rakish face. As he walked towards us I noticed he had a slight limp. There was something familiar about him, and I suddenly realised that this was Antony Armstrong-Jones – Lord Snowdon, Princess Margaret's husband. I couldn't believe I was there, in the private company of a member of the Royal Family and a Member of Parliament.

'This is Norman,' Jeremy continued. 'I want you to keep an eye on him while I am away. Look after him. Ring him sometimes. I'll give you the number when I've got somewhere sorted for him in London.'

Tony smiled. 'I'd be pleased to,' he said.

Although he was friendly and polite, I felt uneasy. Why was Lord Snowdon being asked to keep an eye on me? And what was he doing in this flat in Dulwich? At the time, I knew nothing of the rumours that he was bisexual and had had many affairs and liaisons with men. The other men in the flat were huddled together in a group, laughing and chatting in a flamboyant, extrovert way. Now I might instantly recognise them as gay and describe them as camp, but back then I didn't even know those words. They just seemed like people who felt free in each other's company, with no one looking on or judging them, happy to be themselves in their own safe space. Tony was perfectly charming and very attentive to me. He couldn't have been nicer, which helped me to feel more relaxed, although he never did call while Jeremy was away.

Drinks were handed round and then we left and drove down to Stonewalls, an impressive house in Oxted, where Jeremy lived in a ground-floor flat with his mother, Ursula. As we turned onto the drive, Jeremy said, 'Don't forget what I told you. You are a cameraman. Your name is Peter.' He gave me a fake surname, too, but I've forgotten what it was. 'You live in Colchester,' Jeremy added.

'I don't like to lie. Your mother would be hurt if she found out. Please, why do we have to do this?' I stammered.

'It's too late now. Stick to the original plan!' Jeremy said, with a hint of force as he swung the Rapier up the drive and parked in front of the house.

His mother met us in the hall. 'Supper will soon be ready,' she said. She was perfectly pleasant, but as our eyes met, a chilly feeling came over me and I sensed she didn't like me. She was austere, looking at me unsmilingly through her spectacles, but was quite different when she spoke to Jeremy. 'Come in by the fire. Have a drink, Jay. You look washed out.'

He hugged her and made himself busy pouring sherry for us and gathering up newspaper cuttings from the top of the piano that Mrs Thorpe had saved for him. Jeremy skimmed through these as he and his mother drank and chatted, and I sat, silent and tense, awkwardly taking sips from the tiny sherry glass with Mrs Tish at my feet. Suddenly Mrs Thorpe said, 'Do get your friend to sign the visitors' book.' She turned to me. 'You must sign the visitors' book, dear.'

My heart sank. I was supposed to be Peter So-and-so, I had got that. But as for Colchester? I'd never heard of it. Mrs Thorpe left the room to get the book, and Jeremy glanced at me.

'Where's Colchester?' I whispered.

'Essex!' he hissed.

Mrs Thorpe returned, and I scribbled a totally fictitious entry in the visitors' book.

We ate supper sitting on the sofas. It was boiled eggs with soldiers, which didn't do much to soak up the alcohol from all I'd drunk in Dulwich and the glasses of sherry when we arrived. The conversation was desultory, just the murmurs and abbreviated sentences that are habitual between close family members. It was clear that Mrs Thorpe absolutely adored her son.

Exhausted after the long, emotional day, I could make no sense of what they were saying, and my head was beginning to spin. I asked if I might go to bed, and Mrs Thorpe took me across to my room.

The flat was a rather odd place. The reception rooms were

very large, but the bedrooms felt cramped. My room was warm and comfortable, but it was tiny, and it felt peculiar and unreal to be in someone else's house. Tired as I was, I knew I would have trouble sleeping so I took some pills – Tuinal and Librium – then went to the bathroom to wash.

As I came out Jeremy called from his bedroom to ask if I had everything I needed. 'Are you going to sleep all right?' he asked.

'I expect so,' I said, trying to be polite.

'Let me get you something to read.' He came to the door and handed me a book he said he thought I'd enjoy. It was called *Giovanni's Room*, by James Baldwin. 'Don't worry about your problems,' he said. 'Everything is going to be all right.'

As I got into bed and waited for the pills to take effect, I started reading the book, which was about a homosexual relationship between two men. Despite my tiredness, I found myself drawn into a moving account of the turmoil in a young man's emotions as he tried to discover himself. I had no idea that this story of homosexual love might be relevant to my own future. Neither did it occur to me to wonder why Jeremy had given it to me or even had it in his possession. I read on until the pills kicked in and I began to feel very drowsy.

A knock on my door brought me sharply back to wakefulness. The door opened, and Jeremy, clad in a dressing-gown, came in. He was carrying a towel, and I thought he must be on his way back from the bathroom.

'Are you all right?' He spoke softly.

We hadn't talked about what he was going to do to help with my problems, and I assumed this was why he had come to my room.

'I'm very worried,' I said, as everything came flooding back to me. 'I don't know what's going to happen to me. What's going to happen in my life?'

Jeremy sat beside me on the bed. 'I want you to know that, from now on, you are safe. You are not to worry about Van, about money, about going back to that awful clinic, or anything. Poor frightened rabbit. That's what you look like. But you need never worry again, poor Bunny.' He put his arm around me and drew me close.

I was so full of pent-up emotion and anxiety that this tender gesture somehow released all of my unhappiness and I burst into tears. Jeremy slipped out of his dressing-gown and climbed right into the bed wearing just his pyjamas. He began stroking me gently and comforting me. It was a strange experience, to be so physically close to him under the bedcovers. No one had ever comforted me like that before. It felt so good to be cared for by him.

But then Jeremy's embrace became tighter. He turned me over onto my front and I felt him pull down his pyjama bottoms and start rubbing something onto his penis. Before I knew it, he was inside my body, penetrating me with a savage sexual need. It was extremely painful. It felt almost as if he were cutting into me with a knife. I thought he might be going to kill me, and I struggled, but he held me down with great force as he thrust violently into my body. It hurt so much I was gasping with pain.

'Sssh! My mother!' Jeremy whispered, touching the wall by the bed.

I was in such agony I don't know how I didn't scream but I really didn't want Mrs Thorpe, who was lying in bed on the other side of the wall, to hear what was going on. So, I just bit the pillow in complete shock at what Jeremy was doing to me.

As abruptly as it had begun, the horror was over. Jeremy got off me and wiped himself with the towel. I was sobbing but he said nothing, put a finger to his lips and left the room. I lay there, weeping, wishing that the pain would stop. The brutal sex had taken me completely by surprise. I'd never thought of penetration taking place between two men. I didn't even know it happened. When Brian had got into bed with me in Oxford, it had just been drunken fumbling and sloppy attempts to kiss me, which I had batted off. How could I have been so childishly naïve? I can only say that those were very different times. The clues about Jeremy's sexuality had been there for me to see when he came to visit Van, but I just didn't put two and two together when he gave me his card and invited me to contact him. I had had only the utmost respect for Jeremy Thorpe, never imagining someone like him would do anything illicit or illegal. Above all, he had seemed so friendly and so caring when I arrived in London, as if he had my best interests at heart. I'd begun to feel uncomfortable when he asked me to lie about my name but what could I do? With no transport and no money, I was trapped at his mother's house, a vulnerable young man who had just come out of a psychiatric hospital, exhausted, utterly alone, and befuddled by the cocktail of prescription drugs I was taking.

Mrs Tish heard me crying and crept out from the corner where she had been hiding. I felt so upset that she had witnessed the horrible thing that had just been done to me.

She was shaking, clearly terrified. I took her into my bed and held her tight, comforting both her and myself. Eventually the pills came to my aid, and I slept. It was a brief respite. I woke in the middle of the night to find Jeremy standing over the bed, and once again I was subjected to the agonising ordeal of penetration. I desperately wanted him to stop, but when I tried to struggle, he held me down harder and seemed to become more excited. Every now and then he would whisper, 'Sssh, it's all right!' in a soothing tone, but I think he was just trying to keep me quiet because of his mother.

Years later, at the Old Bailey trial, the courtroom rocked with laughter when I said it had felt as if Jeremy was trying to cut me in half. I don't think, today, that anyone would laugh. What happened to me was rape. There was no discussion beforehand. I was forced into non-consensual, illegal, agonising sex by a man in a position of considerable power and influence whom I thought had been trying to help me.

I wondered whether Jeremy assumed I was gay and therefore thought I would be expecting what he did to me, as if that would somehow make what he did all right. I don't think that was the case. I think he could tell that I was young for my age, just a very innocent country boy. He knew that I was in a fragile mental state, fresh out of hospital and full of very strong drugs. Because of this, he was able to take advantage of me, knowing I would be too weak to fight back and too respectful of his prestige and power as an MP to speak out about what happened.

As soon as Jeremy had climaxed and wiped himself off, he made a speedy departure, leaving me curled up in tears. I got up and went to the lavatory, where, horrified to find traces of blood on my pyjamas, I was violently sick. I ran a bath, trying to wash away the mess, the distress and the guilt. A dark, cloying despair took hold of me. Jeremy had been so kind earlier. I'd felt so safe in his arms, able to let go and cry. Why had he suddenly changed into a monster?

As morning broke, Jeremy walked through my bedroom door a third time and I held my breath in fear. 'Breakfast will be ready soon. How would you like your eggs?' he said, smiling breezily as if nothing had happened. I was so confused, I couldn't speak. He said not to worry and left.

Still in pain, I got up and went outside into the garden, avoiding Jeremy and his mother, who were talking in the kitchen. It was a claustrophobic place, that garden. Terraced, and with high stone walls all around it, which presumably the house was named after. I felt so trapped. A numbing, disabling panic rushed through me. I wanted to leave, but there was no place for me to escape to, except my mother's house. After the night before, the thought of seeing her made me feel ill. Jeremy's behaviour had brought back to me those horrid times with her in the bathroom, as well as the day I had caught her in bed with Phil. She was the last person I wanted to see.

At breakfast, Mrs Thorpe gave me a blank look. I felt horribly ashamed, wondering whether she was aware of what had happened. She asked where my luggage was, as if suspicious. I stammered, wondering what to say, but Jeremy stepped in, telling her my bags were at the air terminal. Then she asked me whether I had been to Malta before. Jeremy spoke for me: 'Oh, yes. He's very good at his job.'

I, who had never held a camera in my life, quailed at the

thought of having to face more questions, but Mrs Thorpe had tired of the subject and began talking about Jeremy's sister Camilla. I was close to tears and Jeremy must have noticed. He got up from the table. 'We'd better go now. Thanks, Urs.'

'Yes, you had. I'm on the bench today,' Mrs Thorpe replied.

'I didn't notice a dog,' I blurted, misinterpreting what she had said. The 'bench' I was most familiar with was to be found at a dog show. The dogs were lifted onto it for the judges to inspect.

Mrs Thorpe frowned. 'Dog? What do you mean? I'm a justice of the peace.'

I quailed again and Jeremy ushered me to the door.

'Well, safe journey, Jay dear.' Mrs Thorpe turned to me with a bland little smile. 'Goodbye. Do make sure he doesn't overwork, won't you, dear?'

She followed us out to the car and said, with cold politeness, 'Do come again, Peter. It's been a great pleasure having you.'

It seems obvious now that she must have known of her son's proclivities, and why he had brought me home. I'm sure, looking back, that he must have taken other young men home to have sex with them. But the conventions of that time and of her class, and also the illegality of the situation, meant this could never be acknowledged.

I was in a daze as Jeremy drove off towards London. He ignored me, focusing intently on the road ahead. Along the way, we picked up Jennifer King, his secretary, and she took over the driving. Jeremy joined me in the back seat. I waited for him to say something, but he just pulled a pile of papers out of his briefcase and studied them in silence.

Once we arrived in London, Jeremy suddenly became all warmth again, instructing me to go to Sloane Square Underground station. 'About three hundred yards down the King's Road there's a tobacconist with a board that has notices of rooms to let. You can get a place to live while I'm away in Malta, and when I'm back we'll find you a permanent base. Don't worry about the rent. I'll take care of that,' he said. Then he left for the Houses of Parliament, telling me to meet him later in the day at a Lyons Corner House near Westminster Bridge.

I stood on the road looking at the car driving away. I could have escaped and never seen Jeremy again but I still had nowhere to go. I was so shattered, on a sort of numb auto-pilot from exhaustion and the effects of my medication, and Jeremy had told me he would look after me. Now he seemed to be doing just that. He was so positive, so strong, so energetic, it just seemed easiest to go along with his instructions. I blocked out the horror of the night before. I seemed to have no other option but to visit the King's Road, where I saw a room advertised at 21 Draycott Place. Then I wandered around for a while before heading to the Corner House near the Houses of Parliament, where a smell of hot tinned tomato soup lingered in the air. Jeremy came to meet me, all smiles, and ordered for us. I told him about the room.

'Good. I'll give you a cheque. No, wait a moment, cash would be better.' He handed me some money. 'That's for the rent. And I want you to go to Gieves, on Savile Row,' he said. 'Get yourself any clothes you want. And shoes. Charge them to my account. Mr Mackintosh will deal with everything for you.'

I couldn't believe this was the same person as last night.

He seemed completely focused on helping me. Shaky and disoriented as I was, I felt so grateful, and hoped this was how things would continue.

The room at 21 Draycott Place was small and drab, but the landlady, Mrs Flood, had a dear little dachshund called Pandora and said she didn't mind me keeping Mrs Tish in the room. She seemed very impressed when Jeremy Thorpe, MP, turned up later that evening.

'Not exactly the Ritz,' he said, looking round the room. 'But it will do. Somewhere to come and be alone,' he said, before immediately initiating another session of brutal penetration. I was still sore from the night before, but I knew I wasn't strong enough to fight him off. And if I did protest, what would happen? Would he be angry and throw me out of the room onto the street? I didn't want that. I had nowhere to go, and I knew I couldn't have coped. I just lay there, in awful pain, and tried to pretend it wasn't happening. Just like before, when it was over, Jeremy behaved as if nothing had happened.

'I'm sad I have to go,' he said, 'but that's how it must be.' He gave me an envelope with more money in it. 'That should last until I return in ten days. If all else fails, Jennifer will give you more.'

He must have noticed how miserable I was, but he ignored it and I couldn't work out whether he was pretending nothing had happened or if in his mind everything was perfectly fine.

'I wish there were more time. I'll write to you. I'll send a postcard . . . Oh, now don't be a silly Bunny!' he said, affectionately.

I hated him calling me that. It felt so demeaning, but what could I say? I felt I was nothing, such a lesser being next to this successful, important man, who was so much older and wiser than me and who was doing so much to help me. When I looked at him blankly, he laughed and leaned in to give me a kiss on the lips. Another new experience, which I found very unpleasant. 'You are so ignorant of love. Aren't you?' Jeremy whispered.

Was this love? If so, it was nothing like I had imagined. I felt terribly confused. He gave me another kiss, then put his arms around me and gave me a warm, affectionate hug. For that one moment I felt safe. His arms seemed so strong and protective around me. I loved the sensation of being cared for, that all his power and energy were on my side. It was what I craved, what I needed.

When he left, I watched from the window as he got into the car and drove away, and I held on to the feeling of warmth that the hug had given me. In spite of the horrible things he had done to me, I felt he genuinely cared and would look after me. As the Rapier disappeared around a corner, I turned back into the room and began rearranging things to try to make it feel a bit more welcoming.

CHAPTER SIX

No Such Thing
as a Free Lunch

FOR THE DAYS that Jeremy was away, I wandered around the streets, not knowing what to do or where to go. London felt very formal, people walking briskly and purposefully past while I felt lost and aimless. In 1961, London still had one foot in the post-war years of austerity and rationing. There were still bomb sites – gaps of rough ground covered with rubble and weeds where homes and offices had succumbed to the Blitz. Jeans, soon to become ubiquitous, were still considered fit only for cowboys in the early sixties. Women wore tweed skirts, twinsets and headscarves. Men who worked in the City wore bowler hats and dark suits, the trousers of which sometimes had a thin stripe. Politicians and men of Jeremy's ilk wore similar suits, often with the addition of a black waistcoat, which added to the air of formality and strict social etiquette.

Out walking near my room, I was approached by a man. In his thirties and very well groomed, he stood out from the dowdy pedestrians in his exquisitely cut grey suit. With a dazzling smile, he said, 'Hello! I haven't seen you before. Where do you live?'

'I'm sorry?' I said, not used to strangers coming up to me like that.

'Are you all on your own? You seem a bit down. Look, why don't you come and have a coffee at my flat? It's not far,' the man said.

He seemed friendly, and, in the slightly bemused and foggy state that came with the heavy doses of medication I was taking, there seemed no harm in taking up his offer of a coffee, especially since I had nothing else to do.

I had barely walked in through the door when, without even speaking a word to me, the man pushed me up against the wall and tried to get intimate. He was much slighter than Jeremy, and I found it easy to push him away. Horrified, I ran out of the flat.

Back in my little room, my mind swam with confusion and doubt. The man's behaviour might well have been normal within the secretive gay community of London. Perhaps there were signals, of which I knew nothing, that passed between men on the street, who might then go back to someone's home for a sexual liaison. Perhaps when I had looked at his suit, returned his smile and made eye contact with him, I had inadvertently given him the wrong message. But I was completely innocent. I lay on my bed feeling shaken, my confusion increasing. What was this world I had come into? This life, where people who seemed so charming, so respectable, just wanted to have sex with me?

My small, empty room only emphasised how completely lost I felt. I was used to open countryside, to getting up at the crack of dawn to do farm work or look after horses and feeling physically tired after a long day. Now I was confined as I had been in the clinic, except that here I was alone. I sat on the single bed in mute despair, just as I'd done in the remand centre when my mother had turned her back on me. I felt trapped in a way that was both familiar and distinctively new. It was more complicated this time. My mind flashed back to the feeling of elation when Jeremy had greeted me so warmly, then the horror of being raped, but every time I thought about all this I came to the same conclusion: I didn't know what else to do. I didn't know who else to turn to. I felt as though, because Jeremy had taken charge of my life, he *was* in charge. He had made decisions for me, and I had let him because I knew of no alternative.

I took more pills and told myself I was fine. After all, I was better off than Brian and Jane from the clinic. Dr Letomondia had told me clearly to seek help from Mr Thorpe. 'We should feel lucky we're in this position at all,' I said to Mrs Tish, stroking her to ease my anxiety.

Following Jeremy's instruction I went, with some trepidation, to Gieves on Bond Street. I didn't really want to but my shoes were worn out and I didn't have enough clothes to put on clean, fresh things every day. When I got to Bond Street I lingered outside for some time. Through the window I could see a grey-haired man, and wondered if he might be Mr Mackintosh. He was, as I discovered when I finally plucked up the courage to go in. He quickly put me at ease. 'Ah, Mr Josiffe, Mr Thorpe has telephoned about you. I am to give you whatever you require,' he said. 'All you need to do is sign for it.'

I didn't want to be greedy, so I chose some shoes, shirts and underwear. I'd noticed that Jeremy had worn an expensive brand of underpants and vests, in a very fine cotton Aertex with tiny holes in the fabric. I chose the same brand – Sunspel. I remembered how Jeremy had told me, very clearly, that I must get whatever I wanted. I noticed a pair of rose-pink pyjamas, which were quite wonderful. My old pyjamas were tatty and worn, so I chose those silk ones, too. I had never owned anything so lovely. As I signed the invoice and headed back to Draycott Place with several carrier bags, I felt spoiled and special. No one had ever done anything so generous for me before. I slipped back into the fantasy of Jeremy as a caring friend, pushing away the thought that I might have to endure more of the rough, painful sex.

Jeremy's extravagant gesture in sending me to Gieves reminded me that I should feel fortunate and I tried to shake off the feeling of loneliness and uncertainty. I was relieved when, ten days after Jeremy had left for Malta, Mrs Flood knocked on the door to say a gentleman was on the telephone for me. Jeremy was back. I felt glad. I really wanted to see him again, to feel that strong, protective hug.

'Are you happy?' Jeremy asked, when I picked up the receiver to talk to him.

I said yes, but I also tried to tell him how odd it felt to be cooped up and how I missed the countryside and being with horses so much.

'But I want you to stay here, in London. I want to keep you safe. I'll see you this evening. We'll go out for a meal.' I could hear the smile in Jeremy's voice, and the fact that he wanted me to stay near him somehow cheered me up.

We went to the Reform Club. I'd never been anywhere quite so formal. The place was full of middle-aged and elderly men, all of them with an aura of authority and importance. When I visited the lavatory, I had to wash my hands alongside a number of these dignitaries and had a strong sense that they were looking down their noses at me. My sense of inferiority was somewhat mitigated by the Vichyssoise that was served up. This soup, I would learn, was the best thing about dining at the club, and on our many visits to dine there I always looked forward to it.

That first evening, when we had finished our meal, Lord Reith, the dour and very tall Scotsman who had been director-general of the BBC, came over to greet Jeremy. I'd only ever seen photographs of him, but now, being a friend of Jeremy's, he joined us at our table for a glass of port. They began talking about some matter at the Treasury, about which I knew nothing.

I sat quietly, looking around the room, until Lord Reith said, 'Our young friend doesn't seem very interested. Perhaps he should give his opinion.'

Jeremy jumped in quickly, 'Oh, this is my ward. He lives in the country and wouldn't have any opinion.'

This was the first time he described me, dismissively, as his ward. Another lie, which he repeated many times. Jeremy's manner towards me was reserved in front of Lord Reith and the other people in the club, but when we were alone in his car he became all warmth and animation. I loved this. It reminded me of his energy and enthusiasm when he had first met me at St Stephen's Hall. Back at Draycott Place he changed again, becoming suddenly distant and businesslike. Right away, he wanted sex with me. It didn't hurt quite so much this time, but although I hated it, I didn't even think about resisting now. It seemed to be something I would have to endure if he was going to be my friend and help me. Then he left.

That evening set the pattern for the next six weeks. During the week, Jeremy would see me four evenings out of five. When he finished work, he would drive to Draycott Place and toot the horn on his car. I would throw down the keys and he would let himself in and come up to have sex with me. I never initiated this, and he never asked if I would like to, or if I minded. That was just how it was. I had been brought up to respect my elders and betters and never question them, so I didn't. Jeremy was eleven years older than me but the age gap somehow seemed much larger. I was a vulnerable medicated young man. He was an MP. How could I challenge him? Although I got used to the sex, I continued to loathe it. I hated the smell of his sweat, which was pungent after his long day in the House; he had nodules on his balls; and his breath smelt awful. It reeked of garlic and cigarettes. I never had any sexual feelings towards him, and after the painful penetration, which happened every time we were in my room, I would feel numb and dead, as if I was just a vessel for his pleasure. When he had satisfied himself, he would make a swift departure to drive home to Stonewalls, leaving me to lie in the dark and wonder who the real Jeremy Thorpe was. The kind, affectionate friend or the cold, sexually driven man who had just been with me on the bed?

Longing for a few moments of affection, I would ask if I could drive down to Battersea Bridge with him on his way home. He would park on the Embankment, and we would have a few moments together, talking, before I got out and walked home with Mrs Tish. But often he would ask me to fondle him sexually while we were parked and sometimes even while he was driving. This was less traumatic than the penetration, but I never enjoyed it. Even if I had liked Jeremy in that way, I was on so many prescription drugs that my libido was low. Also, I was terrified that someone might look into the car and see what we were up to. Especially if that person was a policeman. I could never forget that sexual intercourse between men was illegal. And it remained so until the Sexual Offences Act was passed on 27 July 1967.

We could both have ended up in prison if we were caught. Jeremy's political career would have been destroyed if he was found out, but he never asked me not to tell anyone about us. I suppose he just assumed that I wouldn't. He was undoubtedly fond of me, but I think he knew that, in me, he had found someone so damaged, so desperate for affection, that I could withstand anything. I was a far safer option than casual pick-ups and, despite my dislike of the sex, I was immensely proud that he trusted me with his most intimate secret.

I focused on the part of Jeremy that was caring. Sometimes, sitting close together in the car, or dining at a secluded table, he would be so affectionate. He would talk about how he'd like to have a farm in Devon, where we could live together, and where I might keep horses. It made me feel so happy to hear that he understood about the things I loved and really wanted to share them. In those private moments, the outside world seemed to slip away, and I forgot the doubt and unhappiness I felt about the way he was using me for sex, and the dismissive comments he made to his colleagues about me. It was so easy to believe him, to picture the perfect life we might have, as long as I firmly blocked out the sex. I think, in my youth and with my inexperience of the ways of the world, these shared moments of dreaming about the future made me begin to love Jeremy. We seemed so close then, and I really believed he shared my aspirations.

The only other person who I'd felt so connected to was Sarah. We had stayed in touch but her mental health had continued to deteriorate. She had undergone a leucotomy operation. This infamous neurosurgical treatment, also known as a lobotomy, severed connections in the brain's prefrontal cortex. At the time it was an accepted procedure for curing mental disorders. When she was in recovery at the Bethlem Royal Hospital in south London, Sarah had asked for me. With her parents in Australia, she had no one to visit her so when the hospital staff contacted me I rushed to see her.

When I arrived, Sarah was sitting listlessly in her room. Her head had been shaved at the front and a line of awful stitches ran across her skull. Her eyes were blank, and the personality I remembered seemed to have gone, a common side effect of this procedure. But she remembered me. She knew exactly who I was, so I did what I could to help. I visited several times, bought plants, and together we made a little garden. Sarah loved this and would work on it happily. I always felt very low and insecure when I returned to my lonely digs in Draycott Place, and would make an effort to focus on Jeremy, how stable and capable he was.

I kept in touch with Sarah, but her situation made me

relieved to be out of psychiatric care. This feeling was heightened when Jeremy invited me to go to the House of Commons. I'd sit in the gallery to watch him speak and feel incredibly proud of my connection with him. He was so talented, so charismatic, this influential politician who was making his mark as a Liberal MP. He made such an impact as he stood up to address the House, with passion and conviction. And he was my friend, this man. He was helping me – or so I believed – to move on to a new start in life. This made everything seem right, though I always struggled to reconcile the positive feelings with his uncontrollable need to possess me sexually.

Now I can see that, right from the beginning, Jeremy was a Jekyll and Hyde character. I was on the receiving end of affection and manipulation, of rare tenderness and frequent abuse, a very unhealthy combination. The moments of tenderness and connection bound me to him, making me believe he loved me and genuinely cared about me. He was very generous, but only when it suited him. Sometimes I had no money to buy food. Sometimes he would give me valuable gifts – like a pair of sapphire cufflinks, which he later accused me of stealing. This randomness had the effect, I think, of making me more anxious to please him and made me even more dependent on him. The way he liked to call me 'Bunny' and the dismissive comments he made about me to people like Lord Reith increased my feelings of low self-worth. I see now that this was about control.

Back then, I didn't think like that. My thoughts were muddled: my naïvety and vulnerability silenced my instincts. Still practising my Catholic faith, I believed that God was looking after me. I trusted that if I kept my faith everything would turn out all right in the end. But being involved in a homosexual relationship went completely against Catholic teachings – it was, and still is, considered a sin. I was riddled with guilt, shame and the fear of being discovered and arrested. These emotions fogged my own feelings, making it impossible to understand how I really felt – whether I loved Jeremy, whether I was homosexual, or whether I was just trapped in a relationship that I had never wanted or asked for. I would go to Mass every morning at the Catholic cathedral in Westminster and take Communion. In confession, I told the priest several times about Jeremy. He always listened before declaring that what we were doing was a mortal sin. He told me I must stop the relationship and say twelve Hail Marys to absolve myself. That was quite a lot of Hail Marys, but while I dutifully said them, the relationship continued.

When I visited Sarah, I confided in her because I knew I could trust her and that she wouldn't think badly of me. When I told her everything, she was shocked, saying she hated Jeremy and asking how I could care for a person like that, with those 'great big goo-goo eyes'. Jeremy didn't approve of me seeing her. Perhaps he was jealous or maybe he sensed my need to share the secret of our relationship with her, although Sarah was discreet.

A month went by and, with Jeremy's busy schedule, I was left struggling to fill my days. I would have liked to get a job and earn some money, but I needed my National Insurance cards to do this, and when I asked Jeremy for them he just said he was trying to sort it out. With nothing to do, I spent most of my time hanging around the Kardomah coffee bar on the King's Road with Mrs Tish. It was often crowded so I sat in the corner eking out a cup of coffee. One day a girl came up and asked if she could join me. She was wearing one of those rabbit-fur hats that were so popular in the 1960s, which I thought looked like a dead cat lying on her head. But she was friendly and outgoing and we got on well. We spent the afternoon chatting intently, making arrangements to meet up again. When she left, I noticed that one of her high-heeled shoes was missing a rubber tip on the heel, which gave her a disconcerting lop-sided gait as she walked away. She seemed blithely oblivious to it, which I found delightfully eccentric. I really liked her, and from then on we met up often at the café.

I continued to ask Jeremy about my National Insurance cards, and he assured me his secretary was handling the matter. I believed him, assuming he would either ask Van to send my old cards or organise new ones for me. I also assumed, since he said I mustn't worry and he would look after me, that while I wasn't working, he would be paying for the stamps to go on the current card, so I stopped thinking about it. I wanted so much to be cared for by him, and to care for him in return, but as the weeks went by, his Jekyll and Hyde behaviour continued. When he had sex with me he was always so forceful, so driven, as if an unbearable tension had built up in him and he was desperate for release. I longed to ask him to stop but I could never find the right moment to speak up. It was impossible to challenge Jeremy, so I carried on blocking that side of things away.

One weekend, Jeremy asked me if I'd like to visit

Stonewalls again. He went down early, and I travelled to Oxted on the train. Jeremy was waiting for me at the barrier, very distinguished in his coat with the astrakhan collar. It was a dark, foggy evening and there weren't many people at the station. He greeted me with a warm hug, almost as two men who were in a relationship might behave nowadays. I liked this, but also felt rather nervous in case someone saw us, but Jeremy seemed to enjoy the element of risk, and it was impossible to resist his enthusiasm. On one thing, though, I would not be moved. I told him if I was to be under Mrs Thorpe's roof again, she must know my real name. Jeremy laughed. 'Why not, if that's what you want?'

While I was unpacking in my room, he spoke to his mother. I would love to know exactly how the conversation went and whether he explained it was at his instigation I had pretended to be Peter the cameraman on my first visit. Or did he tell her I was responsible for the lie? Was he in some way trying to show her that he was fond of me and that I was an important person in his life? I cannot guess but when I went down, Mrs Thorpe offered me a drink and asked me to sign the visitors' book again and correct the first entry. Leaving the address blank, I just wrote 'Norman Lianche Josiffe' in the book. I had started using 'Lianche' – a Frenchified version of Lynch, my mother's maiden name – to make my name sound more sophisticated. Being with Jeremy and sometimes moving in exalted circles made me feel insecure about my relatively humble origins.

We went out to eat in nearby Godalming and Mrs Thorpe was pleasant to me over dinner, though sometimes I'd catch her looking at me as if to say, 'I really don't like you, but my son does, and I'll grin and bear it because I don't want to lose him.' Those cold looks sent a shiver down my spine. I worried that she knew about the sex. I'm sure she did. Mothers know things about their sons. Later she always denied any knowledge of it.

As the Christmas of 1961 drew near, none of my family members invited me to join them, not that I would have wanted to take them up on an invitation. Instead Jeremy, who was going to spend the festive period in Barnstaple, promised to fix it for me to join him there by arranging for me to stay with his friend Jimmy Collier and his wife Mary. Jimmy was a prospective Liberal candidate and lived in Devon. One night Jeremy took me to meet the Colliers at a club in Mayfair. He told them I was a family friend who'd been ill with a nervous breakdown and asked if they would have me to stay over Christmas. They agreed warmly. It was another little lie, and it all felt rather odd, but the Colliers were lovely, and I was grateful for their acceptance of me. Jeremy stayed with me at Draycott Place that night. He didn't want sex right away, just held me in the most affectionate and tender way as he talked about his plans. 'There's a house in Devon I'm thinking about buying. It's got stables so you would like it,' he said, describing the rest of the set-up, and painting a picture of what I had always dreamed of. Then he talked at length about his ambitions to succeed his beloved Jo Grimond – whom he affectionately referred to as 'mein Führer' – as leader of the Liberal Party, opening up to me in a way he never had before. I felt he loved me. But then the inevitable sex. I wanted to cry out and tell him to stop, but, as usual, I bit my tongue and kept quiet.

Just before I left London, I paid a visit to the Kardomah to see my friend with the fur hat, whom I'd been meeting up with regularly. We swapped cards and talked about what we were doing for Christmas. Somehow Jeremy's name slipped out. She was visibly shocked. 'I know Jeremy. We've been going to dances for some time,' she said.

I didn't tell her anything about the nature of my relationship with him, and pretended I didn't know him all that well. She explained that she liked him and thought they might have a future together, which made me feel sorry for her: I couldn't see that her feelings were reciprocated. Jeremy wasn't interested in women. In fact, he'd told me that having sex with a woman was like making love to a cold rice pudding. He must have been using my friend as a 'beard', as the saying goes, so that he would look heterosexual. Voters seemed to prefer family men, not bachelors, and certainly not homosexuals.

Christmas with the Colliers was warm and friendly. Their house was decorated with Christmas trees and cards, and I loved feeling like a part of their cheerful family. I thought of my family and found myself wondering what my mother was doing and felt glad when Jeremy rang to say that he missed me. On Christmas Day, he arrived at the Colliers' for a late lunch and on Boxing Day we drove to Barnstaple to meet him for another big lunch in the hotel. Mrs Thorpe was there too but Jeremy kept his attention on me, chatting away and touching my arm. I felt uncomfortable with him doing this in front of her and the Colliers. In those days people didn't really show effusive affection, things were much more formal, but he was in a jovial mood. After the proprietor had welcomed us, Jeremy set about impersonating her. She was very proud to have him staying in the hotel and would put on a refined voice when talking to him. Once she was out of earshot Jeremy would pretend to be her, saying, 'Oh, Mr Thorpe, Mrs Thorpe! Are you all having a good time?' He had her down to a T and everyone fell about in stitches. When he was in a mood like that, his energy was infectious.

As we were about to sit down to eat, Jeremy said, 'Oh, before we start, I've bought some shirts for you, Norman. Come upstairs and try them on.'

When we got to his room, there were no shirts. While his mother and the Colliers sat waiting to eat, he pushed me into the en-suite shower room and had sex with me. He hadn't done this to me for a few days, and it really hurt. Afterwards, I could feel blood running down and my mood plummeted. All the affection he had shown me before lunch and the love I had begun to feel for him back in London seemed cancelled out by his inconsiderate, selfish action. Maybe if I had enjoyed having sex with him, or maybe if homosexuality wasn't illegal, I wouldn't have minded. As it was, I felt dreadful, thinking of the others sitting downstairs around the table and knowing I would have to go down and face them. Jeremy had no such qualms. He just rushed out, telling me to hurry up. I stayed in that horrid shower room, with its ghastly eau-de-Nil tiles, trying to wash myself clean and, when I finally joined the others at the dinner table, sick with shame, I was terrified they might somehow be able to tell what had just happened.

Jeremy, of course, was suave and relaxed, laughing and joking with Jimmy. 'Ah, never fear, old chap. Come the next election, you'll be a candidate, all right!'

'And one day soon, you'll be Party leader!' Jimmy said to Jeremy.

CHAPTER SEVEN

A Proposal and a Confession

AFTER CHRISTMAS, I stayed on with the Colliers, helping Jimmy with his constituency work. I went out with him to do some door-to-door canvassing for the Liberal Party. The next weekend, Jeremy returned to Barnstaple and leaped on me in that awful bathroom. This time I fainted, which, I think, gave him some cause for concern, although he wasn't particularly nice to me when I came round and seemed rather annoyed.

When I returned to my little room at Draycott Place in mid-January, I felt more confused and numb than ever, and wondered where 1962 would take me. Every day I ended up walking aimlessly with Mrs Tish, or whiled away the hours at the Kardomah. Most evenings Jeremy would appear, tooting the horn and coming up for sex. His career at that time was going from strength to strength. He was busy working out a strategy to target selected constituencies, and by March 1962, the Liberals had succeeded in winning the traditionally Conservative constituency of Orpington. Jeremy's ultimate ambition, which he worked tirelessly to achieve, was to gain a Liberal majority in each Tory stronghold, one by one. When I mentioned I wanted to find work and asked after my National Insurance cards again, he just told me he was still working on getting them back from Van. Knowing he was so preoccupied, I carried on waiting, without realising that I was slipping into a complete limbo. I was still heavily medicated, taking pills throughout the day. It seemed I lived my life as a part of Jeremy's, and I felt I had no direction of my own.

Another couple of weeks went by, and then there was a knock at my door. I opened it to see Jane, swathed in a pale blue dressing-gown. I hadn't seen or heard from her since the day she had tried to kill herself at the flat in Oxford, the previous autumn. She told me she had been staying with her son Gilead in Notting Hill but had somehow found my address and persuaded Mrs Flood to rent her a room. A few days later, her son, who lived in London, sent over her clothes, which included a sheepskin coat. I knew how mentally unstable Jane was and worried about what she might be up to.

Remembering her unpredictable and manic behaviour in the past, I didn't want to get sucked into her world and did my best to avoid her. One evening, though, she wheedled her way into my room and tried to seduce me. I sent her packing. She was such a slight woman, very petite, and I had no problem evicting her from my room. Although she was my elder, she was not my better, and I knew how deranged she was. Very disgruntled, Jane left Draycott Place the next day, taking all her things with her and without paying any rent.

Two days later, I was visited by the police, who said Jane had accused me of stealing her sheepskin coat. This was ridiculous. She was so small I could never have fitted into any coat of hers, but the officers insisted they wanted to interview me. When I told Jeremy, he was very protective and insisted the interview take place at his Bridge Street office, as he was my 'guardian' and must be present.

The night before, I couldn't sleep for fear Jeremy's and my relationship would be discovered. As soon as I arrived at Bridge Street I told Jeremy we must stop what we were doing: 'It is illegal, it is immoral, and the police will definitely find out!'

He laughed at me. After what he had done at the hotel in Barnstaple, on Boxing Day, I knew he liked to live dangerously. Now, he pulled me towards him and kissed me. He was just unbuttoning my trousers when the police officers knocked on the door. We leaped apart. I was absolutely terrified, but Jeremy was blasé, and the officers sat down to conduct the interview.

As I was writing my statement, Jeremy had to leave for a division in the House of Commons. One of the officers remarked that I seemed much more relaxed and talkative in Jeremy's absence. In his report he said that I seemed 'rather a weak personality, apparently labouring under considerable mental strain and completely dominated by Mr Thorpe . . .' I'm sure I did look strained. I was almost passing out with the fear of discovery.

Once the police learned both Jane and I had mental-health problems, they decided not to pursue the case. Jeremy sent me back to the Colliers for a few weeks where I carried on helping Jimmy with his political work, handing out pamphlets and stuffing envelopes. I liked working with Jimmy. It was a relief to be away from Jeremy and I loved being in Devon, but I missed horses. Being in the countryside made me long to ride again, so I decided to put an advert in *Country Life*, with some slight exaggerations: 'Ex-public schoolboy, 21, wishes to live with a family and work on a farm. Skilled with horses. Former Badminton competitor. Willing to undertake any work. Pocket money only expected.' Jeremy insisted I gave his address, and I got quite a few replies, but it was clear that some of the respondents were expecting more than my equestrian expertise – they were hoping for sexual favours. One letter, from a man who owned a zoo, stated that he would love to share his place as 'I have always wanted a young man with me.'

Jeremy found these replies very amusing, presumably because he knew I was firmly under his control. Then I saw an opportunity that I really wanted to take up in France, studying dressage. Jeremy wrote to me about this, and enclosed one of the responses to my advertisement, which had included a photograph of the gentleman who was hoping to employ me.

This was the famous 'Bunnies' letter, which was later to be published in *The Sunday Times* just before the Old Bailey Trial. The tone was very warm and affectionate. Jeremy expressed great delight that I was feeling more optimistic about life and was looking forward to finding enjoyable work where I could keep my little companion Mrs Tish by my side. He assured me that whatever might happen, he and the Colliers were there to support me, almost like a family. With all this to look forward to, there would be no more psychiatric hospitals for me. Jeremy finished by saying that

'Bunnies' – referring to his nickname for me – would no doubt be heading off to France, and as a postscript he added that he missed me.

Sadly, the position in France came to nothing, and I began to sink into depression again.

By now I had been languishing for almost four months and I felt trapped. Several times I found myself in tears at the Colliers'. They found this difficult, and I didn't like to get upset in front of their children so I was pleased when Jeremy gave me the opportunity to canvass for him in his north Devon constituency. He introduced me to his agent, Lilian Prowse, and through several weeks in the spring of 1962 I was sent to Lynton and Lynmouth, where I stayed with a dear old lady and trudged around the two towns delivering leaflets. Then it was back to Barnstaple for more leaflets and off I went to Braunton and Saunton.

I found digs with a family, who were dyed-in-the-wool Liberals. Betty, the daughter, was about to get married to her young man and everyone in the family was happily pre-occupied by the news. I envied the couple. They were able to be completely open about their happiness, which made me think of Sarah and how the Horsman Baileys had dis-approved of our closeness. I missed her terribly, but it felt good to be helping Jeremy and the Liberal Party. There was a purpose in my life, even though I wasn't earning a proper wage. I enjoyed visiting the farms and houses and meeting the inhabitants. I spent a couple of weekends with Jeremy at the hotel in Barnstaple, but I saw less of him now. His career was on the up: he was being groomed for leadership of the Party and was adamant he would be successful. This time apart from him made me realise how claustrophobic and demeaning our relationship was. Although he was helping me, he hadn't given me my National Insurance cards so I was totally dependent on him and everything stayed on his terms.

In late March, Jeremy took me to visit Percy Browne, the Conservative MP for Torrington in north Devon. I had met him once before, when he, Jeremy and I had travelled together, leaning against piles of newspapers, in the guard's van of a crowded train to Devon. I'd just jumped on at Paddington to say goodbye to Jeremy, and the train left unexpectedly, so I'd had to stay on until Reading and get off there. Percy and Jeremy were laughing and joking, and it was great fun to be with them in that guard's van. It was lovely to meet Percy again. He was the epitome of an English gentleman. He loved horses and had ridden in the Grand National, and we found much to talk about. Jeremy, who didn't have a special love for animals, must have felt rather left out. When Percy mentioned that a Major Jocelyn Hambro and his family, who lived in Somerset, needed a groom to replace a girl who had been killed in a riding accident, he asked whether I'd be interested in helping out. I leaped at the chance, hoping it would give me independence from Jeremy and put me back on track for a career with horses.

The Hambros were a very wealthy banking family, who lived in a farmhouse with sprawling grounds at East Hollacombe on the edge of Exmoor. Jeremy dropped me off, having told Major Hambro that he was my guardian. Another lie that I would have to live with, but I didn't mind this time. It may have been my connection with a Member of Parliament that had got me the job, but I was delighted to be taken on by the Hambros. I felt slightly ambivalent, though, about being demoted to the position of groom. With my abilities as a rider I was perfectly capable of a more senior job, but it was wonderful to be looking after horses again, close to the wild landscape of Exmoor, which was perfect for riding out.

I was made to feel welcome. The Hambros invited me to all their social activities, including their ritual of washing and changing for a sickly concoction of gin and undiluted orange squash in a tiny cocktail glass every evening at six o'clock. I was invited to all the hunt balls and Pony Club events. I enjoyed doing the 'Twist', the latest craze for young people, and won several competitions for the best perform-ance of this energetic dance with my favourite partner, a local girl I sometimes rode out with.

Back in the early 1960s, the isolated farms and houses around where the Hambros lived were not on the national grid and they had to use a diesel generator for their electricity supply. One of my responsibilities was to start this on frosty mornings, and also in the evenings when it began to get dark. I had to prime the engine with diesel, pull the cord, and then keep holding on until it was chugging away. As the twilight thickened, I would hear other generators starting up from farm to farm across the moor. Sometimes when I was alone there in the dusk I would think of the girl groom who had worked for the Hambros before me.

The Hambros had bought, very cheaply, an ex-racehorse

called Suzie Wong to use as a hunter. She'd been 'de-nerved' – a procedure to prevent horses feeling any sensation in their feet and thus stop them going lame. This was supposed to prolong the mare's racing career, but she hadn't been successful on the track and ended up at Exeter sales. The day after the sale, the girl groom rode Suzie out and put her into a gallop on one of the long grass verges near East Hollacombe. The mare, who could feel nothing in her feet, stumbled, and broke her front cannon bones. She bravely tried to gallop on, lurching and staggering, and the groom fell off and hit her head, suffering a fatal injury. Suzie was later shot, and the girl was buried in the local churchyard. Nobody at the Hambros' seemed to dwell on this tragedy – but I couldn't help thinking of the sad fate of Suzie and her rider in those rare quiet moments when I wasn't kept busy with my work.

Mostly, though, I just felt so good to be back doing what I loved, out in the fresh air with horses again. After a couple of months, I lowered my doses of antidepressants and sleeping pills. I felt I didn't need them now. Jeremy some-times visited, collecting me and driving us to the Colliers' for lunch some weekends, but we saw a lot less of each other. I felt lighter, more independent, back in the countryside and stronger in myself. Gradually things became strained between Jeremy and me, perhaps because we were in less touch, or maybe Jeremy felt he was losing his grasp on me now I had started this new life. After one of these visits, we had just arrived back at the Hambros' house when Jeremy said, in an irritable tone, 'I can't stand your name.'

'What do you mean?' I asked.

'Josiffe!' he replied, with a sneer. 'Awful. It sounds Jewish. Like Joe Sieff – that Marks & Spencer's man.'

As he made this unpleasant anti-Semitic remark, we were looking out of a window at the part of Exmoor called East Anstey Common. 'Look over there,' Jeremy continued. 'Just over that hill is Rackenford, where Lord Eldon lives.'

I nodded, well aware. Lord Eldon was a big landowner and a very important person in the area.

'John Scott, the 4th Earl of Eldon,' Jeremy continued. 'Scott. Now there's a good name. A simple name.'

It was a brief conversation, but it stuck in my mind.

The next time Jeremy came down, a few weeks later, he was in the same sneering mood. Driving to the Colliers' after lunch in his new Rover, he pulled over into a layby. 'Light me a cigarette,' he said.

I got one of the horrid unfiltered Turkish cigarettes he loved from the packet and lit it for him. He took a few puffs, stubbed it out and began to kiss me. His breath smelt so strongly of the acrid smoke, and this, mingling with an overpowering whiff of leather from the new car seats, made me feel sick. Something in me just snapped. For the first time ever, I pushed him away.

'I don't want this any more,' I said. 'I can't bear it.'

Jeremy stopped kissing me, but I knew he was angry. He started the car and drove in silence to the Colliers'. When we arrived, Mary said I looked ill and sent me upstairs to lie down. On the way back, Jeremy pulled over into a little layby. He grabbed me and pushed his mouth against mine but, once again, I recoiled. Opening the door,

I jumped out of the car. Jeremy got out too. I stood facing him, my feet anchored to the ground. Out in the fresh air, I felt stronger. With a new-found determination and clarity, I looked him in the eyes and said, 'We have to finish this relationship. And you must give me my National Insurance cards, stamped and up to date. The Hambros are asking for them.'

As I mentioned the National Insurance cards, I realised it was this issue that had made me angry enough to stop Jeremy's advances. He had gone on putting it aside long enough. Suddenly it felt like my most urgent priority to get them back. They were the key to my independence. As I stood there in front of Jeremy, I was sharply aware of how dishonourable it was for him to ignore the matter. All along I had assumed that Jeremy, who had promised to get my cards back from Van and sort everything out for me, would have been paying for my stamps each week. I later discovered that this had never happened. As time passed, and the amount to be paid accrued, I think Jeremy became increasingly unwilling to pay out and bring the stamps up to date. He preferred to ignore the situation and now he couldn't believe I was confronting him.

'I'll sort it out,' he snapped. 'But you must keep seeing me.'

'I don't want to. Please, just let this stop, and I can go forward. I need to be able to work and I can't do that without my National Insurance cards,' I told him.

Jeremy's face turned to stone. 'I've got the home secretary and the director of public prosecutions on my side,' he said. 'You can't hurt me.' He got back into the car, a cold saturnine smile on his face.

I told him it wasn't my intention to hurt him. I just wanted us to finish, and I wanted what was my right. 'You must give me my cards,' I begged, reluctantly getting into the passenger seat.

His smile vanished and he turned pale with anger, absolutely furious. We split up, then and there, in the car. He dropped me off at the Hambros' and drove away, leaving me terribly shaken.

After that, everything at the Hambros' changed. They might have sensed that Jeremy was angry with me and perhaps they also twigged that something suspect, and indeed illegal, was going on between us. I would go down to breakfast, and the atmosphere would be frigid. No one would speak to me. I hated being treated like that, and I knew I had to get away.

I moved into a guesthouse in Minehead and found work at a riding school but they asked for my National Insurance cards. When I telephoned Jeremy about this he said, 'Yes, of course,' but the cards didn't materialise so I had to leave. Without wages, I couldn't pay for my room, and without the National Insurance cards I couldn't claim unemployment benefit, or the dole, as we called it then. With no money and no prospect of getting another job, I felt as though I had lost my identity. I sat in the bleak little guest room, waiting to be thrown out, and felt myself dissolve into a whirlpool of anxiety. I tried taking a higher dose of my pills but they did nothing to calm me. In a state of complete panic, I went to see a doctor in Minehead.

Dr Keith Lister welcomed me into his surgery with a warm smile. There was a photograph of his children on the desk, and a lovely one of his wife on the mantelpiece. When he asked me what was wrong, I couldn't speak. 'You can talk to me,' he said, so gently. 'You've got all the time in the world.'

And then it all came spilling out. The whole thing, Jeremy, the sex, the National Insurance cards.

Dr Lister couldn't believe me at first. Then he was horrified. 'You must come and stay with us,' he said, when I told him I couldn't pay for my room.

It took a moment for his kindness to sink in but when it did I felt overwhelmingly grateful. Dr Lister came to the guesthouse to pick me up, and I think he must have paid my bill as I never heard any more about it. He drove me to Worthy Manor, his beautiful home at Porlock Weir, and installed me in a room that had once been a chapel with a four-poster bed and two little windows looking out over the sea.

'You've been through the most dreadful trauma and your mind and body need to relax. I'm going to keep you sedated for a while so you can recover.'

I didn't know anything about this method of treatment, or even if it was legal to do this to someone, but I trusted Keith, as he asked me to call him. I felt completely safe with him, and this time my instinct was right. He gave me some pills, and I fell into a deep sleep, staying in that room in a semi-comatose state for almost a month, listening to classical music and the sound of the waves. Keith or Estée, his wife, would take me to the bathroom in the morning and stand outside while I washed. The children – they were such dears – would bring me my meals and push little drawings of horses under my bedroom door to cheer me up.

Slowly, I began to recover and the Listers would bring me down from the chapel for lunch, sitting in the garden at a big wooden table. Keith didn't put me back on medication, reassuring me that I didn't need it: I just needed a steady routine and a safe space to recover. When I got stronger, Estée let me ride her chestnut mare, who lived out in a field. The horse improved my mood quickly and the routine of schooling her helped me feel able to cope and not worry so much about the future. During the summer we took her to a few shows and I loved the trips in the horsebox with the whole family. They began to feel like the family I'd always wanted but never had.

When I told Keith about my friend Sarah, who, having recovered from her operation, was now living with her parents in Hampshire, he encouraged me to keep in touch with her. In July, Sarah came to stay for a week. Arriving in a twinset and pearls, with a chic Alice band covering the scar where her ash-blonde hair was growing back, she looked so beautiful. She seemed much happier, though she still wore the white cotton gloves. Her hands were still sore and she explained that she never took the gloves off.

Sarah took me sailing, borrowing a boat, and as the week passed I found myself becoming deeply attached to her. When she let me, very gently, hold her poor, ravaged hands, as I had done when I'd first met her, I knew then that she loved me. Two days before she was due to leave I asked her to marry me. It seems crazy now – we were two such lost souls – but I had dreamed of us being together so often, and it felt natural to hold on to the one person who seemed to understand and to truly care for me.

To my delight, Sarah said yes, but told me she would have to ask her parents, who were on holiday in south Devon, so we drove down to meet them. They welcomed us with tea and cakes, and I revealed I had come to ask for Sarah's hand. They gave their agreement, though they suggested it should be a long engagement. We drove back to Porlock in a state of elation, although when we told the Listers, they seemed quite upset. Keith, I think, was horrified. With hindsight, of course, they were right to be concerned. Both Sarah and I had mental-health problems. I was so young, and I just thought that everything would fall into place. I wasn't thinking about how I would support Sarah or where we would live. I just embraced the idea that we would be together, able to look after each other. I could put Jeremy behind me and maybe my life would get back on track, become more conventional, more normal and finally be drama-free.

The next day, Sarah left to go home, promising to telephone and to write until we saw each other again. I was very hopeful about our future together, until a few weeks later a letter arrived with the news that she was going on a cruise to Australia. Her father felt it was a bad thing for us to rush, so he was sending her to stay with her grandfather, who held a high-level post in the diplomatic service. She left for Australia almost immediately, and about a month after we had got engaged, she wrote to tell me that she had met someone called David on the boat and they were going to get married. By the time her letter reached me in September, they were already married. I never saw her again.

I simply could not handle this brutal and unexpected rejection by the person I felt most connected to, even with the support of the Listers. I fell into a new low of misery and, with appalling timing, Mrs Tish chose this moment to attack and kill the Listers' ducks. My little dog was very much in tune with my mind, and I think she was put out because I'd been so preoccupied with Sarah. She'd been doing some rather odd things, but nothing to compare with this awful slaughter. The lovely flock of runner ducks were the children's pride and joy, and though Estée said it didn't matter, I sensed that Keith was very cross. I didn't want Mrs Tish to kill any more poultry, and I felt desperate to stay in the Listers' good books and keep their support. I had no one else to rely on. Desperately wanting to make amends for the disaster, and in a sudden fatalistic state, I made the impulsive decision to take Mrs Tish to the vet and put her down.

I loved Mrs Tish more than anything else, and I thought if I made this sacrifice the Listers would see how sorry I was, and how much I cared about them. But they were aghast with my dramatic and unnecessary gesture and I soon realised it was the worst thing I could have done. I was devastated to lose my little companion, who had been at my side through so many difficult times, and I felt terrible remorse for what I had done to her. I was utterly grief-stricken and I didn't even have a photograph to remember her by. I wrote to ask Jeremy if he could send one, and he replied, expressing sympathy but telling me that he would not be able to comply with my request as he feared he had glued the photo into an album and would not be able to detach it. Though he wished me well in the closing lines, I found his tone in this letter slightly detached and dismissive.

And things were *not* going well.

My mental state was deteriorating fast. Unable to shift my mood, the Listers began to distance themselves from me and I ended up spending most of my time in my room, crying. Keith would check on me, but he looked so disapproving it was impossible to talk to him. Estée and the children stayed away.

After a few days of feeling completely hopeless, I attempted to do away with myself by cutting my wrists up in the beautiful chapel bedroom. There was blood everywhere, all over the carpet, the bed and the other furniture. When Keith discovered me, he was furious but, as the good doctor he was, he went straight into action to bind up my wrists and stop the bleeding. When he was sure I was safe, he looked at me and said, 'This is it. You have to go.'

I had never seen him so angry before. I understood then that by bringing such chaos into his beautiful home, upturning the life of the happy family, I had tested him to the limit.

I packed my bags and, with no other option, I rang my mother. We hadn't spoken for a long time, but she said, reluctantly, that I could stay with her. She had moved to another house in Bexleyheath and was still in a relationship with Phil, who spent a lot of time with her. When I arrived, she was dismissive, calling me a failure. I explained a bit about Jeremy and how he had my National Insurance cards, and she insisted that I demand them back.

Jeremy sounded pleased to hear from me. 'Come up to town!' he said. 'We'll have supper.' It was as if our break-up had never happened. He still didn't give me my National Insurance cards, and as I was too weak to fight off his advances, our sexual relationship resumed. I was back living the lie. I upped my doses of antidepressants and sleeping pills and slipped back into a state of groggy confusion.

Jeremy now had a small flat at Marsham Court, near Whitehall, and often I would stay the night. We'd have the usual beastly sex, and then he'd make me drag a camp bed out of the wardrobe and sleep on it in the sitting room. Apart from the sex, Jeremy now rarely wanted to be close to me and liked to sleep alone. While I still hated the sex, I longed for emotional intimacy and felt so unwanted. When I travelled back to my mother's house on the train, I would feel defiled and ashamed. The guilt and shame played on my mind so I returned to church, to the confessional, but the priest refused to give me absolution. 'You cannot take Communion again until you stop doing this thing with this man. You must get away from him,' he said. I explained why I couldn't, but the priest was adamant. Deeply upset, I decided to stop going to Mass.

The strength and confidence I had gained by being apart from Jeremy dissolved, and I was quickly back at his beck and call. I had no work, still waiting for the cards, but Jeremy just ignored the subject. He had become very focused on thrill-seeking, his appetite for sex and risk-taking on the increase. He liked to go to the Waterman's Arms on the Isle of Dogs, a pub run by Dan Farson, the journalist and biographer of Francis Bacon, the artist. Dan was a homosexual and his pub was a haunt for men wanting sexual liaisons. There, Jeremy would pick up sailors. If I was staying with him on one of those nights, I'd be invited to join a threesome, and when I declined – and I always declined – I'd be turfed out. I would either walk the streets or take shelter in a grimy phone box.

One evening, Jeremy returned to his flat with a hulking Swedish sailor and, as usual, I was asked if I'd like to participate, and said, 'No, thank you.' It was pouring with rain outside but I didn't fancy the phone box, which usually reeked of urine, so I asked to borrow Jeremy's overcoat to keep me dry. While he and his one-night stand had sex, I went for a long walk, heading down to St James's Park. Much later, as I was strolling back through the rain, a car began following me. I heard the window winding down and then Jeremy's voice trying to entice me into the car. Not satisfied with his lusty pick-up, he'd gone out in search of another man and hadn't recognised me in his overcoat.

My life continued to spiral down into this peculiar, seedy reality. By the autumn I'd had enough of the camp bed at Marsham Court. Jeremy suggested I move back in with Mrs Flood, offering to pay the rent. I didn't really want this, but it seemed better than living with my mother, who made me feel wretched.

The weeks dragged by and, dreading the inevitable feeling of limbo, I focused on small highlights during the day. I resumed my coffee-bar chats with my friend at the Kardomah. She wasn't working, so being with her made me feel my situation was normal. However, she still insisted that Jeremy was her boyfriend and kept grilling me about my friendship with him. 'Oh, I know him quite well!' was all I was prepared to say. Then one evening she invited me back to her flat for supper.

When I arrived at my friend's flat, just a few doors down from 21 Draycott Place, the wine was flowing freely. After a couple of glasses, the potent mix of alcohol and my medication made me throw caution to the winds. When she complained that Jeremy had treated her in rather a cavalier fashion, I found myself blurting out that he had done exactly the same to me. I told her we'd been having a physical relationship, and he had been using me for sex. I thought that our similar experience might make her feel better, but I couldn't have been more wrong. As soon as the words were out of my mouth, her face turned scarlet. Completely disinhibited by the mix of alcohol and medication, I tried to tell her I was only speaking the truth. Somehow, I managed to blurt out how Jeremy had told me having a woman was like making love to a cold rice pudding.

'You're a horrible, horrible person!' she screamed.

I could only say how sorry I was, then run for it.

Now I find it hard to believe what I did next, but I was out of my mind. I was a young, broken person, highly medicated and desperately unhappy. Over and over, I had yearned for the affectionate side of Jeremy, loving how he had snuggled up to me and talked about the Devon farm we would have. Now all I was left with was the humiliation of his sexual assaults and the degrading way he handed out just enough money for me to eat, as though he was giving me scraps. I stumbled through the streets of Chelsea, battered by frantic thoughts, panicking about what would happen if my friend told Jeremy what I had said. It was unthinkable. In my wild, irrational state, I could see only one way out of this awful mess. I must kill Jeremy, and then do away with myself.

I had a vague idea that I would go to the House of Commons to find Jeremy and kill him, but in my drunken, drugged-up haze, that was as far as I had gone with my plan. I had no idea how I was going to do it and decided I needed some peace and quiet while I worked out my next step. I found myself in Victoria, at St George's Square, and decided to book myself into a hotel so I could think. As I stumbled up to Reception, I was astonished to see Mary Collier, Jeremy's friend, with whom I had stayed in Devon, behind the desk.

'Norman?' she said, rather flabbergasted.

Not only was I the last person she was expecting to see, but I must have looked in a frightful state. She explained that the hotel was owned by a friend of hers, and that she was helping out for a couple of days. I asked if I could have a room and she asked where my luggage was. I explained that I didn't have any as I wasn't going to be staying long. Rather confused, Mary organised a room for me. In my deluded state I fixated on my friend from the Kardomah, deciding to ring her and tell her what I was going to do. I told her where I was, blurting out my plan. 'I just can't stand all this any more. And I know you can't, either. I'm going to kill him. And then I'll kill myself.'

I cut the call and sat on the bed as I tried to pull my thoughts together. I had a bullet with me – my lucky charm from Foxholes – but I didn't have a gun. My muddled musings hadn't gone much further when there was a knock on the door. Two police officers were outside, with an anxious Mary Collier just behind them. My friend must have dialled 999 just after we spoke.

'We understand you intend to kill a Member of Parliament,'

one of the detectives said, as Mary stood appalled behind them.

'I've thought about it,' I stammered, absolutely terrified.

I looked at Mary. She knew all about my mental-health problems and I hoped she might speak up and say something to support me, but she stayed silent.

The officers took me to Canon Row police station in Westminster. I showed them my bullet, explaining I didn't have a gun to go with it, and they must have realised pretty soon that I was in no fit state to kill anybody. I told them of my relationship with Jeremy although I did not admit to anal penetration because it was illegal, instead explaining that there had been sexual relations. The police, probably concluding that I was completely mad, kept saying I had no evidence. I insisted that I did. Eventually I was sent home and told I must bring the evidence to my local police station the next morning to make a statement.

That night I had no sleep. Still drunk and with my mind completely at sea, I moved on from wanting to kill Jeremy. Instead, I had an urgent desire to tell the police the whole truth about our relationship. With a burning, misplaced clarity, I believed the burden of keeping the secret and upholding Jeremy's lies would be lifted if I confessed. Arriving at the local police station with a bundle of letters from Jeremy, I realised I was still a bit drunk.

A detective sergeant and a detective inspector were waiting for me and I jumped straight into the story, telling them how Jeremy had charmed me, tricking me into letting him have sex with me, and that ever since then we had been having homosexual relations. The officers looked sceptical.

There was nothing for it but to tell them in graphic detail about Jeremy's sexual behaviour. They listened, poker-faced. It was 1962. Jeremy was a Member of Parliament. With a clear mind I would have never made this confession, acutely aware of the potential consequences of this truth, but in that moment I was just thinking of me, of my life going forward, and how I needed to be free of the limbo I was living in.

When I showed the officers the 'Bunnies' letter and another that Jeremy had sent me, where he called me 'my angel', writing that all he wanted was to share a Devon farm with me, their manner changed. Becoming very interested, they insisted on taking them from me. I also had with me some of the correspondence I had taken from Van, including the postcard from Jeremy about Princess Margaret's marriage and how Jeremy wished to 'marry one and seduce the other'. They took that too.

With obvious embarrassment, the two officers told me that I must have an anal examination to confirm that I was telling the truth about the penetrative sex. This practice was a nineteenth-century evaluation, thought to determine homosexual conduct through the tone of the anal sphincter or the shape of the anus. Doctors or police officers carried out these examinations using either their fingers or a metal instrument. Although forced examinations are still carried out in some countries today, they have long since been discredited in the UK and stopped, now considered a violation. Unfortunately for me, they were still part of British practice then, and a police surgeon came in and told me to take my trousers down. He carried out the examination with a horrid metal instrument, which was very cold. Not only was it uncomfortable, it was incredibly humiliating. The examination confirmed what I had said about the homosexual activity.

At the end of it all, the officers told me I was free to go but when I asked for my letters to be returned they were adamant that they must keep them. Perhaps I should have been stronger, but I didn't push the point, and I didn't ask why they wanted them. I had just been physically examined in the most humiliating way and I did not want to stay another minute longer.

It was early evening by the time I left the police station and I walked out in a sort of trance. I was in a strange, cold state of calm after the frenzy of drugs and alcohol, the long-winded questioning and the horrific anal examination. The urge to do away with myself was gone but I couldn't bear to go back to Draycott Place and possibly face my friend from the Kardomah again. I knew I was in no state to spend time with my mother so, ironically, I went to Jeremy. I knew enough to say nothing about my interview with the police and I had a gut instinct that the officers wouldn't contact him, which they didn't. I later discovered that they passed the matter upwards through the chain of command until it reached MI5 but absolutely nothing was done.

CHAPTER EIGHT

Billy

IN DECEMBER 1962, heavy snow started to fall. The country was plunged into a white-out, with blizzards that made snow-drifts twenty feet deep, covering all the cars and transforming London into a glittering white world. Temperatures plummeted as low as −20, and lakes and rivers – including the Thames – froze over in one of the coldest winters on record. It became known as the Big Freeze of 1962–3.

Too cold to go out, I became more aware of how trapped I was. I had never wanted the life I was leading, having sex I didn't enjoy only to be turfed out onto the lonely camp bed afterwards, bruised mentally and physically. Jeremy was becoming tired of my company, too. At night, he went out to pick up one-night stands so I'd spend hours walking the streets, wrapped up in layers that did little to keep out the cold, yet reluctant to return to either Marsham Court or my depressing room at Draycott Place. In the mornings, I no longer had the option of going to Mass, so if I was with Jeremy I'd squeeze oranges and make him coffee, keeping silent while he read the morning papers and made telephone calls. Without looking up from the paper, he might ask me to fetch something, as if I was his servant. Apart from that, he ignored me. He made me feel as if I didn't exist – as if I were a lesser being, someone of no account who was simply fading away to nothing.

One breakfast time, something inside me snapped. Breaking the silence, I asked Jeremy, once again, to sort out my National Insurance cards. As usual, he ignored me. I asked again, loud and clear. Without looking up, he mumbled that while I had been in Devon he had sent me replacement cards. I told him I had never received them, and asked once more but then Jeremy got irritated. It was clear he was not prepared to help me.

I did think many times about going to the Employment Office to get a new card for myself but it would have not been stamped, and I would have had no right to sickness and unemployment benefits so it seemed pointless. Jeremy's latest lack of cooperation spurred me into action. In January 1963, I found an advertisement in *Horse & Hound*, which had been placed by a Swiss veterinary surgeon called Dr Choquard, who lived in Porrentruy on the Swiss–German border. He needed someone to look after and school his dressage horses. I liked the sound of that, so when Jeremy was in a better mood, I told him about it. To my surprise, he offered to pay my fare and organised a passport.

On the morning of my departure, early in the New Year, he went off to the House of Commons and I packed up all my things in a suitcase, including some letters from him that were still in my possession. The maid who looked after the flat gave me an odd look as I left. Goodness knows what she thought of my staying there with Jeremy. 'Going away, are you, sir?' she asked.

'Yes. For good,' I replied.

I took the boat train from Victoria, under the dismal grey sky. After crossing the Channel, then catching a train to Paris, I trundled across France into Switzerland where the snow was deep, and finally reached Porrentruy. I'd fallen asleep and was woken up by a train guard shaking me, telling me it was my stop. Jumping off the train, I landed in thick, soft snow, and started shivering immediately. It was well below freezing, and I was unsuitably clad in a light Prince of Wales check suit and oxford shoes. Further down the platform, cases were being stacked on a truck. I hurried over, but my suitcase was not there. The train left and I stood on the platform without my belongings and with no sign of anyone there to collect me.

By now, my hands were completely numb and I was shivering violently. I took a taxi up to Dr Choquard's house, a tall gloomy building just outside the village. An old housekeeper who spoke no English greeted me. She did not understand when I tried to explain about my luggage and ushered me into a dingily lit room. I waited alone, listening to the ticking of a clock and an occasional rustle from the Delft porcelain stove that heated the place.

Eventually Dr Choquard, a rather dishevelled man, appeared. He shouted for his supper and snapped in broken English that he would show me the horses when we'd eaten. The housekeeper brought cold meats and pickles, and I tried to tell Dr Choquard about my missing luggage, but he didn't listen. He just informed me that I had been employed to school his horses to Prix St Georges standard – the beginning of the top levels of dressage – and carried on eating without saying anything more.

For our tour of the stables Dr Choquard donned a thick coat and a pair of snowshoes that were rather like tennis racquets. I explained I had no outdoor gear, as all my things were in the missing suitcase. He gave me a pair of snowshoes and, still without a coat, I followed him to the stables. I have never seen a sorrier sight than those poor animals, and couldn't believe anyone, especially a vet, could keep horses like that. No one had been removing droppings from the stables, so they were caked with dung. They were bedded on shavings, which had become so dark with ordure I thought they were peat. There was no fresh water and some of the horses' hoofs were curling upwards from lack of trimming. All were thin and wormy. I expressed my concerns to Dr Choquard, but he ignored me, turned his back and returned to the house.

I stayed with the horses, clearing the droppings from under their feet and breaking the ice on the water barrel so I could fill their buckets. I spent a long time brushing the dirt off them and when I finally returned to the house, I was filthy, my suit covered with muck and grime. The house was in darkness except for a thin light under the housekeeper's door. I knocked. 'Where is my room, please? And have you a clothes brush?' She put her fingers to her lips and led me up interminable stairs to a small room. As I lay down, I felt like some lonely character in an Ibsen play.

The next morning the housekeeper's son brought the news that I was sacked: 'The vet does not want you to work for him as he has a strong sense you are a homosexual,' he said.

I was shocked by the vet's audacity, but I told the house-keeper's son not to worry because I didn't want to stay. My gut feeling was to get out as quickly as I could. I wanted no more to do with Dr Choquard. He had no compassion for his poor horses, and none for me, either.

The housekeeper's son was kind and helpful. He explained there was a train to Paris in an hour and discovered that my suitcase had been put off by mistake at a different station. I didn't want to stay a minute longer, so I asked him if he would redirect the lost luggage to Marsham Court. 'Please make sure the horses get wormed,' I said to him as I left. The suitcase never arrived, and I expect the poor horses struggled on until the worm burden finished them off.

I was glad to escape that hideous set-up, but on the stop-over in Paris, I wandered through Les Halles with just half a franc in my pocket, wondering what to do next. I sank into despair. My mother was no longer prepared to put me up. She had made it perfectly obvious I'd made all the wrong choices and would just have to get on with it. I walked down to the Seine thinking of the boy in Sartre's *Roads to Freedom* who climbed over the railing and dropped into the cold grey water. I just didn't have the courage to do it.

The only person I could turn to was Jeremy. I thought he would be furious at my swift return from Switzerland, but when I rang him from Victoria station he insisted I take a cab to Marsham Court. He met me at the door of the flat and threw his arms round me. 'Poor Bunny!' he said. 'You look absolutely broken. You must stay here. Rest, and we'll talk tomorrow.'

He was all kindness and consideration, and even refrained from trying to have sex that night, which was a welcome change. To my surprise, I felt glad to be back, far away from the dark, sinister Swiss house. But the mood quickly changed when I asked him to help me retrieve my lost suitcase. Without a job, I didn't have the money to get it back myself and without the suitcase I had no clothes. When we learned how much it would cost to retrieve it from Switzerland, he refused to help. Sometimes he could be very mean about spending even small amounts of money and, with his disregard of risk, he seemed not to care about the letters. Perhaps he thought they would be safe from prying eyes in a Swiss left-luggage office, and he could just forget about them. Whatever his reasoning, Jeremy wouldn't budge on the matter. The suitcase stayed in Switzerland.

Now Jeremy became even more distant from me, his sights firmly fixed on more one-night stands and rough sex. He never spoke now about living on a farm in Devon with me, and was no longer at all affectionate. All I was left with was the forceful sex and the awful feeling of low self-worth when he behaved as though I didn't exist. For the sake of my sanity, I knew I had to find another way to get out of this unwanted life. I read through *Horse & Hound* again, and found an advertisement for someone with dressage experience to go into partnership at a riding school at Comber, Northern Ireland. Dressage was mainly a German thing in those days, but it looked set to become much more popular in Britain. It sounded absolutely perfect for me, and when I rang the owners I was delighted when they asked me to come over for an interview.

Jeremy wasn't pleased. He had served in Northern Ireland when he was in the forces, and he'd told me he didn't like the people there. I took this with a pinch of salt. If Jeremy didn't warm to someone, he made no effort to be polite, which of course put people's backs up and went on to confirm his initial impressions.

Earlier in our relationship I would have listened to Jeremy, not questioned him. Reluctantly, I would have let the idea go. Now I felt compelled to fight for this opportunity. I knew this job could help launch my career with horses and also give me independence. If I'd had my own money or my National Insurance cards so I could earn, I would have just left for Northern Ireland, but I needed Jeremy to fund the ticket there. Feeling like a nagging child, I persisted, bringing up the subject at every chance I got. I was just desperate to get out of the seedy life I was leading, always at Jeremy's beck and call. He kept ignoring me, so eventually I let him know how I really felt. I confessed that while I loved him, I found sex with him unpleasant. And I had to move on. 'I need to be free,' I said finally. Only then did he take notice and, after much discussion, agreed that I should go over for the interview.

I left London and took the ferry to Belfast. As I watched Ireland come into view, I hoped the trip wouldn't be a repeat performance of my arrival in Switzerland but Jean Mitchell, one of the owners of the riding school, came to meet me with a colleague, giving me the warmest welcome. The facilities at their yard were impressive, with brand-new stables. Half of the school was covered so it could be used in all weathers, which was almost unheard of in those days. I was excited, and as soon as they had seen me ride, the owners asked me to stay, offering me the job. I was delighted, but had to explain that I was ill-equipped for the job as my riding clothes had been lost on my trip to Switzerland. The owners promised to kit me out with some new things, and also offered me a partnership in the business explaining that they were really keen to get the enterprise off the ground and were sure I was the right person to help. I couldn't believe it. Not only was I thrilled by the idea of settling into a respectable career with horses, but the people were friendly and professional. I felt myself relaxing.

I lived in a caravan for a few days and once my accommodation was ready, I moved to a little apartment above the tack room. I loved being there because I was close to the horses and could hear them moving about and snorting through the night, reminding me of my time with Listowel. It was unheated and cold but in the sixties everyone was used to living without central heating and I treated myself to some jumpers and wore them to keep warm.

Advertisements for the riding school went out in the local newspapers, and within a couple of weeks I had six livery horses to look after and was fully booked up to teach dressage lessons. Dressage was such a novelty in Northern Ireland in the 1960s that I soon became a celebrity. A girl called Tessa White from the BBC recorded a radio interview with me for the equivalent of the *Today* programme. Tessa and I got on very well, and one day she brought a friend, William Lowry, to meet me. Billy, as he liked to be called, worked as a sales rep for her parents' business, the corn merchants White, Tomkins, and Courage, which is now the leading oats brand, White's. He was also a great horseman and on the day we first met, he, Tessa and I went for a ride.

Billy was easy to get on with and the next day he came

round to the yard and took me up into the Mountains of Mourne. We sat looking at the dramatic landscape, enjoying bread and cheese and a bottle of wine, speaking non-stop, finding out about each other. Billy lived with his mother, four brothers and a sister, at Rokeby Hall, a lovely old Victorian mansion out in the country. One of his brothers was a horse-dealer who ran a breaking and schooling business selling lots of horses to England. Billy loved horses, too, and most of our conversation focused on this common ground. After that, we saw each other most days. As well as our shared interests, Billy made me laugh with his gentle but wicked Irish wit. I soon sensed that our closeness might become physical, and knew if this happened it would be entirely different from being with Jeremy. Billy was just so kind and warm. He listened, he understood, and from the very first moment I met him, I just wanted him to hug me.

Everything was going so well except that I didn't have my National Insurance cards. One day Joan took me aside. 'Norman, I've had the "brew" on the phone,' she said. (The brew was her Northern Irish way of saying the 'Bureau' – or the Employment Office.)

'They've seen you riding past their office, and they've asked me where are your cards,' she asked, her tone clipped.

I assured her they would be arriving soon, but the situation preyed on my mind because I knew they wouldn't. I could have said I'd lost them, and asked for new ones, but I would not have been entitled to any benefits. I would have had to explain where I had worked before, and who my employer was. Jeremy's name would have come up and if the officials had started asking why he was keeping the cards, this would have opened a terrible can of worms. I had no explanation for why Jeremy was holding the cards except to keep me available for sex. Homosexuality was illegal. If our relationship were discovered, his career would be ruined. I didn't want to get him into trouble, but I felt trapped. Billy and Tessa picked up on my anxiety and I told them a bit about my situation. Being straight-thinking and honest young people, they told me to ring Jeremy right away and get my National Insurance cards sorted.

I rang Jeremy several times before I got through to him, at which point he told me he would look into my cards but, by now, I knew he wouldn't. For a few more weeks, Joan didn't follow up the issue. Business was increasing and I hoped she and the other partners would just forget about the cards until Jeremy had finally sorted them out. In the meantime, I focused on the horses. One of the clients asked me to take on a mare called Miss Kop, who would make a top-class show hack, 'if only she could let someone stay on her back long enough to prove it!'

I took these words of warning as a challenge and agreed. Miss Kop was thin, wild-eyed and nervous, but I liked her. I would go into her box in the evenings and spend time reading to her. Every spare moment I would make a fuss of her so that she got used to my company and learned to trust me. As she settled, I began to lunge her each day and then I would lean over her back, getting her used to my weight, and ease her gently into the idea of carrying someone.

One lunchtime I quietly got up on Miss Kop's back while she was in her box. She exploded, but I hung on and when she finally stopped leaping about she looked round as if she was surprised to find me still on her back. When I finally got off she pushed her head against me as if to say she was sorry for being so rude. I repeated this for a couple of days. There was always an initial explosion and then she'd settle. One morning I tried riding her in the school and she bucked without stopping for ten minutes, until she was exhausted. I decided to take advantage of this exhausted state and asked the groom to open the gates so we could ride out.

We walked along the quiet lane past the forge, where the blacksmiths looked at us in surprise, all well aware of Miss Kop's reputation. We carried on slowly, taking a short reconnoitre through the town. All went well, until outside the chip shop and without warning Miss Kop suddenly jumped about ten feet in the air and threw herself over backwards, much to the consternation of the fish-and-chip lunchers. By some miracle I was still aboard when she got up, and we trotted off along the high street as though nothing had happened.

As we headed home, a car came up behind us. It was Billy, laughing his head off. He'd been in the chip shop buying some lunch for us and had seen everything. 'There was a great *craic* in the shop when Miss Kop got up and you rode her away,' he said, visibly impressed. I couldn't remember when I had last achieved anything that might warrant admiration and his reaction triggered a feeling of empowerment. I was good with horses, really good. They didn't see me as weak or vulnerable or someone they could manipulate. Those magnificent creatures respected me, and so did Billy.

That evening Jeremy phoned, wanting me to meet him in London the following day. Thinking this was my chance to get the National Insurance cards, I caught the early plane and was in St Stephen's Hall at Westminster by lunchtime. As we ate, Jeremy remarked on how well I was looking, and how much I had changed. He said he, too, had changed, and he wanted us to try again with our relationship. All I was thinking about was the closeness that was developing between Billy and me. I really didn't want to go back into a relationship I had got used to enduring. As we sat there at lunch I realised that it would suit Jeremy to see me occasionally and, as far as he was concerned, we were now in an ideal set-up. But the more he told me he wanted me back, the more I realised he had no intention of discussing my National Insurance cards, let alone giving them back. He didn't even mention it and when I brought it up, he changed the subject.

After lunch Jeremy took me back to his office in Bridge Street, continuing to tell me he wanted me back, that he was sure we could make a go of it. When he locked the door and tried to have sex with me, I told him no. I wasn't to be inveigled any more – and that was what Jeremy had been doing. He had been bailing me out, helping me, finding me jobs and places to stay, which, on the surface, sounded exceptionally kind and decent. However, his generosity was insincere and random. He used luxurious treats and bouts of tenderness as currency. I had foolishly believed them to be gestures of genuine affection but they simply gave him leverage, making me a puppet in my own life. I had come to depend on him, yes, but only because he held the means to my making a living and standing on my own feet.

Now I had had space from him I was more and more aware of the unhealthy dynamic. As he was pressing his body up against mine our relationship flashed through my mind with new clarity. When I had turned up in London just over a year before, hoping a powerful stranger could help me, I was naïve, young, vulnerable and utterly desperate. Jeremy had masqueraded as someone dependable, someone on my side, when actually he was a master manipulator. He wanted to control me and now I had almost broken free of his grip, the matter of my National Insurance cards was the last remaining puppet string he could tug. I pushed him away, telling him firmly that I had met someone else and that I didn't want to continue our relationship. As I said this, I felt a sudden flicker of sadness for Jeremy. I had become so much stronger and I could tell that this shocked him. For a moment he looked at me, still hoping I'd give in, and then he snapped, 'You will be sorry. And I'll make you come back.'

I told him no. 'Give me my National Insurance cards, properly stamped, and I will be more than happy to see you sometimes but not for sex,' I said, before telling him to unlock the door. I suggested we part as friends, and he complied but with rather bad grace.

I was back in Belfast by 10 p.m. and Billy was waiting at Comber. There was no one else around, and I was so pleased to see him that I hugged him. We had never hugged before, but he immediately responded, holding me very close. I felt my stomach flip over. It was a tense, electrifying moment, something I had never experienced before. Everything about him was a world away from Jeremy and it was incredible to be held so lovingly.

Things continued to move slowly between Billy and me, and it might have taken a very long time for us to get closer, but when I had an accident, everything changed. One day, as I mounted Miss Kop ready to start work in the school, I must have landed heavily in the saddle. Miss Kop reared and went over backwards, rolling on me. I hit my head on a stanchion, and the next thing I knew, Billy was standing over me, white-faced. I got up, feeling dazed. Miss Kop stood glowering at me from the other end of the school. 'Norman! Norman! Are you all right?' Billy asked.

'Yes,' I said. I walked over to Miss Kop, talking quietly, and, despite Billy's protests, I mounted her again. I couldn't let her defeat me. Billy stood by the gate, shaking his head, but Miss Kop seemed to have settled. I put her into a canter, leaning forward to scratch her ears. Her neck lowered to accept the bit, and she began to move in a beautiful outline. Then, out of the blue, she threw six huge bucks and charged at the entrance gate with her head in the air. Billy shut it to stop her, but she kept going and went to jump the gate from four strides out, catching her foot on the top and flipping over in a rotational fall. As she struggled to get free the gate crashed down on both of us. It was a nightmare of flailing hoofs, sky, brown earth, splinters of wood, then indescribable pain and all went dark.

I woke to warmth and quiet voices, and smelt polish, ether and disinfectant. A nurse was telling me not to move.

I opened my eyes and everything came flying back. 'The horses!' I said. 'What about the horses?' The nurse told me they were being taken care of. 'Your friend's looking after them. He'll be in later.'

I tried to sit up. 'No, no!' the nurse said. 'You've hurt your back. Stay still. We're waiting for the result of the X-ray.'

I tried to move my head and felt a searing pain, lost consciousness and came round to find a doctor standing over me.

'I'm afraid you have fractured six vertebrae in your neck and the top of your back. You must remain totally still,' the doctor said.

'I must get back to the horses,' I said, but the doctor shook his head and said I mustn't think about it.

I stayed in the hospital for five days. Billy was a constant visitor, but I found the confinement impossible and decided to discharge myself. The doctor told me this was very foolish, but I signed a paper accepting full responsibility for my actions and walked slowly out. I couldn't bear being restrained, the hospital too much like the psychiatric clinic, and although I was still in pain, I wanted to get back to the yard, back to the horses.

Somehow I managed to do the yard work. As I couldn't use my arms to lift things, I tied sacks round my legs and shuffled along on my knees to drag the water buckets across the yard. But I couldn't bring the horses in from the field, as I was unable to raise my arms to fit the head-collars. A couple of weeks passed and then Jean made another request for my National Insurance cards, which, of course, Jeremy had not sent. When I said they had not arrived, she was understandably furious, warning me that unless I sorted it out, I would not be able to keep working.

I felt terrible that I had let her down and worried about my future. With my injuries still severe, Tessa persuaded me to fly to England with her and visit the London Clinic for a proper medical assessment. The clinic advised that if I wanted to make a good recovery I should be in traction for six months. I told them this was impossible, as I had to work and was unable to claim sickness benefit.

I was angry now. The accident had made me realise just how important it was for me to be able to claim sickness benefit. I took my X-rays from the clinic and went to see Jeremy, feeling resentful of the way my job was now on the line because Jeremy hadn't given me the cards. 'It's a matter of urgency!' I said. Jeremy just smiled, assuring me he was doing everything he could to chase the matter up. I wanted to scream, utterly exasperated, but there was nothing more I could do. I returned to Comber.

For a while Jean didn't follow up. As my broken vertebrae gradually healed the pain lessened, and my life settled down again. After about six weeks, I got back into the saddle, and it wasn't long before I was schooling show-jumpers again. Spring turned to summer and a local man who owned a pet shop offered me a ride on his super show-jumper, Karinga Bay, who had qualified for the prestigious Guinness competition at the Dublin Horse Show. Billy's mare, ridden by one of his brothers, had also qualified, so we travelled to Dublin together. I was thrilled to take part in this high-level event – the equivalent of the Foxhunter competition in England – but I had a bad fall, ending up in hospital. There was some further damage to the vertebrae I had injured before, and now the bones became fused. I was told I was lucky not to have been permanently disabled, and to this day I have a slight sideways twist in my neck.

I stayed in hospital for a couple of weeks, wishing I could

get back to the horses, but whenever Tessa and Billy visited and I asked after the horses and the yard, they always changed the subject. When I finally got back to Comber I understood why. All the boxes were empty. In my absence, the liveries had all been taken elsewhere. Jean and the other owners had decided that, without me to teach dressage, school show-jumpers and run the yard, the business wasn't viable. Becoming disillusioned with the whole plan, which was inevitably not helped by my lack of National Insurance cards, they had closed it all down. They must have been furious with me. They didn't tell me they were going to close the business and never contacted me again. I was heartbroken.

Billy stayed overnight with me in the on-site caravan, as my accommodation was now locked up. In despair, we both got very drunk and ended up passing out in a stupor on the bed. Next morning, he disappeared, coming back to say he'd spoken to his mother. He asked whether I'd like to come and stay with them at Rokeby Hall until I'd found another job. It was so kind of him to offer this and, not knowing what else to do, I agreed.

It was the best decision I had made in a long time. The big old house was surrounded by fields and stables full of horses. Billy's family were friendly and easygoing, welcoming me as if I was a long-standing friend. Billy and I shared his room and, to my surprise, no one seemed to think there was anything unusual about our friendship or that we were sharing a bed. If anything, they seemed pleased that he was so bright and full of fun in my company. Although nothing had happened physically between us, it felt like there were no barriers for us any more. Perhaps Billy's family were innocently oblivious or maybe they didn't mind but there was a feeling of security about the set-up. Knowing I couldn't get another job because I couldn't ride until I recovered from my injuries, I relaxed, hoping by the time I was physically fit again, Jeremy might have relented and given me the cards.

Billy and I spent all our time together, chatting in our room or walking in the fields. We shared happy suppers with his family and he introduced me to his friends. On the way back from an evening spent listening to music and drinking wine with neighbours, we drove past the moonlit lough on the Newtownards peninsula in a state of tremendous gaiety. Billy had an extraordinary voice, very deep, and behind each word there was always a hint of laughter. The wine had gone to our heads, and everything we said made us dissolve into hysterics. When we got back, rats were running about in the yard. They often appeared, attracted to the spilled horse feed, and there was a dustbin lid hanging up for the purpose of scaring them. Laughing wildly, we made a terrible din as we whacked this with a big stick and afterwards heard the rats scuttling away. Then we stumbled around topping up the horses' water buckets and chortling with glee when one of us tripped up.

When we crept into the house, everyone else had long since gone to bed so we tried to be quiet, tiptoeing up to our room, but it was completely dark. We ended up crashing around, knocking some hunting boots to the floor and making a terrible din, but nobody seemed to wake up. Too drunk to undress, we collapsed on the bed and fell asleep. About an hour later I opened my eyes to find Billy sleeping with his arms around me. I woke him, and we brushed our teeth, undressed and at last were in bed comfortably. We talked for a while, and then, as though it were the most normal thing in the world to do, he made love to me. There was no roughness, no urgency, no penetrative sex. Billy was all tenderness and care. Afterwards, when he lay beside me snoring gently, I felt so totally clean and happy. This was how it was supposed to be. Nothing could be more different from my traumatic experiences with Jeremy. I felt no shame now, just the most glorious peace and relaxation after our gentle, sensual lovemaking, and I fell into an incredibly deep sleep.

I woke up to find Billy standing over me with a mug of coffee. 'Morning,' he said. 'How are you?' I couldn't look at him, suddenly afraid that he might think we had gone too far.

He lit a cigarette and gave it to me. 'It's all right,' he said. 'Things haven't changed.' He took my hand in his and held it tightly. 'I really meant last night. I'd felt it a long time, and I couldn't pretend any longer. I love you.'

I felt so safe. 'I do too, Billy. I'm sure and I'm so happy,' I replied.

He asked if I would like to go for a ride that morning, but I felt doubtful. I was still feeling fragile after my fall and hadn't been on a horse for the two months since. 'Do you think I should? Remember what the doctor said?' I asked.

'I think it would do you good. We need only walk,' Billy replied, squeezing my hand.

When I went down to breakfast, the whole family were there and I felt the colour rush to my face. Had they guessed what had happened last night? They were all laughing at us, saying, 'Who was drunk, then, last night?' I wanted to run from the room but Billy grinned and told them all to shut up, and I realised they were just teasing us for making so much noise on the stairs. In all the time I lived at Rokeby Hall, sharing Billy's room and his bed, there were never any sly comments, or accusations of anything untoward between us.

After breakfast we tacked up Billy's show-jumper and a big black thoroughbred. I clambered on with the help of a mounting block and we rode off down the drive. Billy's mother watched us go, looking concerned, but we were careful as we quietly rode through the lanes and across the fields. It was beautiful to be looking through a horse's ears at the lush green fields alongside the bright gold expanse of the stubble where the corn had just been cut. And beautiful, too, to have Billy by my side – someone I loved and who shared my passion for horses. I remembered how Jeremy had said that to share a Devon farm with me would be paradise, but it could never have been anything like this.

A few weeks later, I was able to ride properly again. One splendid day, Billy and I went hunting with three of his brothers. Five of us, all together. We mounted our horses in front of their huge old house, and as we hacked down the drive, I felt as though I had slipped back in time to the golden years before the First World War. Life at Rokeby Hall went by like a happy dream, but as the autumn of 1963 turned the leaves brown, I began to wonder what my next step would be. Billy was adamant that I could stay with him for as long as I liked, but I didn't want to be dependent on his family's kindness. I needed to be able to fend for myself.

I called Jeremy again but he told me he didn't want to see me, and put the telephone down. I was livid. I changed tack, catching the next plane to London. Going straight to St Stephen's Hall, I sent up a green card requesting a meeting with Geoffrey Johnson-Smith, a Conservative MP who was parliamentary private secretary to the minister for pensions and National Insurance. I mentioned that this was not because he was the MP for my constituency, but because Jeremy Thorpe, MP, was refusing to give me my National Insurance cards. Mr Johnson-Smith saw me immediately. I didn't need to say anything about the sexual stuff, as he already looked quite horrified and promised to look into the matter right away. Finally, I felt I was getting somewhere. I flew back to Belfast and Billy met me at the airport, his eyes shining expectantly.

'How did it go?' he asked.

'Well, I've done my best and I think it might pay off,' I said, feeling proud of how strong I had been. I knew Billy was pleased, but when I mentioned that things might take time and that I didn't feel I could go on staying with his family, Billy shook his head. 'But you can. You can stay as long as you want. Nobody minds.'

I loved him so much, but I explained I knew that our relationship would suffer if I continued to live at Rokeby Hall. I felt he would begin to find me a drag if I was totally dependent on him and his family and I didn't want to feel like a burden, or be dependent on anyone any more. I remembered the Listers and how everything had gone wrong. I couldn't bear to lose my footing again. He kept assuring me that he would look after me, and it would all be fine. I so wanted to believe him, but my inner voice kept telling me otherwise.

Instead of burying the issue of my National Insurance cards, I fixated on it because now I had something to lose: I had a life with Billy. I decided to return to England so I could keep chasing the issue until it was resolved. I looked for a job, hoping I might find one with employers who were less bothered about my cards. *Horse & Hound* were advertising for someone to teach and school show-jumpers at the Pennwood Riding Stables near Wolverhampton, so I flew over, met the well-known owner, Fred Harthill, and he took me on.

Telling Billy was heartbreaking. I kept putting off the date of my departure but the Harthills were impatient for me to start. The last evening at Rokeby Hall was quite dreadful. We had a sleepless night, smoking endless cigarettes and talking as I tried to reassure him that as soon as I had settled into the job, got my cards sorted, and found somewhere to live he could come and join me. Then we made love. I was booked on the night ferry from Belfast, so Billy drove me to the docks. I stared at him as the ferry chugged out into the bay, watching until he was just a dot.

The Harthills made me very welcome, showing me my room and introducing me to the fifty or so horses on their yard. Mrs Harthill burst out laughing when I told her I had worked for Van der Vater. 'Oh, him!' She snorted. 'I knew him before all that nonsense started. He was just plain old Norman Vater – a miner's son from the Welsh valleys,' she said.

It came as no surprise to me that even Van's name wasn't really his. If you wanted to be successful in those early days of dressage and three-day-eventing, it helped to have an aristocratic-sounding name, so it seems he'd invented one. Years later, I discovered that Van did quite well in the end. He moved to the Republic of Ireland in the mid-1960s and ended up on the Irish international eventing team for the 1976 Olympics. He didn't complete the competition as he had a fall on the cross-country section and broke several ribs.

I worked for the Harthills for a couple of months that winter of 1963, jumping some super horses and enjoying teaching my clients, but I just couldn't settle: I was worrying about the National Insurance cards because, although I had taken the matter to a higher level, nothing had happened. Knowing Pennwood would need them, I realised that the only other option I had was to move to the Republic of Ireland because there I would not need National Insurance cards to work.

In early 1964 I applied for another job advertised in *Horse & Hound* – what would I have done without that magazine? The Grand Hotel at Malahide in Dublin was opening an equestrian centre and needed an instructor. It was very grand, with a huge indoor school set in beautiful grounds, and was rumoured to be *the* place to ride in Ireland. Flying to Dublin, I stayed for free at the Grand for the four days of the recruitment process but I didn't get the job. The people at the hotel were lovely and told me to stay on a little longer if I liked. So I asked Billy to join me. When he arrived, we dined and went for a drive. Our spirits soared at being back together but I was suddenly frightened by the intensity of our emotions, and back at the hotel, my mood took a dip. My problems were still exactly the same as they had been before and now I had been rejected from the job, there seemed no way out. Billy kept asking me to go back and live with him but I couldn't bear the prospect of returning to the misery of begging Jeremy for my National Insurance cards. The conversation I had had with the secretary to the minister for pensions and National Insurance had gone nowhere. My only option was to find work in the Republic of Ireland.

Billy was so warm and so loving, but my mood stayed low. I couldn't sleep with him and spent the whole night sitting up in a chair. If I let him near me, I knew I would give in to his tenderness, and then I could never bear to be parted from him again, so I pushed him away. In the end I fell asleep in the chair and woke to the sound of a car starting up below the window and Billy gone from the room. I rushed to the window and watched his little Morris Minor disappearing up the drive. I stood by that window for a long time, desperate for Billy to return, but I never saw him again. I heard later he had got a job in Canada. I must have hurt him terribly, but though I loved him so much, I could not let go of my need for independence. I had to be able to work, and to make my way in life, and it all came back to Jeremy. If he had kept his promises, and sorted out my National Insurance cards, I would not have been in this fix. I could have stayed with Billy and had a good career wherever I wanted. I could have been free.

CHAPTER NINE

Peter Bessell

IN THE NINE years since I'd left school, I'd had countless jobs, becoming used to going from place to place and starting again. When I got a job in Dublin working for Nat Galway-Greer, the well-respected horseman, I hoped to settle for good. During his career Nat won the prestigious perpetual challenge cup on ten occasions at the Dublin Horse Show and I looked up to him. When I saw that he was advertising for someone to help prepare his horses for the 1964 show, I immediately applied, and as soon as he had seen me ride, he offered me the job. I was excited, believing that working for Nat and having access to some of the best horses in Ireland would help me progress and achieve my dreams. When there was no mention of the dreaded National Insurance cards, I dreamed of staying on there indefinitely and building my life up again.

I took a room in a house on the North Circular Road in Dublin and caught the bus each morning to Nat's yard at Dunboyne. It was very easy. Nat's two young horses would be brought out to me, groomed and tacked up with their hoofs polished, and I would school each one for forty-five minutes. The horses were beautifully balanced after all my schooling, and when I took them out into the fields, they jumped the huge hedges with ease. Nat would watch me and told me he liked the way I rode his young horses. 'You were born with beautiful hands,' Nat told me. 'Don't ever lose that! My horses love you.'

As well as getting on very well with Nat, I became friends with his daughter Betty, who was a fine horsewoman, and we often rode out together into the hills. I began going to Mass again, with Betty and her mother. I said nothing to the priests about my time with Jeremy, because I worried it would lead to difficult conversations, but I was happy to be back at church, breathing in the incense and hearing the words of the old Latin Mass. It felt so right to do this in Ireland, where Catholicism was so deeply ingrained. I'd sit on the bus, and as we passed a church you could almost feel a draught passing along as everyone raised their hands to make the sign of the Cross.

Through the spring and summer I took care of Nat's horses with a focus of having them in top condition for the showing classes at the Dublin Horse Show. As the date neared, I was excited at the prospect of riding them at this prestigious event. If I rode well, the show could change my life. Top show-jumpers such as the Italian D'Inzeo brothers would visit Dublin to find their future mounts for international competitions, and with people like that watching, I could really make my name in the equestrian world. I put all my energy into the horses, going the extra mile, wanting them to be perfect, so that they and I would truly shine in the show ring.

A week before the show Nat told me the well-known riders

Jack Gittins and Natalie Tollitt were coming from England to ride his horses at the show. He told me casually, without having any idea of how the decision would impact me. From his point of view, it was normal – they had always ridden for him in the past – but I was really shocked, feeling Nat was being very unfair. I had done all the groundwork and the horses were now going beautifully because of my efforts but he wouldn't budge on his decision. Outraged, I told him I was leaving, unable to bear waiting on the sidelines, watching as two already successful riders took what I felt was mine. I had worked so hard and got so close but it had all gone wrong, and the worst thing was that I had tried so hard and dared to hope. So, just like that, I turned my back on horses, took myself out of the game and stopped trying so that I wouldn't suffer the pain of failing again. When I think about it now, I see how fatalistic I was. I wish I had stuck at it. Instead, my decision led me to step out of the equestrian world for five years.

Life changed completely. Without the structure and income of jobs with horses, money became extremely tight, and without a purpose, I felt aimless. For a while, I embraced this. Dublin is a big city, but in those days it had a village feel to it. Penny-whistle players piped on St Stephen's Green and there were bars and pubs full of lively and interesting people. I discovered a café I came to rely on, run by a delightful Scottish woman in her sixties, who was married to a Pole. Mrs Gaj served good food very cheaply, and customers could stay until she felt like closing. I would drink endless cups of coffee with Mrs Gaj, then wander out onto the streets unable to sleep. Knowing I had no money, she

'The pretty Miss Lynch and the other one'. This photograph was taken in 1921. My mother Ena is on the left, and her sister Josephine seated. I don't see a difference, myself. They both look pretty.

Happy times: my mother looking stylish on a day out with her husband Bertie Merritt in the 1930s.

Aged fourteen on an outing with Bexleyheath Boys Secondary School (far right). My hairstyle is ahead of its time – very Vidal Sassoon. I borrowed the yellow scarf from my brother Edward.

Jeremy Thorpe MP gives his signature wave to admirers
outside the Houses of Parliament in 1967.

Jeremy Thorpe and his mother Ursula
Thorpe (seated) and second wife Marion.

22 Draycott Place: I used to throw down
the keys to Jeremy from the balcony – my
room was directly above the front door.

An early modelling test shot from 1968 by Francis Loney. I kept that plum-coloured velvet shirt for years.

Vernon Dewhurst took this one for Quincy Jones' shop on Shepherd Market in 1969. Stella models a Loewe coat and I am in one of the shop's designs.

Sue with our son Benjamin in 1969. The only picture I have of them together.

My daughter Bryony aged three in 1979, already adept with pencil and paper. Probably making a drawing for her daddy. We were – and still are – very close.

At Chester Square in 1968, as Conway Wilson Young's grandmother Hilda Wertheimer looks down.

Prima ballerina Margot Fonteyn. I met her in 1969 and she was a good friend through a difficult time.

Artist Francis Bacon taking some refreshment on a train – perhaps recovering from our brief liaison. We met at the Colony Club in Soho in 1966.

Romany Surprise, a little horse with the heart of a lion that I used to show-jump and event with great success, takes the Normandy Bank at Romansleigh near South Molton.

A relaxing hack on my lovely Blue Slipper in 1976, with rescue dog Chino leading the way. (I always wear a riding hat now – those were very different times!)

On Dartmoor, near Kestorway in 1976, riding Rosetta. Chino went everywhere with me. The most faithful and loving confidante, she could have written her own book about our time together.

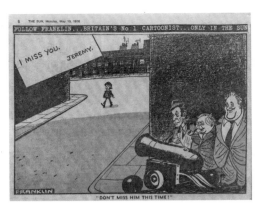

A cartoon by Franklin from May 1976, after the Newton Trial. Jeremy Thorpe out shooting bunnies.

David Holmes, Jeremy Thorpe's Mr Fixit.

Emlyn Hooson, the Welsh Liberal MP, looking the epitome of decency and respectability.

Andrew Gino Newton, the would-be hitman. His dress sense says it all.

George Deakin – one of the accused.

John Le Mesurier about to give evidence in June 1979. Not the amiable actor and star of *Dad's Army*, but a carpet salesman from Swansea.

Jeremy Thorpe is heckled by Brixton Gays as he arrives at the Old Bailey for the judge's summing-up on 18 June 1979.

About to give my evidence in May 1979.

Peter Bessell leaves the Old Bailey after taking a hammering from the defence counsel.

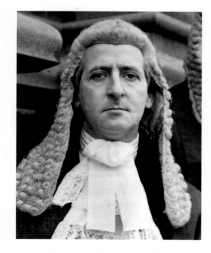

'It is no worse than shooting a sick dog'

A horrible headline, one of many.

George Carman, Jeremy Thorpe's defence counsel, rather resembling a grumpy spaniel. Both his bark and his bite were savage.

Pumpkin time at the farm.
With my grandchildren Jay,
Jasmine, Ebony and Holly
in 2020.

The beautiful Coppelia,
one of the horses I showed,
winning with me at
Honiton Show in 2004.

On the sofa with
my Affenpinschers
in 2019: a typical
evening at the farm.

would sometimes invite me to eat with her at her mews cottage in Ballsbridge, making me promise to have at least one meal a day in the café.

I also discovered Bartley Dunne's, the oldest gay bar in Dublin. It was dark and intimate, with little velvet-curtained booths to sit in, and often Ray Charles's song 'Take These Chains From My Heart' would be playing on the jukebox. Homosexuality was illegal in Ireland, just as it was in England, but there was nothing secretive about Bartley Dunne's. Although the gardaí would be standing outside the door around 10 p.m., they never arrested anyone. I think they were there just to stop anyone getting beaten up.

Bartley Dunne's was owned by two brothers, Barry and Gerald. They were both straight, but perfectly at home with the gay clientele. They loved to make me laugh, always greeting me with a very formal 'Good morning, sir!' when I arrived. I'd spend afternoons there, enjoying long and point-less discussions with a mad, happy cross-section of people. Barry and Gerry always closed the bar between three and four – the 'Holy Hour' as they called it – so I would head to Mrs Gaj's for tea, meeting up with another wonderful crowd, including the Irish folk band the Dubliners; Lady Longford, the historian and prominent agitator for social justice; her nephew Valentine Lamb, who was editor of the racing news-paper the *Irish Field*; and members of staff from Teilifis Éireann, the national broadcaster. We would discourse on all manner of subjects.

Distracted by other people who also weren't working, and still stubbornly steadfast on giving up a career with horses, I found my attitude towards life shifted to one that was more reckless and hedonistic than before. The Swinging Sixties were under way. The age of free love had reached Dublin and I was more than willing to participate. It became normal for me to stay up half the night drinking and talking to people. I didn't go looking for a job, and the relaxed atmosphere of Bartley Dunne's set me free to enjoy sexual liaisons with men, including an older man called Maurice. Though he wasn't part of my usual younger crowd he always wanted to buy me drinks. I assumed he must be a businessman because, if he managed to get me on my own, we would have long chats and he would try to make me see that my lifestyle was getting me nowhere. He was very kind, and only had eyes for me. On a few occasions, after I'd had quite a lot to drink, he came back to my room, and we slept together. There was something vulnerable about him and even though I wasn't attracted to him, I didn't mind having sex with him. Our occasional liaisons were such comfortable affairs that they seemed harmless. One evening Mrs Gaj saw me with him, and told me he was Maurice Dockrell, who had been the Mayor of Dublin, and was now a TD – the Irish equivalent of an MP. This should perhaps have made me wary, but Maurice was a gentle soul, not at all like Jeremy.

It was at Bartley Dunne's that I also met a young man called John, who had a big flat where he lived with a group of friends, all sociable young people. John and I started an intense affair, and he asked me to move in with him. None of us had any money so we pooled what we had. If we were desperate we would go to an upmarket restaurant that served unlimited free snacks at the bar, order Guinness and stuff our faces with canapés. On one of our escapades we tried to steal a fireplace at the beautiful eighteenth-century Weavers Hall in the centre of Dublin, which was about to be knocked down. The gardaí interrupted us, asking what we were up to, so I told them boldly, 'We're saving this fireplace for the nation!'

It was the time to be young and wild and, for a while, I felt thoroughly happy living in the moment with others doing the same. Sometimes I would skip lunch to treat myself to a cup of coffee in the luxurious Gresham Hotel. One morning as I was gazing around at the beautiful interior, Elizabeth Taylor and Richard Burton walked into the lobby, with a stunning young man. When the film stars left, the good-looking man made a beeline for me and we started chatting. He explained he was Elizabeth Taylor's secretary and had come to Dublin with them on their yacht. He told me, with twinkling eyes, that they'd returned to the yacht to be with their pet dogs, so he had the afternoon off. When he asked me to go back to his hotel with him I was happy to agree. We left the Gresham and arrived at the Hotel Pelletier where he was staying. This was a temperance hotel – alcohol-free and rather strait-laced. It was also right opposite my flat so the staff knew me and my flatmates as they had seen us throwing loo rolls out of the windows to unfold like streamers. They looked a little surprised as I walked across the lobby with Elizabeth Taylor's secretary, but I smiled at them before heading up to the secretary's room where we spent a most pleasant afternoon together.

But by the end of 1964, the carefree existence began to fray and I found myself longing to go back to England. With no skills except with horses, I didn't know what sort of job to try for and John and I were arguing a lot. We split up and suddenly I had nowhere to live and no money to pay for rent in a normal set-up, where I wouldn't be sharing with so many others. Mrs Gaj became worried about me, trying to cheer me up, and Maurice, who I was still sleeping with occasionally, tried to advise me, though without much success. A kind friend, Cara Proby, whom I'd met during the happier times earlier in the year, found me a small flat but I couldn't afford the deposit.

Not knowing what to do, I turned to the Church and confided in a priest, Father Sweetman. After Mass he invited me to the Priests' House for a glass of sherry and I told him everything, becoming very emotional as I described my relationship with Jeremy. I felt very ashamed, wondering what he would be thinking. My voice caught in my throat as I said how I longed to return to England, but that it was impossible. I felt like a stammering, hopeless broken record. 'This National Insurance card issue haunts me at every turn, blocks me from choices I want to make,' I said. 'And now I'm about to be homeless.'

Father Sweetman listened intently, then said, 'You must write to your friend in London to get the cards back, but in the meantime, we have a fund and we can help you with rent for a flat.'

The relief was huge. One man's kindness countered another's control, and with the money provided by the Church I was able to move into a new flat. When I wrote to Jeremy, he didn't reply. A few months went by but then something happened that provoked me to write another letter, this time to Jeremy's mother, Ursula Thorpe.

One night when Maurice had just left my house, two men in trench coats and trilby hats knocked on the door. Shocked, I knew even before they pulled out their identity cards that they were police detectives.

'That man who just left. Why was he here?' one of them asked.

'What business is it of yours?' I responded, confused and rattled by their arrival.

The detective frowned. 'There's things going on with you,' he said, 'and we want to know what it's all about.'

I immediately panicked, assuming they were asking me questions because of something related to Jeremy. 'This is nothing to do with that man,' I stammered. 'It's because of who I am, isn't it? Why do I have to be in Ireland? Because of Jeremy Thorpe! This is about him, isn't it?' I said, beginning to shout.

I ranted on about Jeremy, as I remained convinced they were there because of him. They obviously thought I was deranged and took me to Harcourt Street police station, where the police doctor gave me an injection, which knocked me out.

I came to in a cavernous, dingy ward in the Grange Gorman psychiatric hospital, strapped to an iron bed, and surrounded by toothless, unshaven old men who laughed and gibbered and pulled me about. It was like a scene from *Gormenghast*. I still sometimes dream about that night, and wake in a panic, struggling to escape. Terrified and helpless, I screamed until a male nurse came into the ward. I tried to tell him there had been a terrible mistake.

'That's what they all say,' he replied.

'No, really, there has been!' I exclaimed. 'Can I see somebody in authority?'

'Tomorrow,' he said, giving me another injection. I dread to think what happened to me, lying there out cold while the inmates frolicked around me.

In the morning I was relieved to see that the old men were all asleep on their beds, and when another nurse came, I told him I wanted to see the person in charge. He took me to an office, and I waited there in my hospital gown until someone finally brought me my clothes and took me to a psychiatrist.

'I am telling the truth,' I said. 'This is all a mistake.'

The psychiatrist listened to my explanations and told me that the gardaí had probably come because they were afraid that my association with Maurice Dockrell might compromise the Dáil – the Irish Parliament. 'It won't be anything to do with Jeremy Thorpe. Is there anyone who can vouch for you?' he asked.

I told him to contact Mrs Gaj and it turned out that she had already been trying to telephone the hospital, as one of the detectives had come to her restaurant for his break and told her what had happened. She came straight to Grange Gorman and got me out, but after this shocking experience, my mental state began to go downhill very quickly.

Through the long, dark nights of the winter of 1964, with no money and no job, I became anxious and obsessive. I kept dwelling on the memory of being committed to Grange Gorman and couldn't help thinking it was connected with my relationship with Jeremy. I started imagining what would happen if our homosexual relationship leaked into the wrong hands and worried about being arrested or thrown into a psychiatric hospital again. I remembered my suitcase, which had been languishing in a lost property office on the continent for almost two years, with all the letters Jeremy had written to me inside it. I had forgotten about it, while I was enjoying myself in the summer, but now the letters became all I could think about. If they were found, it would be a disaster for Jeremy. He might end up like I had, with policemen on this doorstep, arrested and taken away, his shining political career in ruins. I didn't wish him harm. I didn't want him to go through something similar to what I had experienced, especially when he had so much more to lose.

Other famous men before him had suffered hugely when their homosexuality had been discovered. In 1953 John Gielgud, who was newly knighted and at the height of his fame, about to direct himself in a prestigious West End production, was arrested in a public lavatory in Chelsea. He was charged with 'persistently importuning men for immoral purposes', his conviction causing a sensation. Although he carried on acting, he suffered a nervous breakdown and never spoke of it publicly. The home secretary at the time, David Maxwell Fyfe, had been outspoken about his homophobia, stressing that the police were to arrest anyone who ignored that homosexuality was a criminal offence. The same year Alan Turing, the mathematical genius who broke the Enigma code, had been convicted, stripped of his security licence and given hormone injections as a result of admitting he was homosexual. Turing had committed suicide two years later.

When I think back to the persecution that men have suffered for being homosexual, I am appalled. For three hundred years, since Henry VIII's 1533 Buggery Act, the punishment was death and the crime was categorised with bestiality. In the 1960s, the sentence was prison or sometimes hormone injections, but either way, the resulting publicity could ruin a reputation, a career and sometimes, like Turing, led to suicide. Homosexual crimes were thought so obscene, they were often described as 'gross indecency', and even in the new liberal age, homosexuality was still one of the biggest societal taboos. The more I thought about the letters, the more mentally unstable I became. I tried to hold myself together, but in March 1965, I made a last-ditch, desperate appeal for help. I wrote to Jeremy's mother.

I believed Ursula Thorpe knew about our relationship. How could she not, when she was so close to Jeremy? She adored her son. If she knew about the damage the letters could do, she would be extremely worried so I hoped she would talk to Jeremy, and if she did I knew he would listen. I hoped that if I wrote to her she would make sure the suitcase was returned to me and then, perhaps, something would finally be done about my National Insurance cards.

Once I started the letter, everything just poured out. I began by saying I had been having a sexual relationship with Jeremy for five years, beginning with that first visit to Stonewalls. I continued with a description of life at Draycott Place, the misery of those lonely nights on the camp bed, and my realisation that Jeremy was not the caring friend I longed for but was just using me for sex. Then I came to the issue of the missing luggage. I asked Mrs Thorpe to plead my case with her son, asking him to pay the money to recover it from lost property and assured her that I would repay this as soon as I had the funds. My letter rambled on, my emotions unravelling as I filled seventeen pages. I stressed that I didn't want to cause friction between her and Jeremy and that I knew how close they were. On the last page, I said I hoped she would understand, and begged her to believe me, as I was desperate for help.

This letter was proof of how anxious I had become. I was asking for help about more than just the retrieval of the letters. My rambling, desperate letter went off in the post but I heard nothing. I couldn't sleep for despair and would instead roam the streets aimlessly. One night, I came home in the early hours to find a small card on my doormat. On it was written, 'Please ring me, no matter what time of night you come back.'

It was from someone called Peter Bessell. I had never met him, though the name was vaguely familiar, and I wondered if this might have something to do with my letter to Mrs Thorpe. Mr Bessell was staying at the InterContinental Hotel and, feeling apprehensive, I telephoned him at 3 a.m. Mr Bessell was asleep but roused himself enough to invite me to have breakfast with him later that morning.

Arriving at the InterContinental at 9 a.m., I felt very shaky, wondering who this man was and why he wanted to meet me so urgently. When I saw Mr Bessell, who was thin with reddish hair and a deeply lined face, he didn't explain who he was, or give me the chance to ask. Instead, he began haranguing me. Although I didn't know who he was, he seemed to know a lot about me. He told me what an appalling thing I had done by writing to Mrs Thorpe and how, as a result, the home secretary, Sir Frank Soskice, had issued an extradition order for me.

'Great,' I said. 'I can't think of anything I'd like more than to be back in England.'

Mr Bessell was visibly shocked. In fact, he looked horrified. When he said he was a Liberal MP, I began to feel suspicious, realising this was clearly some kind of cover-up operation instigated by Jeremy. I was pretty sure the extradition order was a lie, intended to intimidate me, and I did not want to be fobbed off again.

'I've got to go to the airport now. Come with me, and we'll talk,' Mr Bessell said.

I agreed, hoping I would find out what was going on. As we waited for a taxi, Mr Bessell became flustered, and as one pulled up, he ordered me not to mention Jeremy's name in our conversation. 'Call him JT,' he whispered, before we got into the car.

In the back of the taxi, I explained about my relationship with 'JT' but Mr Bessell insisted that 'JT' denied any knowledge of me. I mentioned the missing suitcase, with the letters and my shirts marked by the laundry with the Marsham Court address, and Mr Bessell's stance changed. He listened with great attention and I could tell he was beginning to believe me.

Mr Bessell asked me to have coffee with him at the airport and we continued talking. I told him about the situation with my National Insurance cards. 'I guess you think I'm some kind of blackmailer. I'm not. I just want what is mine,' I said.

'And this is why you've stayed in Dublin all this time?' Mr Bessell asked, putting two and two together. 'Because you can't get work in England?'

'Exactly. I don't need National Insurance cards here,' I explained.

'I understand you don't have any money,' Mr Bessell said, his manner less hostile now.

'I'm living off the kindness of the Church, as Father Sweetman has been looking after me,' I replied.

It was almost time for Mr Bessell to board his plane, and as he got up, he promised to write when he had spoken to Jeremy, and gave me five pounds to get a taxi back to Dublin. At last, I felt I'd made some progress, and that someone was going to sort things out for me.

A few days later Mr Bessell wrote, care of Father Sweetman, to say he was doing what he could about the cards and in the meantime he would pay me a retainer equivalent to the unemployment benefit I could have claimed with fully stamped cards. He kept his word. Every week for the next year, I received five pounds in cash in an envelope (it would be worth around eighty pounds today), along with a note on House of Commons paper: 'Here is your retainer for this week.'

My lost luggage from Switzerland finally turned up two months later but I was horrified to see that both the locks were smashed, and it was held shut by a belt. Inside were my riding things and a few other clothes. But no letters and also no shirts. I riffled through it, double checking, feeling through the lining, tipping the contents out on to the floor. Panicking, fearing someone had stolen them and might use

163

them for blackmail, I rang Mr Bessell but he told me not to worry about the letters. He insisted the suitcase had come straight to Dublin from Switzerland but I was convinced he was lying.

CHAPTER TEN

Aversion Therapy . . . Why?

IN THE LATE spring of 1965, with a little money in my pocket again, thanks to Mr Bessell, my life found a new direction. A Norwegian designer, Lisbeth, caught me doodling in the pub one day, loved the little figures I had drawn and asked if I would be interested in designing some clothes for her. I was surprised but delighted. I had no experience of tailoring or clothes design, but ever since the days at 26 Brampton Road, with the William Morris wallpaper and my mother's requisitioned curtains, I had been fascinated by the way that different fabrics flowed and fell into different shapes.

Lisbeth's boutique was in a seventeenth-century house, which had once been a bulb exchange, where people went to buy and sell the latest, very valuable, tulip bulbs from Amsterdam. It was high-end, and sold some exquisite tailored Irish tweeds for men and women, but mostly evening dresses. Each of these was usually of chiffon, hand-made, with as many as 150 hand-cut buttons. Her designs for these dresses were beautiful, but rather rigid and Scandinavian. My sketches were much softer and more flowing, and I designed a series of dresses that Lisbeth wore to dances and parties. I seemed to have an instinct for what would work, and just knew that if something was cut on the bias, it would fall in a certain way. Everyone loved my designs, and Lisbeth asked me to join her in her business as a designer.

Through designing I also started compèring fashion shows in Dublin. One, held on the top floor of the InterContinental Hotel, had a large number of beautifully tailored heather-coloured tweed creations. My job was to describe the outfits. Knowing that if the audience had more fun, they would write great reviews and order more of the clothes, I livened it up a bit. As more and more tweed came on to the catwalk, I said things like, 'Oh, not more bloody tweed,' and when the models paraded some hand-knitted Aran sweaters, I remarked, 'Ah, every stitch a prayer!' The Irish audience fell about with laughter, knowing I was just teasing, and afterwards two men from the audience I didn't know came up to tell me how much they had enjoyed my commentary. Vernon Dewhurst and Jeremy Bailey were in Ireland to take colour photographs of the country for postcards. 'Colour photographs?' I said. 'Impossible job. It's always raining!'

They roared with laughter, because of course that was exactly what they had been experiencing, and from then on, the three of us became great friends. Shortly after this there was a fire at Vernon and Jeremy's studio, and all the negatives for the postcards were lost. Deciding to become fashion photographers instead, they took some test shots using me as a model, and encouraged me to take this up more seriously, believing I would be very successful. I dismissed the idea at first but enjoyed the buzz of the shows and being surrounded by creative people.

Since Mrs Tish, I had been moving around too much to

have another dog but in 1966, I found a whippet called Emma. She was a slender, beautiful little creature and I loved the feel of her smooth, silky coat and the grace of her long limbs.

Although the National Insurance matter was still ongoing, Mr Bessell continued to send weekly retainers. Glad of his assistance, I felt settled in the world of fashion and design but my love-life was more complicated. Ever since my relationship with Jeremy, I was afraid to trust anyone and found the idea of emotional intimacy impossible. Only Billy had been different. I kept getting into unwanted situations with both men and women – first with Lisbeth, who was married but separated. We started having an on-off affair even though I wasn't in love with her. She was very unhappy, equally insistent, and as we were working so closely together it became impossible to refuse.

In the age of free love, casual sex was very normal. Everyone was doing it and I had got used to dysfunctional relationships. I thought, wrongly, that by sleeping with her I might ease her pain and help her to forget. And then there was Adam, who had left his wife and children to come to Ireland to be with his lover Martyn, but now found himself attracted to me. I wasn't attracted to him but he was as insistent as Lisbeth, both of them convinced they were in love with me. Weakened by my low sense of self-worth, I liked to please. It never worked. I always felt empty and regretted it but I kept doing it all the same.

Every time I reached another unwanted climax, I recalled a brass nameplate I had recently walked past. It advertised the services of a Dublin physician, who, I had heard, practised a form of aversion therapy for homosexuals. I didn't want to be another Adam, going from person to person always hoping to find the right one. I hated myself for being so morally weak, sleeping with people I knew I didn't want to be with. Nothing fresh or clean, no genuine love. I spoke about the aversion therapy to Lisbeth, and she thought this might be a good idea, hoping it would help our relationship.

By the sixties, the concept of homosexuality being a pathological medical or psychological condition was well established. In 1961, a short social-guidance propaganda film was released in America called *Boys Beware*. It detailed how homosexuality was a disease, the narrator saying, 'One never knows when a homosexual is about. He may appear normal and it may be too late when you discover he is mentally ill.'

Horrendous things, like testicular transplantations, had taken place in the 1920s, after pioneering doctors declared that homosexuality was rooted in a man's testicles: the cure was to swap them for 'heterosexual' testicles. From then on, other treatments had been developed, including gay 'conversion camps' (where men were isolated, hypnotised and told to pray until their homosexuality subsided), electroconvulsive therapy, hormone injections and even lobotomies. Then there was aversion therapy and I had heard horror stories about men being shown gay pornography; if they were aroused, they were given a drug that made them vomit.

When I went to see the Dublin doctor, he assured me that his method was based on rest and hypnosis. There would be no vomiting, no electric shocks: 'You will emerge after a week at my clinic completely cured of any homosexual tendencies.'

I was rather alarmed to discover that the price for this

week of rest and relaxation would be three hundred pounds – about four thousand today. There was no way I could afford that, but Lisbeth was very keen for me to undergo the treatment, and offered to help pay.

I booked myself into the clinic and was given some injections that put me into a semi-conscious state. I remember almost nothing of what happened during my stay except being led, occasionally, along a very brightly lit corridor so that I could use the lavatory. Looking back, I am horrified by this. Anything could have been done to me while I was out cold. Perhaps all sorts of horrid things took place that I have just blanked out. Or maybe I had no treatment. The doctor could easily have been a quack, and I just spent a week in deep, peaceful sleep while he counted up the money he had made. Certainly, any hopes that I would emerge as a bona-fide heterosexual male were dashed when I stepped out on to the street at the end of the week and felt an instant attraction to a good-looking man who was walking towards me.

My relationship with Lisbeth continued until, out of the blue, she decided to close the boutique and travel to Afghanistan. I asked why, as the business was doing well, but she wouldn't say. After she'd left, friends said she might have been pregnant, and Mrs Gaj agreed. I never heard from Lisbeth again, and I sometimes wonder if, somewhere in the world, I have a child who knows nothing about me.

I carried on having meaningless relationships with men and found myself living a life I didn't want. I met a young Vietnam draft dodger from Buffalo in the US called Murray and we soon became lovers. We spent a lot of time at Bartley

Dunne's, and when he said he was going to London for a weekend, he asked me to go along. When a girlfriend of his from the US joined us, he ended up going back to Buffalo with her, and as I had a few days before my return flight to Dublin, I hung around in London. I was in the Salisbury pub in Soho one night and met a man who took me to the Colony Room Club on Dean Street in Soho. This was a notorious haunt with garish green walls, mostly frequented by alcoholic folk, many of whom were gay. The painter Francis Bacon was a founding member, and artists and musicians, such as Lucian Freud and George Melly, went there to drink. Princess Margaret was also famed for frequenting the club. It was known as somewhere for anyone who felt like a misfit or an outsider.

I returned on subsequent evenings to the club and sat on a bar stool drinking and talking to the owner, Muriel Belcher, who had become very fond and protective of me. Whenever the more louche members approached me, she cried out, 'Keep your hands off this beauty!'

On one of the nights, I had an awful lot to drink and was picked up by Francis Bacon, who took me back to his house. We downed champagne in his filthy, paint-spattered studio before having sex. I tried to sleep next to him but his snoring was so bad I curled up in the studio. It reeked of turpentine, but the fumes helped me go to sleep. The next morning, Bacon, who had assumed I had gone, was irritated to find me in the studio and, no longer drunk, exclaimed, 'You're not my usual type.'

I returned to the Colony Room Club that night, and Bacon arrived, already drunk, and immediately invited me back to his. 'What would be the point?' I said, turning him down.

One-night stands and drinking sessions felt normal after a couple of years but I felt less and less content. The original feeling of liberation had worn off and the parties I went to, although glamorous, only made me feel more aware I wasn't where I wanted to be in life. One party, the most spectacular of them all, left me longing for a change.

In the summer of 1966, my friend Cara Proby and I were invited to Luggala, the Guinness family seat, ahead of a huge party that our mutual friend Tara was throwing. Tara, the heir to the Guinness fortune, who tragically died in a car accident in London the following Christmas, was extremely popular, known for throwing big parties. He lived his life between London and Luggala in the Wicklow Hills, a striking Gothic house, white and pristine as a wedding cake.

Cara and I went to visit just before the party and sat down to tea with Tara, his mother Baroness Oranmore and Browne, and their friends, siblings Julian and Jane Ormsby-Gore. Jane went on to become the editor of *Vogue* and is thought to have been the inspiration behind the Rolling Stones hit 'Lady Jane'. Over tea, the atmosphere was full of a relaxed bohemian contentment, with toys scattered everywhere for Tara's young children, and we chatted about the plans for the forthcoming party. When we finished, a strange and timeless household ritual took place as the maids came in and tipped tea leaves over the seagrass carpet, before sweeping it all up.

The party was spectacular. Internationally famous interior designer David Mlinaric, who had designed the exquisite interiors at Luggala, decorated the marquees with garlands of flowers. Outside he had hung swings from the trees with ropes of flowers twined around them and the whole place was floodlit. Tara hired two private jets to fly guests from America including the pop band the Lovin' Spoonful who were to play for the guests. Mick Jagger and Marianne Faithfull were also there. They looked so beautiful. All the beautiful people were there: I saw fashion designers Ossie Clark and Michael Rainey, and actress Anita Pallenberg, Rolling Stone Brian Jones's girlfriend, among the crowd. Everywhere I looked there were famous faces.

I kept on drinking with everyone, but I couldn't shake off a feeling of melancholy. All around me successful, wealthy young people were dancing, high as kites on drugs and alcohol, but I felt I could never belong. How could I ever be a part of this happy crowd? I felt so inadequate having achieved so little in life.

After the party, I tried to pick up my mood, but I was stuck in a deep melancholy and I began to worry about my future again. I carried on living in Dublin but as friends started to move to London, I longed to return. This feeling was exacerbated by a series of unsettling communications with Mr Bessell throughout 1967 that I would later discover were connected to Jeremy's success. That January, Jeremy had become leader of the Liberal Party. After the 1966 election, the Liberal leader, Jo Grimond, stepped down. By then Jeremy was the highest-profile member of the Party. After the twelve Liberal MPs voted for either Eric Lubbock, Emlyn Hooson or Jeremy, Jeremy won the majority and was declared the new leader. It was all over the news. I wasn't in the least bit surprised, and he catapulted even further into the limelight.

He was younger than the other politicians and his attitude of engaging with the reporters and the public alike made him very telegenic. Footage of him athletically jumping over fences to speak to adoring crowds of Liberal supporters would flash across the news, and pictures of him smiling with his arms flung into the air would be printed in the papers.

Mr Bessell, who had carried on sending the retainers, suddenly started suggesting I move to America, inviting me to work in one of the restaurants he was planning to open. I asked him what I would do there. 'Cooking and washing-up,' came the reply. He said he would arrange a visa for me. He was persistent, and although I didn't want to go, I agreed, but the visa didn't materialise and the plan just fizzled out. This played on my mind. It was such a peculiar offer and Mr Bessell never properly explained why he had suggested it, always insisting he was just trying to help me.

All this made me feel determined to get back to my life in England. When Vernon Dewhurst and Jeremy Bailey moved to London to be in the thick of the fashion industry in the summer of 1967, I hoped I could get freelance work as a model there, for which I wouldn't need my National Insurance cards. Vernon told me he was getting a lot of work for a photographic agency called Studio Five, and he thought I might make a go of it as a model. So, in late 1967, after five years away, I finally returned to England.

CHAPTER ELEVEN

A Model in the Swinging Sixties

STUDIO FIVE WAS the epitome of the swinging sixties. A fashion and advertising agency run by the photographer John Cole, it was tucked into a narrow street in Mayfair. The basement and a small sunlit studio on the ground floor became the launch pad for many huge names in the fashion industry. Now world-famous photographers such as David Bailey and Brian Duffy worked there alongside top models Jean Shrimpton, Joanna Lumley and Twiggy. I went there to meet Vernon, who introduced me to Cole. He liked my look but not my name and thought I'd get more bookings if I changed it. I remembered the conversation I'd had with Jeremy just before I ended the relationship for the first time, about John Scott, Earl of Eldon, and decided to call myself Norman Scott. Scott was easy to remember and pronounce, and sounded very English. The requests to see my portfolio soon came flooding in.

Having no money to pay for a portfolio of photographs, I contacted Mr Bessell, chasing my National Insurance cards so I could get some work. Instead, he sent me enough money for a basic portfolio. Having no other option, I took the money gladly. Through friends of Vernon, I was offered a room to live in, and moved in with my whippet Emma.

Earlier that year, in July 1967, before I'd returned to London, homosexuality had become legal in England, though it remained illegal in Dublin until 1993. I thought that maybe London would feel different once the law changed but it didn't. The attitude to homosexuals was still hostile. During the debates in Parliament to pass the bill, the then home secretary, Roy Jenkins, argued for the law to be changed but his words, quoted in newspapers, didn't feel supportive. 'It would be a mistake to think that by what we are doing tonight we are giving a vote of confidence or congratulation to homosexuality,' he said. 'Those who suffer from this disability carry a great weight of shame all their lives.'

The law still restricted homosexuality too: any homosexual act could only happen between two people over the age of twenty-one and only in private. 'Private' meant that homosexual acts were limited to a house without anyone else inside, meaning that in public, in hotels or in houses with anyone else there at the time, homosexuality remained a crime.

Socially, the stigma didn't ease either. As I made friends and started going out, I was wary of leaving a gay club as the pubs closed because people would catcall and shout threats. Sometimes I'd go to the Coleherne Leather Bar in Earls Court and the gay discothèque on the corner of the square. The actor Peter Wyngarde was a regular and used to park his large American car outside, filled with gay men. Most Fridays anyone coming out of the club would get chased by anti-gays and fights would break out. I'd walk the long way home to avoid any trouble, afraid I'd be beaten up.

Staying close to friends, although I didn't feel liberated now the law had changed, I did feel a sense of defiant pride. Even though it wasn't always easy, I was glad to be living in London in the heart of the sixties.

One of my first photoshoots was with the photographer Francis Loney. I travelled to his studio in Clerkenwell, where I sat in front of a grey background wearing a plum velvet shirt with puff sleeves and tailored trousers I'd borrowed from nearby shops. 'I'll do anything you want but don't ask me to be butch!' I said.

Francis roared with laughter. We got on so well, and I felt relaxed as he giggled, instructing me to pose and look in different directions. 'You're a complete natural,' he said, when he had finished, which gave me great confidence.

Soon I was invited for test shoots that weren't paid but the photos helped fill my portfolio. On one shoot I met a girl called Stella. As we posed in high-collared jackets in Liberty prints, we discovered we had a mutual love for interior design and became friends. She introduced me to her boyfriend Jack, who was a graphic designer. Cara Proby also moved to London, setting up a boutique right next to Studio Five. I began to feel settled and happy to be in London, excited about what modelling could offer. The problem was, though, that most of the photoshoots I did were unpaid test shoots that didn't amount to anything. I went to endless castings, often with Stella, and every now and then I'd get booked for a job. I was the face of a few outfitters, modelling their clothes in editorial features for magazines or photographs in their shop windows and catalogues.

In between castings and shoots, I would hang out at Studio Five. There was a real buzz, people always coming and going, and everyone would congregate at Emilio's café on the corner. It was an eclectic mix. There was a group of friendly girls with skirts that were very short, and tops that were very low, who turned out to be prostitutes. They'd smoke in the doorway, waiting for the punters, and chat with me, but if someone saw a policeman, they'd shout, 'The old Bill's coming!' and all the girls would run off. There was also a large elderly woman, Grace Baby, who had once been a motorcycle rider on the Wall of Death. Toothless and cheerful, she lived on the nearby Peabody Estate and liked to sit outside Emilio's with her fat Jack Russell.

Sometime in 1968, friends came over from Ireland and invited me to supper with a girl called Kat at her flat in Earls Court. Kat worked at the Courtauld Institute of Art. We got on really well, and within a matter of days, Kat introduced me to two people with whom I went on to have significant relationships. I now believe one to have been the love of my life.

First, I met Sue Myers, Kat's flatmate. She was a beautiful girl with high cheekbones and huge eyes who worked with Kat at the Courtauld as a restorer. They had recently been to Florence as part of the huge mission to help restore artefacts – mostly religious carvings and paintings – damaged in the devastating floods of 1966. I'd meet the girls at the Courtauld, and when they went home, they'd invite me over. Often they would work on artefacts into the evening so I would make them cups of tea and cinnamon toast as they painstakingly repaired cherubs' heads and delicate angels' wings. If we could afford it, we would go out to eat at the Artist Affamé on Brompton Road, where we loved the scrubbed-pine tables and the magic-lantern show, that flickered over the walls, but most of the time, we stayed in their flat, playing Mozart's 21st Piano Concerto on the gramophone through the long evenings, deep in conversation.

Sue was caring and open, talking about her own complicated childhood and relationships, explaining that her parents had separated when she was a baby and she had grown up without a father figure. I listened, learning that she loved horses. As a teenager she had found work with neighbours looking after their horses, and had become romantically involved with two much older married men. Mrs Myers did not approve, and this was why Sue had come to London to work at the Courtauld.

I could relate to much of her chaotic love-life, but I felt unable to tell her so, not wanting to talk about my own complicated past. Instead I made light of situations, told stories about fashion shoots, and favourite horses from my show-jumping days. It was easy to distract Sue as she loved fashion and horses, but she was perceptive, too, and sometimes she would say, 'Are you all right, Norman? You aren't the person you pretend to be, always laughing, are you?' She was kind and intuitive but I didn't feel ready to explain why she might think that.

And then there was Conway Wilson Young. Studying at the London Opera Centre, Conway was wealthy and handsome, with flaxen hair and a chiselled face, lighting up whatever room he was in. He was one of Kat's friends, and

Sue told me that Kat was in love with him but hadn't got anywhere.

The first time I met Conway, in the late summer of 1968, Kat took me to his home in Belgravia. It was one of those beautiful white stucco-fronted houses on Chester Square and Kat explained that Conway was gutting, redecorating and turning it into flats, which he would rent to friends. The world-famous Royal Ballet star and prima ballerina Margot Fonteyn and her mother Hilda Hookham had already moved into the basement. Margot, who was christened Peggy Hookham, had changed her name when she became a professional dancer. Conway, who loved ballet, was financing a film about her life.

When we arrived, Conway flung his arms round Kat, who returned the embrace with affection. Then he turned to me. 'Hello, Norman! Kat's told me all about you,' he exclaimed.

'Hi!' I said, in a rather pathetic way, bowled over by his exuberance and instantly attracted to him.

Conway ushered us in and took us to the library for drinks. It was all rather untidy. I was surprised to see an electric kettle in a corner of the room, and half-packed tea chests were strewn across the floor, full of gramophone records of operas. Paintings leaned against the walls and more gramophone records were scattered on the sofa. I stared at the paintings, all in exquisite baroque and renaissance frames. One was particularly beautiful, an enormous turn-of-the-century oil painting of a woman standing in a long ivory satin-and-lace dress, with strings of pearls. I gazed, mesmerised, at each pearl, the lace ruffles, and the woman's slight smile.

'She's beautiful, isn't she?' Conway said, glancing at me

before making a space for us all to sit in between the records. He chatted to Kat but kept flashing smiles at me, and I was so affected by this I had to get up and go to the window. Looking down over the mews and the garden, I saw a tall, monk-like man watering the roses.

'That's Keith,' Conway said. 'He's having one of the flats and he's a writer, helping me with my film about Margot.'

That evening we watched Margot perform at the Royal Opera House and afterwards we ate tortillas and drank rough red wine in a Spanish restaurant before returning to Chester Square. Sensing that Kat resented my presence, I made my excuses and got up to leave but Conway came to the door with me. 'May I see you tomorrow?' he asked, pressing my arm.

'I'd like that,' I replied.

In the morning, I returned to Chester Square and found Conway frying bacon and boiling an electric kettle in the library. As I sat down, another fair-haired young man came into the room, smiled and left without a word. I asked who he was, and Conway said dismissively, 'Oh, that's just Peter Sylvere.' I thought nothing more about him.

We piled the bacon on plates and sat in the library, eating, surrounded by dust sheets. The morning passed quickly as Conway talked about his family, his schooldays at Eton and how he had become involved with ballet and opera. I sensed a vulnerability and loneliness about him, in spite of the busy social life he led and his enthusiastic demeanour. That afternoon, after lunch, we went to Mr Fish, the popular clothing shop run by Michael Fish, the British designer. The kipper ties and colourful, dandyish clothes were at the forefront of the peacock revolution in men's clothing, which broke right away from the staid traditions of the past. We tried on many wonderful shirts and ties, teasing each other and laughing. I tried on a stunning leather coat, but the price tag was far more than I could afford.

When we arrived back in Chester Square, a large orange box was sitting on the hall table.

'For you,' Conway said.

Inside the box was the leather coat. He had bought it for me and had it delivered ahead of us. 'You're having it, and that's final,' he said. 'You looked so good in it.'

Conway was a whirlwind of energy. There was something about this that reminded me of Jeremy – the ability to pick me up, spin me round, and carry me along – yet the two men could not have been more different. Conway's generosity felt completely genuine.

As we were walking through the house, he explained he had to leave that night to go to Portugal to visit his mother. To my surprise, he asked me to house-sit for him.

'I'll be away for about three weeks, depending on my mother,' he said. He broke into a smile. 'You make me very happy, Norman.'

'I make *you* happy?' I said, laughing. '*I* haven't been so happy in ages.'

Kat looked furious when I told her I was going to move in at Chester Square, while Sue seemed a little unsure about the possibility of me and Conway starting something. 'Norman, be careful. Don't be hurt – but if you are, I'll be here for you,' she said kindly.

I packed a bag and took Emma over to the house. She

bounded around, shards of light showing up the dust in the huge rooms. I put Mozart's 21st Piano Concerto on the record-player and let the music flood out of the bedroom window, then Keith invited me to join him and some friends for drinks in his sitting room, where a log fire burned in the grate. Margot arrived soon after and her dark eyes sparkled as she spoke about her involvement in the Panamanian revolution. She had been caught steering a boat that was involved in her husband Tito Arias's attempted coup and had been imprisoned for a time but she made little of this, which was very charming. Later, I walked around seeing the house finished in my mind, all the while very aware that my own money had run out again. It seemed crazy that I was living in this opulent world but was always broke. My retainer didn't go far and the modelling payments were so unreliable. If I'd had my National Insurance cards I could have taken a job, perhaps in an art gallery, and kept modelling as a sideline.

In the first days of Conway's absence I thought about him a lot but then a postcard arrived from him, mentioning that Peter was with him. I felt stung and confused because Conway had been so dismissive of him earlier. I thought I'd been invited to house-sit because of the chemistry we had, not just because it suited him to have someone there. Disappointed, I went out to the Salisbury pub in Soho and got talking to an American called David. We instantly found common ground in our love for antiques. David invited me to eat with him at the Savoy Grill and, having nothing else to do, I agreed. He was very handsome and well groomed but something about him made me a little tense. When he asked for my number, I gave it to him, unable to stand the awkwardness of saying no.

The next morning David rang, inviting me to go to Surrey with him for a few days. When I declined, he changed the invitation to tea at Fortnum & Mason. I agreed, though again I felt a certain reluctance. As soon as I arrived, David gave me an expensive silver watch in the shape of a stirrup and announced he was keen for me to go back to America with him. I was reluctant to accept the present, and not convinced by the idea of going with him to the US. David bristled, telling me I could make a life for myself there and he would look after me. He seemed a clean, proper man and he was promising me the world – a better life. It was flattering to be made to feel so wanted but when he invited me back to the Savoy, again something made me hesitate. I told him I had to go back to check on the builders at Chester Square instead and his face fell.

That night I took sleeping pills, drank some Scotch and got into bed but, to my surprise, David rang. 'Can you come for a nightcap?' he asked. I told him the pills were making me feel woozy.

'Well, can I come over? Even for a few minutes?'

I was still politely protesting when the phone went dead. The doorbell rang at some time during the night so I staggered up, disoriented by the sleeping pills mixed with Scotch.

David was at the door.

'David, I'm sorry, but I'm so sleepy,' I said, hoping he would understand and go away.

'That's OK. I just wanted to see you.' He came in and

looked around. 'God, this is a huge old place. Does it belong to you?'

'No. A friend.'

'A lover?'

'No,' I said.

'Why don't you show me around?' David said abruptly.

Feeling lethargic and heavy-eyed, I gave him a tour, but the rooms went in and out of focus. I told David I had to lie down. Suddenly I saw a terrible coldness in his stare. He followed me to the bed, knelt over me and there was a tremendous crack as he hit me across the face. I shouted out, asking what was wrong, and he hit me again. My head swam, stars circling in front of my eyes.

David's voice came as though from miles away: 'If you won't come back to the States I'm going to make sure *he* won't want you . . .'

He hit me so hard I blacked out. When I came to, he was standing by the bed, smoking. His eyes were like steel. I couldn't move – my wrists and ankles were tied.

'Perhaps you like pain?' he said, and stubbed out the cigarette on my stomach. I screamed at the searing agony.

'Shut up, or I'll kill you.' He lit a match and dropped it, flaming, on my chest. As the match flickered out, he began masturbating. Moaning, he came all over me, rubbing it into the burns on my stomach and chest, then lay heavily on top of me. Too afraid to move, I became aware that he was crying.

'David,' I croaked, my voice barely a whisper. 'Why?'

He said nothing, untied me and left, slamming the front door. I dragged myself to the lavatory and was violently sick, crawling to bed, shivering. Was it some fault in me, some incurable wickedness, that had made David behave in that vile way?

I crammed a fistful of sleeping pills into my mouth and then I slept, only to be woken by violent retching. I was sick all over the bed and rang the Samaritans – I'd seen their number so often on the taxi adverts that I knew it off by heart. I opened my mouth to speak but was sick again, so I hung up. It was 2.25 a.m. I dialled Sue's number and she came over straight away. I hid the marks on my chest and didn't tell her about David, just that I'd been afraid and had taken pills, and she sat with me, leaving at dawn.

I slept through the morning and the next thing I knew Conway was by the bed, shaking me awake, asking if I was all right. I caught his hand, hungry for the kindness of his touch. 'I'm fine, but why are you back early? I thought you'd be gone at least another week.'

'Sue rang. She was so worried. I caught the next flight and here I am. But what's wrong?'

I felt a mix of emotions. Cross with Sue for telling Conway, I was also grateful to her because the relief of seeing him was huge. I told him about David and he held me close before going to fetch coffee and something to put on the burns. Then he told me to get packed. 'I'm taking you to the opera in Bayreuth. Then on to the Mozart festival in Salzburg. No buts. We're going! Tomorrow!'

I agreed, touched by his effort to cheer me up, grateful to him for taking me away to forget, to move on. That night we slept side by side and by the following morning we were on a coach ride from Orly to Paris. Conway kept trying to make me laugh and I couldn't help but join in. He was able to lift my spirits easily, his spontaneity for my benefit, which I felt really touched by. I blocked out David's attack and felt liberated, my feelings for Conway intense. When we boarded the overnight train from Paris to Bayreuth in Germany, I felt relaxed and invigorated: Conway's enthusiasm was infectious.

We threw our bags on to the bunks and went to stand in the corridor for a smoke before the train departed. We said little, the air charged with nervous energy. Oblivious of the other passengers, I put my arm around Conway as the train began to move, breathing in the subtle lavender fragrance of his Caron cologne as the train rocked slowly out of the station. Watching the lights of Paris disappear into the darkness of the horizon, I felt his heart beating strongly against my body.

Taking some iced beers to our compartment, we settled down to talk, getting into our separate bunks before saying goodnight. I had been nervous in case Conway wanted sex, but he was respectful and didn't try anything on. I lay there trying to sleep but as the train thundered through the French countryside I found myself replaying the horror of the previous night. Hours later Conway asked if I was asleep and I mumbled no.

'Norman. Please don't worry. Enjoy these few weeks. We'll return to Chester Square refreshed and things will be fine,' he said. Then he added, 'I think I love you.'

I felt the same way, that day marking the beginning of a whirlwind romance, falling in love as we travelled across Europe, watching night after night of opera. In Bayreuth, wearing dinner jackets in the blistering heat at the end of summer, we saw Wagner's *Ring Cycle, Tristan and Isolde,* and *Parsifal.* In the intervals, champagne flowed, fountains played, and everyone talked in muted voices. Then it was on to Salzburg for performances of *Don Giovanni, The Magic Flute, The Marriage of Figaro* and other works by Mozart.

Our relationship started as an emotional one before we became physical. I opened up about Jeremy, about my childhood and all the twists and turns of my life, and he told me about his past, too, but most of all we had fun. When we took the train to Salzburg, we found ourselves in hysterics, triggered by the stoic expressions of the other passengers who all sat bolt upright and silent on the grey plastic seats. In the town we lunched next to matrons with blue-rinses, wearing mink coats, who were clearly unimpressed by our outbursts of laughter. We stayed up late that night, chatting about how we could do up Chester Square together, and the next morning raced each other through a field of bright yellow flowers before heading out to the first opera. One afternoon, towards the end of our stay, as we were changing to get ready for a performance of *Fidelio*, Conway suddenly said, 'I can't stand this any longer. Please, come to bed with me.'

He pulled me to him and it was heaven. Nothing sordid or furtive or rough. We made love. With him, I found a totally new dimension of being cared for and of caring. Afterwards, I wanted to stay lying there with him but his beloved Christa Ludwig was singing in *Fidelio.* As the music washed over me, I thought how well Beethoven understood life and its tragedies, but beside me, Conway was squirming with anger. As we walked out into the foyer afterwards, he was seething with rage, muttering that the performance had been bloody awful, but then his mood changed. We met his friend Heidi Pappas, the daughter of an opera singer, and suddenly Conway was all smiles. 'Wonderful, wonderful!' he said to Heidi, and when we parted, she said to me, 'I can't think when I've seen him happier. You must be good for him.' Then she lowered her voice and said, 'But don't be hurt by his outbursts!'

For a while I didn't understand Heidi's warning. When we returned to Chester Square, we were closer than ever. We slept in the big empty bedroom surrounded by dust sheets, listening to the autumn rain pattering down, Emma curled up asleep between us. Looking around the room, I began to laugh. 'Remember what you said while we were away?' I said, pointing around the empty room, impersonating him. 'Our bedroom will be palest grey. The walls will be covered with silver-framed Keith Money original sketches of ballet stars and all along one wall we'll have fitted wardrobes – enough for all our clothes. We'll have a log fire, and under the window, a pale grey washbasin.' I laughed when I looked at the unplumbed bath that sat like a wrecked ship in the middle of the room. 'And on our bath there will be gold taps! Look at us now!' I exclaimed.

Conway hugged me. 'Thank you for making me see how unimportant things are. Material things, I mean.'

I loved him so much at that moment. I might have been of no use to anyone else, but I could raise his spirits. I could be strong for him.

Over the next weeks, I advised Conway about decoration and furnishings for the house and he took me to his childhood home at Barham in Suffolk. It was about to be sold and he wanted to retrieve hundreds of books from the library there. As we walked into the huge Regency hall at Barham, Mrs Prentice the housekeeper followed us with the luggage and I realised I had stepped into a very different side of Conway's life. In London he was known as flamboyant and outspoken, but here I sensed a heavy, oppressive atmosphere. It was very formal and the house felt neglected. Regency sofas and beautiful drapes were covered with dust, and forgotten portraits gazed down from the walls. As we walked through the house, I listened spellbound as Conway told me more about family. His mother was a Nast from the Condé Nast family and his late father's family were the Wertheimers, who were friends of the painter John Singer Sargent.

Conway's paternal great-grandfather was Asher Wertheimer, the renowned twentieth-century art dealer who commissioned the largest-ever private portrait collection by Singer Sargent of himself and his family, which was hung in the family's London house until it was bequeathed to the Tate, the New Orleans Museum of Art and the Smithsonian. Singer Sargent visited the Wertheimers many times and always referred to their dining room as 'the Sargent's Mess'. During the First World War, when anti-German feeling was widespread, Conway's grandfather and great-uncle changed their surname to Conway, which was where his first name came from.

'The painting of the woman in pearls that you love in Chester Square is by Singer Sargent. It's of my great-grandmother, Flora,' Conway said, explaining that the painting had been redone a few years after the original he had. The new one was painted deliberately dark and mournful to portray the tragedies that had happened in the interim: Flora's two eldest sons had both died in 1902, one poisoned by a bad oyster on honeymoon, the other fighting in the Boer War.

A grim-faced Mrs Prentice interrupted Conway as she walked past us and set the tea tray down in the next room with a clatter. 'I *had* packed the silver . . .' she said.

I felt irritated on Conway's behalf, but he just grinned.

We sat in Conway's mother's sitting room, which was smaller than the other rooms, with a deep-green velvet sofa and chairs, and a painting of her as a young woman by Cecil Beaton on the wall. We chatted, Conway talking about his childhood memories of coming home from Eton, and then we set to work in the library. I watched Conway as he opened the shutters and the room was flooded with light. Stepping out on to the lawn, which swept down in a long slope towards the house, I looked back at it all. The mass of Virginia creeper that covered the walls was turning crimson, glorious in the late-afternoon sunlight, and I pictured Conway playing on the lawn as a little boy, rolling down the slope towards his mother, who would be waiting for him at the bottom. I thought, with envy, that this place had known him for so much longer than I had. It had been a stable base for him, something I had always longed for as I moved from place to place, leaving at a moment's notice with my bag of belongings in my hand. I truly hoped that our love would last, and that a shared future would grow from our hopes and dreams.

Sitting together, we spent the day sorting through hundreds of volumes under the watchful glass eyes of a stuffed white crane that glowered at us from the corner of the library. It was a mammoth task, with occasional bouts of bickering over which books we should take before piling them up and wrapping them in brown paper and string.

At dinner time, Mrs Prentice laid our places at opposite ends of the very long mahogany table. She slammed down the serving dishes, obviously itching to get back to her cottage and complain to her husband about the young men who had invaded the house. We found it all terribly funny, shouting down the table at each other to pass the salt as Mrs Prentice looked on sour-faced until she stalked off, leaving us alone.

That night we slept in his mother's huge 1930s bed, with a fur rug draped over us. Conway's head rested on my chest. I wanted to wake him and tell him how much I loved him, but I had a sudden fear that he might be irritated by that. In the morning, I crept down to make tea, but when I reappeared, he was very disgruntled at being woken.

'Why didn't you let Mrs Prentice do the tea?' he snapped.

I was stunned. 'I like to do things for you, Conway.'

'Well, I wish you'd leave me alone.'

At once, his mood changed and, gripping my arms, he said, 'I'm so sorry,' and explained he was just stressed and emotional about having to say goodbye to his childhood home. I brushed it off but things began gradually to change. Over the next few weeks, Conway's little explosive rages became more frequent. He was aggressive towards the builders at Chester Square and I often had to step in. It seemed I was the only person who could cope when he got angry. I treated him like a fractious thoroughbred horse. I didn't get upset, just stayed quiet, ignoring the outburst and waiting for him to calm down. Sometimes I would find one of the lovely books in the library and sit quietly reading until he came to me, and we could talk through whatever the problem was.

He continued to say that he loved me, but I knew he was beginning to find my sleep problems irritating. I was either wide awake all night, or in a drugged stupor after taking my pills. I became uneasy when visitors kept coming to the house and disappearing into the library with Conway. I thought he might be seeing other men, although Margot assured me this wasn't the case, telling me she had never seen him happier. Looking back, I think these people may have been coming to buy cocaine. Conway used it sometimes but I never joined him. It didn't seem like a good idea, given all the prescription drugs I was taking, and now I wonder if his cocaine use contributed to his violent mood swings.

After a couple of months of living together, Conway suddenly said he wanted time alone. He just came into the library where I was and blurted it out. Things had been tense but I had no intention of ending the relationship. I loved him and was devastated, trying to talk him out of it, but he had made up his mind. I packed my bag and we stood on the step in the late-afternoon sun before I went. He said he was sorry about everything, but it was probably for the best. I left, feeling completely broken.

Not knowing where to go, I instinctively returned to Dublin, back to the community I had felt part of, far away from Conway, leaving Emma with Sue. The penny whistlers were still playing at St Stephen's Green and Mrs Gaj was thrilled to see me, asking how I had been, but it was so depressing to be back, feeling I'd achieved nothing. I booked into a hotel, and telephoned Sue to check on Emma. Reluctantly she mentioned that Conway had told her he did not want me back because he feared he would destroy me.

I called Chester Square from the hotel lobby and the phone was picked up at once. A man answered and told me Conway was in the bathroom.

'Who are you?' I asked.

'Oh, just a friend.'

Instantly suspicious, I gripped the receiver. 'Ask Conway to ring Norman Scott at the Shelbourne in Dublin.'

The man laughed. 'Oh, you're Norman! I can see your photograph on the bedside table.'

I felt suddenly cold, as though my feelings for Conway had turned to stone.

I rang again and this time Conway picked up. He sounded impatient. 'Norman – what do you want? Is something wrong?'

I told him I wanted to come back, that he couldn't let go of me that easily, it made a mockery of all we had shared, but he refused.

'You don't mean this. Let me come back, talk to you,' I sobbed, my face running with tears.

'No. It won't work. I have to go now. Goodbye,' Conway said. The phone clicked and he was gone.

I leaned against the wall with the receiver in my hand until the operator said, 'Are you holding?' I hung up and went to drown my sorrows and got chatting to an old acquaintance, Brian. We had drinks, then got into the car to drive somewhere else and he made it clear he wanted sex.

I refused, explaining I needed a friend, but he began masturbating instead. What was this sordid world I was a part of?

When Sue told me she was coming to Ireland to look after me, I felt relieved. Waiting at the ferry, I saw her before she saw me, in a red cord jacket and headscarf, holding Emma in her arms. Emma's little head was lifted, questing the air.

We stayed in Ireland for a few days, Sue comforting me as well as anyone could have. Trying to get my mind off Conway, we borrowed horses from friends and rode bareback into the Wicklow Hills. A faint smell of peat hung in the air, and in the conifer plantations, the light streamed in blocks through the trees. This was the real Ireland and all I could think of was how I wished I could have been with Conway, sharing it with him, introducing him to my world, but Sue tried to change my mind. She kept telling me the breakup was for the best, and while she was trying to help, I also sensed her feelings for me went deeper than friendship. Not wanting to lead her on, I explained about Jeremy and Billy and Conway. After she went to bed, I headed into town and had an intense and violent sexual encounter with a man. It was horrible, yet somehow the degradation and pain helped me to forget. Afterwards, I felt a complete revulsion, and from then on, I decided to listen to Sue. I wanted to spend time with her and try to forget Conway.

She offered me a room in her flat at Earls Court so we returned together and, not wanting to bump into Conway, I stayed in the flat. While Sue and Kat worked on more artefacts from Florence, I made them tea and toast. One afternoon, when we were alone, Sue suddenly burst into tears. I hugged her, and from her gasped words I gathered the man she had been seeing had behaved so badly she could no longer endure it. She was like a broken doll, racked with emotional pain, and for once I was needed. I comforted her gladly, sleeping next to her in the spare bed in her room. Our relationship remained platonic, but from then on, we were inseparable.

After a while, Conway and I resumed contact. Things were amicable, and I think we had missed each other terribly, but we kept our distance and I focused my attention on my close friendship with Sue. She would come to Studio Five and hang around the café and we'd walk home together or I'd meet her for lunch at the Courtauld, and gradually I got over Conway.

Out of the blue, I had a letter from Peter Bessell, saying he was going to America and hoped to find a way of helping me permanently, but in the meantime my retainer would go up to seven pounds, as this was in line with the recent rise in unemployment benefit. I was grateful, but every time I heard from Mr Bessell, I thought of Jeremy. I tried not to think about him, both the good times and the bad, and bury the problem of my National Insurance cards, but it was hard to forget him completely. His face would appear on the news and in the papers, and friends discussed politics in restaurants and bars. The previous summer Jeremy had married a girl called Caroline Allpass, which, given what he had told me about his attitude to women, was a surprise. He had met her while on holiday with his friend David Holmes, who was an assistant treasurer of the Liberal Party. There was a story going around that the two men – both gay – had tossed a coin as to who should go out with her, and at the wedding, David Holmes was best man. The political gossip continued when the younger Liberals, discontented with Jeremy's policies, teamed up with disaffected senior MPs to try to topple him while he was on honeymoon. These actions, both in and outside the Party, were seen as treachery and backfired. The executive backed him by forty-eight votes to two. His personal life went on to flourish with the birth of his son Rupert in the spring of 1969. Later in the year the Liberals received a political boost with the unexpected win of a by-election in Birmingham, overturning a Labour seat.

The days of going to the House of Commons or the Reform Club were long behind me. My life was vibrant and energetic and I no longer lived in the shadow of anyone. I was still modelling, doing shoots for clothes designer Michael Fish, and for Quincy Jones, and I hung around Studio Five, surrounded by friends. I valued Sue increasingly, and that autumn, we became lovers.

Sue and I spent Christmas 1968 at her mother's home in Lincolnshire. Partney Grange was a striking Queen Anne house at the end of a long, bumpy drive. Portraits hung everywhere on the walls, and there was a welcoming smell of apples and polish. In the huge old kitchen, photographs of children on ponies and with dogs stood on the dresser, and a blue roan spaniel called Misty lay by the fire. Sue and her mother had a strong bond, and as they made supper together on the first night, there were moments when I felt very alone. Their close relationship highlighted what I had missed out on in my own childhood: the warmth of unconditional, all-encompassing love.

We went riding and Sue showed me the places where she

had jumped her ponies as a child, her beautiful face becoming animated as I had never seen it before. Her mother threw drinks parties and Sue introduced me to the 'regulars', clad in tweeds, twinsets and strings of pearls. She and I did a quick circle of the room, then got drunk. Aware of everyone staring at my velvet suit, silk shirt and black patent shoes, we began to find the whole thing hilarious. In the run-up to Christmas Day we attended more drinks parties and my emerald-green shirts, black velvet trousers and snakeskin shoes from Sid's of Sloane Street continued to shock Sue's mother and her neighbours.

At breakfast on Christmas Day, a few neighbours were present as well as the family. There were small gifts by all our plates. Everyone was cooing, 'Oh, how lovely!' as they opened them. Sue's mother watched me, eyes glittering behind her spectacles, as I unfolded tissue paper to reveal a dark-blue mug with 'STRYCHNINE' written on it. I knew then how deeply she disliked me. I was hurt, but perhaps she feared I would steal her beloved daughter from her, or maybe she worried that Sue loved me and I didn't feel as strongly. It's hard to say how serious Sue and I would have become if things had remained as they were, but a couple of months later everything changed. I came home to the Earls Court flat one afternoon to find Sue on the sofa with a glass of water in one hand and a pill in the other. A friend of hers was there saying, very vehemently, 'No, Sue. Take it. You must do it now.'

I asked Sue if she had a headache and her friend departed, leaving us alone. Sue told me she was pregnant, explaining she had been pregnant for several weeks but had not known what to do. The pill was to abort the foetus. I was devastated that she hadn't told me and explained that getting rid of a child went against everything I believed.

'We can't have a baby, Norman. We absolutely can't,' she replied.

'Why not? We love each other,' I responded.

Sue was just twenty-three, and I was twenty-eight. We were young but I couldn't let her destroy our child. I kept thinking, What if Mummy had done this when she found herself pregnant with me? I held Sue close and told her we would get married. I was so relieved when she agreed. I didn't think about any of the potential stresses or challenges of parenthood, just felt excitement and real happiness at the thought of becoming a family.

Sue was willing to convert to Catholicism and we planned to marry in the crypt of Westminster Cathedral, but her father vetoed this. Instead we wed on 13 May 1969, at Kensington Register Office. It was an odd gathering. Her mother sent a crate of champagne, but did not attend. Neither did my mother nor Sue's father. Some of our friends turned up, including Kat and one of Sue's ex-lovers, as well as some of the prostitutes from Shepherd Market. Our witnesses were my photographer friend Vernon Dewhurst and Grace Baby.

When Grace arrived at the register office, I noticed something different about her.

'Yes, it's a special occasion. I've got my teeth in, haven't I?' she said, favouring me with a dazzling artificial smile

When the registrar asked her for her name he couldn't hear the reply because she had taken the teeth out. 'I'm sorry, madam. How do you spell that?' he asked.

'B-A-B-Y!' Grace spluttered, in her strong Cockney accent, adding, 'Like fucking kid!' The registrar looked very put out.

Afterwards, we ended up drinking gin at the nearby Coleherne, famous for its clientele of leather-clad gay men, which shocked some of Sue's friends and her father when they joined us. Ignoring me, Sue's father spent the rest of the evening with Sue. At the end of the night, he was visibly the worse for drink. He walked back to the flat with us, muttering endearments to her, and as we parted at the door, I heard him say, 'Oh, my darling Zanny, I wish it were me coming upstairs with you!' Zanny was his pet name for her and apparently he'd had a thing for her for years. I find it ironic that when, subsequently, there were defamatory articles about me in the press, Sue's father chipped in to say I was a dreadful pervert.

CHAPTER TWELVE

Benjamin

BENJAMIN WAS BORN on 18 November 1969. He was beautiful, with his soft, plump cheeks and huge round eyes. My heart melted as his tiny fingers clasped my thumb. He was perfect and instantly made up for the stresses of the previous six months as Sue and I had scrambled to sort out our lives in preparation for becoming parents.

Throughout the pregnancy, money had been the biggest issue. For the first few months Sue had carried on working at the Courtauld but my modelling jobs were sporadic and the payments unpredictable, taking months to process. Sue's mother was insistent we claimed maternity benefit as well as milk tokens when the baby came, but the problem was that this was all paid through the husband and I could not get any of these extra family benefits without the National Insurance cards. I made various forays to the Employment Office, but with no proof of my employment history, I got nowhere. Sue's mother could have helped us out, as she was very wealthy, but she refused, getting more and more angry with me.

Sue's brother-in-law, the actor Terry-Thomas, generously gave us a wedding present of some money to rent a home for a year and I found, through an ad in *Horse & Hound*, a little stone cottage at Milton Abbas in Dorset. Still renting the flat in Earls Court, we intended to move permanently to Dorset once Sue had stopped working, so for a few months we lived between London and the country, but money stayed tight.

Kat moved out of the flat, leaving for America, which meant we had to cover her rent as well, and we became increasingly worried about our financial situation. Fortunately Sue found two Czech girls from the Courtauld who needed a room, but soon after they arrived, the telephone bill rocketed, the loo paper began disappearing at an alarming rate, and huge amounts of tea leaves appeared in the lavatory bowl. To start with we didn't understand and, blaming each other, we had huge rows. Then we discovered what was going on. One morning as I was about to go out for a day of castings for modelling work, there was a scratching at the kitchen door. I opened it and was stunned to find an elderly woman in a nightdress. While I was shocked to see her, she seemed perfectly comfortable in her surroundings and, in a thick Czech accent, said, 'I went to the bathroom but I've locked myself out of the bedroom.'

Having no idea what was going on, I unlocked the bedroom with the spare key to find five more Czechs, all total strangers, looking at me in alarm. They had been living there, eating our food, drinking our tea, and using the telephone to call their family back home, without paying a penny. I felt sorry for them, but we couldn't afford to subsidise them all. Sue felt deceived by the girls and told them to move themselves and their family out immediately. Having to cover the rent for the empty room and pay the telephone bill on Sue's small salary stretched us to the limit, and with few modelling jobs coming in, we both got incredibly anxious.

When Sue was too pregnant to carry on working, we went down to the country but she didn't want to give up the flat in Earls Court so the bills kept coming. She kept saying, 'What are we going to do?' and when I didn't know what to say or how to rustle up the money we needed to eat, she would announce she'd have to live with her mother once the baby was born. She didn't want to, back then, she wanted to be with me, but we were sometimes so hungry I resorted to taking the stale bread from our neighbour's duck house to keep the two of us from starving.

Begging Mr Bessell for my National Insurance cards only got me the same response he always gave me, that he was doing everything in his power to sort things out. In utter desperation, I called Jeremy's wife, Caroline. She was shocked when I explained who I was and why I was calling, hoping she would intercede. I was apologetic, telling her I wasn't trying to disrupt their life, just wanted to get out of a desperate situation. I hoped that as a new mother herself she would have some sympathy for our situation, but she told me there was nothing she could do, hanging up abruptly.

The consequences of that telephone call were helpful in the short term, although I wonder whether involving Caroline made Jeremy see me in a different light: not simply as an inconvenience but as a threat to his marriage, his ambitious political career and social standing. Looking back, maybe that three-minute telephone call was the spark for him to decide to get rid of me once and for all.

At the time, though, the result was a relief. Caroline telling Jeremy meant that, soon after, I received a curt letter from Mr Bessell, telling me I was being issued with a temporary emergency card and could claim emergency benefits and register as an unemployed person. I felt insecure about this because it didn't seem to be official: Mr Bessell had managed to skirt round the issue without really resolving it. Without stamps I couldn't claim the full unemployment benefit but I would get social security payments, which were less than that, and Sue would get her maternity benefit. I also received a letter direct from the private secretary to David Ennals, minister of state for social services, confirming that he was looking into the matter. Shortly afterwards we were visited at the cottage by someone from the DHSS in Weymouth. He took details from me and asked why stamps had never been paid for my cards. I was getting so exasperated that I told him this was because I had lived with Jeremy Thorpe. 'As his secretary?' the man asked.

'No. As his lover,' I replied.

The man made a hasty exit.

Finally, though, I got somewhere, and within a week Sue had her maternity benefit cheque. But instead of rationing it, she went into Blandford to buy necessities for the baby. She also came back with a black Indian dress covered in mirrors for herself, four Penguin books and twelve peacock feathers. With all our benefits spent, she breezed back to the cottage and started arranging the peacock feathers as though we had no cares in the world. I couldn't believe it. We were surviving on stolen duck bread and tins of beans. With no other option, and Sue heavily pregnant, we gave up the cottage, which had turned from a country idyll to a desolate nightmare, and returned to London. I did every modelling job I could get to scrape together enough money to pay the rent but it still wasn't enough. The kind landlady of Sue's flat in Earls Court saw how desperate we were and allowed us to rent out the rooms by the night, like a modern-day Airbnb: a constant stream of American tourists came to stay. She allowed us to keep any excess money after the rent was paid so we struggled less but, with no idea of what the long-term solution would be, we were still fraught with worry.

By the time Benjamin was born, I tried very hard to stay positive and strong for both of them. That Christmas we stayed at Sue's mother's, but she cut me dead, refusing to talk to me and even putting me in a separate bedroom from Sue. It would have been awful except for Benjamin. I took him for walks in his Silver Cross pram, feeling great pride.

Back in London when he was still very new, my mother came to visit us and I hoped introducing her to Benjamin would give us an opportunity to connect. When she showed no interest in her grandson, just wanting to drink tea and talk to Sue, I decided to liven things up. I dressed Emma in a baby's bonnet and put her in the pram. Wheeling it in, I asked, 'Don't you want to say hello to Benjamin?'

My mother gave a cursory glance and, without realising, said, 'Oh, yes. Lovely.'

Then Emma, still wearing the bonnet, jumped out. My mother screamed and almost fell off the sofa. I'd rather hoped she might find it funny, but of course she didn't.

This was not the only time that my lovely whippet was called upon to play a role. Shortly after my mother's visit I saw an advert in the *Sunday Times* for 'a friendly, smiling greyhound' who needed a new home. Horace was elderly, and I knew he wouldn't be around for long, but I just had to take him. He was a sweet, gentle dog and he and Emma adored each other. Photographer Michel Molinari spotted them walking with me one day and used them in some wonderful photographs with Tessa Kennedy's young sons Damian and Cary Elwes, and both Emma and Horace went on to do other modelling work.

I was glad of this distraction, as the rest of life was proving very stressful. The situation remained unpredictable, our future hanging on the decisions linked to my National Insurance cards; I got another letter from the DHSS telling me I was liable for seven years' worth of unpaid contributions and without payment I would not be entitled to benefits. This was the equivalent of getting a bill for hundreds of pounds – many thousands in today's money, as the stamps had not been paid for a decade. As I stood reading the letter in the flat, I had no idea how I would ever be able to sort it out. I started taking more pills again and, unable to sleep with the stress of our finances, became fractious towards Sue, who was also experiencing huge mood swings. Suddenly I would find her packing her things and taking Benjamin to her mother's for weeks on end. I didn't like being without them. Benjamin changed every week, without me there to witness his progress, but I reassured myself that they were better off with her mother, who could at least feed them properly.

Fortunately, I received a letter from Mr Bessell, telling me that all legal action against me was being waived but that I could not have full benefit. I realised that, once again, I was being treated as a special case. A minister of state was facilitating the payments to continue the cover-up and the lies. I felt overwhelmed by simultaneous relief that the debt had been cleared and also despair that the situation would clearly never go away.

My doctor prescribed pills for anxiety and suggested that I visit a psychotherapist, explaining that if I were declared mentally ill, I would be able to claim sickness benefit. I really didn't want to do this but had no other option. Sue's mental health had declined, and when she was at home, she rarely got out of bed. Now I believe she was suffering from post-natal depression but at the time I didn't know about this and felt helpless because I couldn't lift her spirits. She was more mentally unstable than I was and, knowing we both wanted and needed Benjamin to be all right, I would leave Sue in bed and look after him. Wrapping him in his patchwork quilt, I'd take him to any modelling jobs I got, often passing Emma and Horace looking very superior as they headed off to their own shoot in a different taxi. When we arrived at the studio, the make-up artists and stylists would make a huge fuss of my little son. Sometimes we came home to find Sue had perked up. She would be pleased to see us, wanting to cradle Benjamin. I'd hold on to these happier moments of feeling like a real family, but I worried about her state of mind. When a friend invited us to dinner, she refused and said she'd rather sleep in Hyde Park. She spent more and more time at her mother's, coming home sporadically for a few days before leaving again, as though she had changed her mind. Then I found something she had written about me, 'He lies by my side in this bed, not stirring. I try to wake him so many times wanting him to hold me. But he is full of sleeping pills. I think how easy it would be to go up to the bathroom and cut my wrists and by morning I would be dead. This whole miserable existence would be over.'

I didn't tell Sue I had seen this but I worried that Benjamin would somehow be affected by the tension and unhappiness. Not knowing what to do or how to make her better, I suggested reluctantly that she and Benjamin should go back to Partney Grange. The truth was I loved her but I wasn't in love with her. We both knew it, and by then our relationship was strained almost beyond repair. Just after she left, through my own actions, the marriage ended.

I was still in love with Conway and had stayed in touch with him. He came over to deliver a wedding present – an electric kettle, evoking memories of the library at Chester Square – and when I asked him how the renovations had come on, he invited me over to see. We ended up in bed.

I told Sue straight away. It was a foolish thing to do and perhaps would have been kinder if I hadn't, but I thought I must be honest with her and I didn't want either of us to go on living a lie. Sue came back from her mother's to talk. Not surprisingly, she was inconsolable and, after a huge fight, she moved out of the flat, leaving for her mother's in floods of tears. I felt awful for her, and for our son, and terribly sad. I hadn't meant to hurt her. She wrote a long letter telling me she still loved me and was coming back to work things out, but then she changed her mind. Over the telephone, she told me that we were finished. Suddenly I had lost both Sue and our son. Just before our first wedding anniversary, she filed for divorce.

Sue refused to see me or let me see Benjamin. That summer she came to collect our things. It was a tense encounter. We had an argument about the furniture and I threw her clothes over the balcony into Earls Court Square. Over the next few days, I became severely depressed and rang my doctor, who came over and gave me an injection to calm me down. His wife, who was Greek, kindly sat beside me while I went to sleep. I woke up to find all the furniture had gone from the room. Only the bed I lay on was left. Sue and her brothers had returned and removed everything, even the curtains and the carpet. They must have lifted the bed with me in it to roll the carpet up.

I prepared for the divorce and the subsequent custody hearing living in the empty, echoing flat. At least I had a bed and a roof over my head. I needed funds for the lawyer, and Mr Bessell arranged for a solicitor who worked for him to handle my case. The solicitor advised me not to attend any of the divorce proceedings as this might be too much for me, given my fragile state of mind, and could jeopardise my chance of gaining access to Benjamin. Instead I talked to him at length, explaining the breakdown of my marriage was a direct result of not having my National Insurance cards. I said that Jeremy Thorpe had them and I needed them back, and the lawyer nodded, reassuring me that things would be all right.

Mr Bessell reiterated these sentiments, suggesting I would benefit from a long holiday. He offered me a world cruise and a stay in Florida, adding that I could take Emma if I wished. I couldn't have done this, as my dog would have had to go into quarantine. Also, I wasn't sure what was behind this proposition, which seemed rather peculiar, so I declined. Mr Bessell persisted, offering me a vacation in the Bahamas with an associate of his. I declined again. Something about these suggestions did not feel right.

I stayed on at the Earls Court flat into 1971, when I was offered fifteen hundred pounds to leave by the agent for a company who wanted to buy the property. The landlady was keen to sell up, so she was happy for me to keep this, which was very kind of her. The lump sum meant I could afford to put a deposit down on a mill house in north Wales I'd seen advertised so I moved out of London, turning my back on modelling. I longed to see Benjamin, knowing I was missing out on so many little changes, but the prospect of Wales motivated me and I hoped I'd get at least partial custody of my son.

The mill house was an amazing place. The water wheel was long gone, but the millstream still rushed past the house, and I loved to hear it when I went to bed at night. My modelling friend Stella and her partner Jack came from London to stay, and we explored the local antique shops together. I bought some wonderful old pieces very cheaply, which looked perfect in the mill house, and many of these items I have kept to this day.

People in the village were wary of me to start with, except for a few kind souls who soon became friends. Keith Rose, who owned the garage, invited me for a drink and Gwen Parry-Jones, a widow who owned the village post office, invited me for supper.

Hopeful that the countryside would provide me with a stronger footing, I dreamed of teaching Benjamin to ride, and making a life for us both surrounded by animals, but it wasn't to be. A few weeks after I'd moved to Wales, full custody was granted to Sue on the basis of my mental state, my lack of financial stability and because I was homosexual. When I read through the statement and the case my solicitor had put to the judge, I was horrified: my solicitor had taken it upon himself to omit Jeremy's name and the whole explanation. With that ruling, I lost my son and it would be two years before I saw him again. I never even got to say goodbye.

In the days after the verdict, I got very drunk with Keith, telling him everything – from being Jeremy's lover to how I had lost custody of Benjamin. A staunch Liberal, as many Welsh people were at that time, he was aghast. He told me to phone Mr Bessell from the garage so he could listen in and be a witness. The next day, with Keith beside me, I rang Mr Bessell and said, 'I am no further forward than I was when you first met me. Surely the money that would have been spent on my world cruise could be given to me now so I can establish myself and create a base for my son.'

Mr Bessell suggested I travel to London to talk to him, telling me he thought it might be possible to raise five thousand pounds. Keith caught most of the conversation, and as I put the telephone down, I was delighted. It seemed at last I might be able to begin again and maybe somehow keep Benjamin in my life, but the money did not turn up. Mr Bessell eventually wrote, explaining that he had not been able to raise it before leaving for the United States on urgent business. He hoped to see me on his return. In fact, Mr Bessell had gone bankrupt and fled to America.

Unable to cope, I got very drunk again, took lots of pills and stumbled up onto the hillside hoping to end it all. Keith found me, and he and Gwen did everything they could to raise my spirits. As I could not pay the rent for the lovely mill house, Gwen kindly invited me to move in with her. Having just been pulled back from the verge of a breakdown, I didn't realise she was drinking heavily, perhaps trying to numb her grief at losing her husband. Both of us were so lonely and desperate we fell into a relationship. We were an unlikely couple, as I was just thirty-one and she was in her early fifties, but we were both in need of the comfort of a physical relationship, so things just developed.

Gwen was horrified by my situation once I had confided in her. She, too, was a Liberal, and thought it a disgrace that the Party leader could have behaved so badly. To her and many others, the government was a body of people for whom society should have the utmost respect. They were the role models, people to depend on and look up to. Until then Gwen had seen Jeremy Thorpe as a beacon of hope – a charming, caring man, who had dedicated his life to the good of the people.

Determined to help me get my National Insurance cards back, Gwen wrote about me to Emlyn Hooson, the Liberal MP for Montgomeryshire. Hooson, who had been chairman of the Liberal Party for Wales since 1955, had contested the Party leadership election of 1967 but had lost to Jeremy. Gwen was delighted when Hooson replied, inviting us to meet him in the House of Commons. She hoped this would solve all my problems.

I was wary, and returning to St Stephen's Hall was unnerving. I kept looking around, praying Jeremy wouldn't appear, picturing his face and imagining how awful it would be, and then, for a terrible moment, I thought I might have to endure that: Hooson's secretary met us, immediately apologising as she gave us the news that Hooson was not there and suggesting she ought to take us to the Party leader, Mr Thorpe. I froze. She looked at me, oblivious, before carrying on to explain that unfortunately Mr Thorpe was in India.

I wondered why on earth she would suggest I meet the very person I had come to discuss negatively, but it transpired that no one had quite understood my issue. When we finally sat down with David Steel, another Liberal MP, who later took over from Jeremy as leader of the Party, he was confused. He explained Hooson had thought Gwen's letter was about me having an affair with Mr Bessell, not Jeremy. I put Mr Steel right.

'Jeremy Thorpe was the man who has created the problem and Mr Bessell was trying to help me,' I said, trying not to sound exasperated.

'I just don't believe you,' Steel said. 'I don't believe this could have happened.'

I explained about my National Insurance cards, and that I presumed Jeremy had not handed them over because he wanted our relationship to remain secret. Steel pooh-poohed this and asked me to leave, but I didn't budge. I hadn't come all the way here to get nowhere again and be accused of lying. I produced the letters Bessell had sent with the retainers.

'Did I make this up?' I asked, handing them to Steel. I have never seen anyone turn so pale. Even his hair seemed about to go white. Presumably not only did he realise I was telling the truth but he recognised the risk the truth posed to Jeremy and, by extension, the Liberals. The next day I met with Hooson and Steel, but despite all the documents I'd shown them, they said there was insufficient evidence. 'You must have actual letters from Jeremy,' they said.

They were shocked when I told them how I had given Jeremy's letters to the police officers who interviewed me back in December 1962, on the night I'd planned to kill him. When I explained the whole sorry saga had been officially written up and filed, both men buckled, shooting each other the same worried glance. I knew as well as they did how dangerous the police report was: it was an official document that stated all the facts. Finally, they took notice. I was invited to a meeting the following day at the House of Lords.

That night Gwen was terribly upset, so I suggested she go back home to Wales while I stayed with Stella and Jack, in their London flat. At first, they thought I was a lunatic and a fantasist, and that what I told them about Jeremy was completely untrue, but as I explained further, like Steel and Hooson they believed me, and just like Gwen, they supported me completely, livid and exasperated on my behalf.

At the next meeting, Steel and Hooson were joined by Lord Byers, a Liberal peer in the House of Lords. It was a short meeting – eleven minutes to be precise. I went through what I had already said and, although I had hoped they would take me seriously, Lord Byers's response was to call me a common blackmailer, suggesting I needed medical treatment. I had been nervous until then, acutely aware of how unsavoury the idea of homosexuality was, even though it had been decriminalised. People still didn't talk freely about it, and having to explain my sexual relationship with not only strangers but Members of Parliament did not come easily to me. But when Lord Byers accused me of blackmail, I was enraged. He was one of the dignitaries Jeremy and I had dined with at the Reform Club, years before, a man who had sat drinking with Jeremy and me, accepting Jeremy's lies about me being his ward. I reminded him of this and, looking him straight in the eye, I said, 'If I were a common black-mailer, you have just morally blackmailed me.'

Shaking with fury, I left the House, my bravado evaporating as I walked quickly away. I was determined to gather the evidence so I could prove that what I was saying was true, but trying to retrieve my letters from the police was an ordeal. The police instructed me to write a statement explaining why I needed to prove my relationship with Jeremy. It took ten hours to get all this down, and by the time I left Lambeth police station at 1 a.m., I felt absolutely drained and helpless.

When I returned to Wales, Gwen was a huge support, rallying around me, and together we consoled ourselves by drinking wine until the early hours. Gwen was traumatised by the concept of political corruption and all of her disap-pointment transferred into energy to help me: she saw me as the archetypal underdog in an unfair world. When I started talking about my dream to have my own horses, she fuelled me with the belief that I could do it and she offered to help. A Victorian house with stables up on Offa's Dyke was for rent, divided into a holiday let and private accommodation. I thought it would make an ideal trekking centre, and Gwen agreed. In fact she was adamant, putting up five hundred pounds to ensure the idea succeeded. She was wealthy, owning several properties in the village, and exceptionally generous, insisting on helping as if somehow her kindness would counter the way I had been treated. I added to the pot by buying a horse and selling it on at a profit so I could buy some ponies, and early in August 1971 I moved in. Gwen stayed at her house, not wanting to come with me, and although our physical relationship ended, we kept in touch. I felt a wave of relief and excitement at the start of this new enterprise, but I was nervous about embracing those feelings, knowing how quickly things could change.

The house was an absolute joy. It was an old Victorian pile with a terrace of overgrown roses in the garden. I got to work, digging a vegetable patch to grow food. I bought two horses and broke in some Welsh ponies and cobs, ending up with nine horses in total that lived in a big field. I advertised children's riding holidays and soon I had lots of bookings, establishing the place as the trekking centre Gwen and I envisaged. I took the children for rides, as well as cooking, cleaning and making the beds, and supervising them as they looked after the ponies. Within six months, the business was paying for itself and I was able to start paying Gwen back.

In early 1972, Gwen came to stay. Although she was pleased

to see how successful the set-up was, she seemed even more worried about my National Insurance cards than I was. She understood now about the corruption, but just couldn't accept it. She was completely disillusioned by the Liberal Party, going into despairing rants. Knocking back glass after glass of wine, she stumbled around, saying, 'If I can't trust the Liberals, who were supposed to be caring, morally upright people, then you tell me, who can I trust? Who can anyone trust?'

I tried to comfort her but her reaction seemed to be almost like another bereavement, on top of the loss of her husband. I noticed she was drinking throughout the day too, and all I could do was try to cheer her up in small ways – by walking with her, and listening, knowing I could not reassure her. When I drove her home, she seemed very down, and told me she would be staying with an aunt for a while.

Three weeks after Gwen came to stay, a letter arrived, which had been forwarded by the postmistress in Tal-y-bont, addressed to Gwen. I rang the postmistress, who said that Gwen hadn't been seen for a while and she had assumed she was staying with me.

Convinced something was wrong, I told her to call the police straight away while I got into my car and drove to Tal-y-bont as quickly as I could. My premonition was correct. I watched from the road as police broke into Gwen's house, noticing her bedroom window was horrifically dark with flies. The officers found the central heating at full blast and Gwen's body lying in the bedroom, in a state of decomposition. She had written a note explaining that she could not cope with the concept of political corruption, as she had always believed in the integrity of MPs and considered them to be protectors of the public interest. Then she had taken an overdose of sleeping pills, washed down with whisky. I was devastated. Sick with horror, I could only think that Gwen's terrible end was because of Jeremy.

At the inquest, I said I believed that Gwen Parry-Jones had committed suicide as a result of getting involved with my problems and her subsequent disillusionment with the establishment. I explained how she had accompanied me to the House of Commons and related absolutely everything we had told David Steel. An open verdict was returned by the coroner, and this was recorded by the local press. In the newspaper, there was no mention of the revelations I had made about Jeremy. Either I was not believed, or the reporters were fearful of picking up the story.

That year, a child lost contact with his father and a woman lost her life, and while there were surely other factors, the catalyst that linked these tragedies together was Jeremy's decision not to give me back my National Insurance cards. For a long time, I believed he had originally held on to my cards to ensure I stayed with him, and when we broke up, to try to lure me back. Then I thought he'd kept them out of spite when I didn't want to rekindle our relationship. At some point I realised his reasoning was more practical than that. Giving me back my National Insurance cards would have provided me – and anyone I chose to share them with – legitimate proof of our connection. It would have shown an unequivocal link that would be much harder to dismiss than whatever I said. For a man with so much to lose, it makes sense that Jeremy wanted to ensure there was no tangible connection between me and him, but the consequences of his decision were ruthless. He had effectively stolen my identity and now my identity as a father, along with the life of a woman who believed in decency and the integrity of the people who ruled the country.

CHAPTER THIRTEEN

Living in Fear

IT WAS MORE than two years before I saw Benjamin again, and by this time I had left Wales and was living in north Devon. I had eventually been granted access of four half-hour visits a year: two hours a year with my son. Sue had cited my relationship with Conway during the custody proceedings and, as a homosexual, I was considered unsuitable to be alone with Benjamin. This meant that these visits had to be at her mother's house, where they lived, and I had to be chaperoned by a probation officer 'in case you harm him'.

I was appalled by this but desperately wanted to see my son so in 1973, when Benjamin was three years old, I arranged a visit to Partney Grange. I arrived before the probation officer and was greeted coldly by Sue's mother. She didn't invite me in so I waited awkwardly in the garden while she rang Sue, who had taken Benjamin to stay with her boyfriend. When they arrived, a fair-haired little boy ran up to me, asking, 'Are you my daddy, Norman Scott?'

When I said yes, he took my hand. I wanted to burst into tears, to pick him up and hold him, but I didn't. Wary of too much physical affection being misconstrued and worried a show of emotion would look like I was causing a scene, I just walked along with my son as though it was the most normal thing in the world.

With the probation officer still not there, Sue walked next to us and we wandered round the garden and outbuildings stooping over the plants in the flowerbeds and looking at the horses. As I watched Benjamin happily stroking one, for a brief moment it seemed everything we had dreamed of in the early days of our marriage was there. I asked him if he liked to ride, and he said he sometimes sat on his mother's horse so I set up a course of small obstacles on the lawn for him. Delighted, he ran round, leaping over them. Every time he hit a jump, I gave him four faults, but whenever he got a clear round, I found some old rosettes in the car, which I'd won at shows, and gave one to him. His face lit up as he clutched the rosette and grinned at me.

The probation officer arrived and the little bubble was broken. When he started asking me what I did for a living and taking notes, I told him that I was considering writing a book about my life. Sue's expression turned sour and she said it was 'all too nauseous'. Her mood changing from tense to fraught, she started walking back. When we got to the house, Benjamin asked why I could not come and live with him and sleep with Mummy. This made me so sad. Out of earshot, the probation officer told me he was amazed at how readily 'the little lad' had taken to me, and that my visits should continue, but although I desperately wanted to see my son, I wasn't sure it would be good for either of us. Before I left, Benjamin gave me a plastic figure of a Native American from a cereal packet. 'It's for you to keep,' he said. 'Will you bring it with you when you come back?'

I felt lost for words at the depth of my small son's dream that was also mine but it all seemed like a mirror of my own childhood. Broken relationships, emotional scenes, interfering officials. I held it together until I said goodbye, then burst into tears. I had nothing to offer Benjamin and my own life had become unstable again.

I ended up moving to north Devon because after Gwen's death I couldn't bear to continue living in Wales. I gave up the house and the horses, and for several months I moved from place to place, either looking after people's horses or temporarily staying with friends. Stella and Jack, who were appalled by Gwen's death, supported me. When they bought the Old Rectory in South Molton, they offered it to me until they'd moved in. It was unfurnished, so I was able to bring some of the antiques from Wales with me. Grateful for their kindness, I hoped the move would work out. Unbelievably, I hadn't twigged that the town of South Molton was in the heart of Jeremy's north Devon constituency so when I arrived there in early 1973, with my dear whippet Emma at my side, it was a shock to discover the Liberal Club was right next door to the Old Rectory. With no other option, I stayed.

I visited the local doctor, Dr Ronald Gleadle, and explained about my mental difficulties and showed him some of the notes about my retainers from Mr Bessell so he would believe I was telling the truth about the problems I'd had. He was very understanding and friendly, insisting that I call him Ron, and prescribed pills for me – 'one to cheer me up and one to knock me down'. For a while I felt level-headed, and with my mental health settled I bought a horse, keeping him at the Town Arms pub, which was down a narrow side street in South Molton. One day I was riding back to the pub when a white Triumph car came towards me. There wasn't enough room to pass, so I moved the horse back. As the driver approached, I looked down and saw it was Jeremy. At exactly the same moment, he looked up and saw me. Shaking, I rode away quickly.

Back at the Old Rectory, I sat at the kitchen table in a state of shock for about half an hour. It was horrible meeting Jeremy like that, after so many years. His face looked cadaverous and sinister, utterly cold and unfeeling. Everything came flooding back to me, and I became overwhelmed with fear and despair. Right in my eyeline was a rack of kitchen knives. I grabbed one, carved 'INCURABLE' into my arm and slashed my wrists. There was blood everywhere, all over the beautiful kitchen. In a complete panic, I rang Dr Gleadle, who came right away and stitched me up on the kitchen table. Concerned about my volatile state, he took me with him on his rounds for a few days and suggested I might benefit from hypnosis with the Reverend Fred Pennington. He was a plump gentleman with a ruddy complexion, and a rather insincere manner. His sessions weren't effective, as I never actually 'went under', but I told him everything, revealing details about my relationship with Jeremy, hoping it might make me feel more able to deal with living so close to him.

Months went by without my bumping into Jeremy. When Jack and Stella were ready to move into the Old Rectory, I rented a bungalow on Exmoor, taking Emma and my horse with me, and helped to pay the rent by looking after the landlord's two point-to-point horses, getting them ready for the racing season. As always, working with horses was the best remedy for my mental troubles and, with the house so isolated, I hoped that up there on the wild moor, I would never have to see Jeremy again.

By mid-1974, I had given up the hypnosis sessions. I'd made friends by going to the Three Tuns in Barnstaple in my free time. They were a lovely crowd of people, really supportive. I talked about some of my past and my problems with them, but didn't go into details about my relationship with Jeremy. However, I had spoken freely about Jeremy to Dr Gleadle, and to the Reverend during his hypnosis sessions, and around this time some alarming things began to happen.

Someone telephoned the Barnstaple social security office pretending to be Michael Heseltine, MP, asking where I lived. When the call was followed up and checked, Heseltine denied this. The social security officer feared the call had been from an imposter wanting to know my whereabouts. This idea unnerved me, and when helicopters started flying above the bungalow as if checking me out, I was totally rattled. By early 1975, Dr Gleadle was prescribing huge quantities of Valium, Librium and Mogadon, and I was drinking a lot of gin in an attempt to ease my fears.

One day when I was at home at the bungalow, I saw a helicopter come into view, landing nearby. Two burly men appeared through the gate two fields away, one wearing a rally jacket and the other a shiny mohair suit. They were definitely not locals. As they approached the bungalow, I drew the curtains and crouched against the front door, which shook as they thumped it, shouting, 'Mr Joseph!'

I realised that was their Cockney way of saying 'Mr Josiffe' but nobody knew me as Josiffe now.

They moved off towards the stables before returning to pound the door again. Eventually they gave up and left. When I told Dr Gleadle, he said the men had probably lost their way and upped my already extremely high dosages of tranquillisers and sleeping pills. A few weeks later, on a February evening when I had just taken my pills and gone to bed, Dr Gleadle knocked on the door. His voice was agitated.

'The documents,' he said. 'Where is the file with all your notes from Mr Bessell that he sent with the retainers, and the correspondence from Mr Thorpe? There's someone who will pay really good money.'

'Is this a good idea?' I stammered, completely taken aback by this sudden visit, and by the doctor's abrupt manner. I had never seen him like that before. He was usually so relaxed and friendly.

'It's a very good idea.' Gleadle spoke forcefully. 'How much money do you want? At the moment, I think the sky's the limit.'

I had no idea what he was talking about. I was so completely out of it on my pills, totally muddle-headed, living in a sort of Hieronymus Bosch bubble. I could barely speak, and couldn't think about anything except that I desperately needed to lie down and go to sleep. Somewhere in the back of my mind I sensed that something odd was going on, but I had no idea why. I offered Dr Gleadle a coffee, so we could sit down and talk things through calmly but he refused. If I had been able to think straight, I would never have given him anything, but he kept demanding the letters.

'The sky's the limit!' he kept repeating. 'Let me have the letters.'

In the end I gave in. I trusted him, thinking he was on my side as he had been so kind in the past. I bumbled around, collecting all the papers I could find. Dr Gleadle took them and, discombobulated, I went to bed and fell into a drugged sleep.

I woke up with a muzzy head and gradually realised what had happened. I searched the bungalow in a frenzied attempt to find any papers I might have overlooked, but there was nothing. Without the papers, I had no proof that my story about the National Insurance cards was true. Panicking, I knew that without this proof, not only would I never sort out the matter but I also became afraid this might be part of a plot to get me committed to a psychiatric hospital. I rushed to the Health Centre and said, 'I must see Ron.' The receptionist looked at me coldly. Since he had asked me to do so, I always called Dr Gleadle Ron when I went in to see him. I'm sure the staff thought we were having an affair.

The receptionist frowned. 'Dr Gleadle has a patient. You must wait.'

Barging in, I said, 'I want everything you took from me last night.'

'Too late,' he replied, showing me the paying-in slips for sums of a thousand and fifteen hundred pounds into deposit and current accounts in my name.

Only then did I realise that Gleadle had taken the letters on behalf of Jeremy but there was nothing I could do. Feeling completely hopeless, I went to the bank to give my signature and complete the formalities. I had to keep myself from falling into another breakdown so, not knowing what else to do, I embraced the money. I bought drinks for everyone at the Three Tuns and a small green Morris 1100. On one of the first outings, when I drove down the lane, the brakes failed. Luckily, I was able to coast, coming to a halt in the hedge. When the local garage investigated, they discovered the brake cables had been cut. At best, someone was trying to hurt me. At worst, they wanted me dead.

I found myself gripped by a chilling fear that I just couldn't shake off. For my safety, I decided to leave the remote bungalow on Exmoor and move in with my friends Janet and Chris, who had room for me in Barnstaple. I took up a part-time job working at a menswear boutique nearby, called Hunky Dory, where the owner paid me in cash. In my spare time I took Janet's dog Rinka for walks. Rinka was a Great Dane and her gentle nature and huge size comforted me. I spent time at the Three Tuns but a few months later, when I was walking back from the pub, I heard a man shout, 'Mr Josiffe!' Then another man appeared, and the next thing I knew, they were beating me up. They broke my teeth and I was so badly battered I was taken to the hospital. When a social worker came to see me, I told her I had been attacked because of Jeremy Thorpe. Far from shutting me up, this incident had made me more determined to speak out.

Although my friends rallied round me, my living situation declined rapidly. Hunky Dory closed so I lost my job, and with no income, I felt I couldn't stay on at Chris and Janet's because I couldn't contribute to living costs. To start with, I moved from friend to friend, staying on sofas and spare beds. Jack and Stella kindly looked after Emma for me in South Molton, and I saw her when I could and also continued to take Rinka for walks, which helped me a lot through this difficult time. Not wanting to outstay my welcome and hating to be a burden to my friends, I ended up sleeping in the men's lavatories in Barnstaple's Rock Park. Rock Park was the pick-up area for all the local dignitaries who were in the closet, and lawyers and businessmen went there to solicit. After they had finished their sordid liaisons in the lavatories, I crept in, locked myself into a cubicle and slept as best I could. Sometimes the police came and flashed their torches around, but they never threw me out.

I was homeless for about six weeks. Chris and Janet, and also Stella and Jack, often invited me around for meals, but when anyone asked where I was staying, I lied. I didn't want anyone to feel obliged to put me up and I didn't want to admit I had nowhere to go. Worrying about me, Chris and Janet sometimes gave me a couple of pounds, which I spent on rough cider to keep warm. The humiliation of not having anyone to call family – of having no one I could go to – made me feel numb. Only Rinka's gentle companionship on our walks lifted my spirits.

One night, I was so desperate for a bath I booked myself into the Royal Fortescue Hotel in Barnstaple. It was so wonderful to wallow in hot water, and to wash my hair, but I felt a terrible guilt because I knew I couldn't pay. The manager, Paul, was a friend of mine whom I'd met on the show-jumping circuit. I felt dreadful when I explained the situation to him, but Paul was very sweet and told me to pay in my own time.

These were some of the bleakest moments of my life. Meanwhile Jeremy was at the peak of his career. Though tragedy had struck when his first wife Caroline had died in a car accident in 1970, he had remarried in 1973. His second wife, Marion, was a concert pianist, who had previously been married to George Lascelles, 7th Earl of Harewood, a cousin of the Queen. Marion was a close friend of the composer Benjamin Britten and his lover, the tenor Peter Pears, so if she knew of Jeremy's homosexual activities, she might not have been greatly shocked. In 1974 the Liberal Party, of which Jeremy was still leader, won six million votes in February's general election. The result was a hung parliament and he was offered a cabinet post by Edward Heath, the Conservative prime minister, if he agreed to bring the Liberals into a coalition government. After discussions, although the prime minister rejected Jeremy's condition of reforming the electoral system and decided not to make a coalition government, Jeremy was in a strong position. Heath resigned and the government changed from Conservative to Labour, but the Liberals had increased their popularity by two and a half times since the last vote. While I pictured him strategising his next move, fuelled by his ambition to become prime minister, I was lying curled up on the floor of a public lavatory five miles away from his picture-perfect thatched cottage in the idyllic village of Cobbaton.

One Sunday morning as I sat in the Three Tuns, I had a revelation. I realised the only thing that would help me was to speak to Jeremy face to face. I'd had a couple of drinks, just enough to give me courage, and asked if anyone would accompany me to Cobbaton, but a loud chorus of 'No!' echoed round the pub. Borrowing a friend's shooting brake, I went anyway, convinced it was a good idea.

When I got to the village, I asked a local which was Jeremy's house, drove right past and stopped. My resolve was wavering, but I made myself turn around and enter the drive. I parked the shooting brake at the top of a steep slope leading to a converted barn, which had big windows and the most beautiful new garage-type doors in wood, possibly walnut or mahogany. Through a window I could see a grand piano.

Walking up to the house, I knocked and a dark-haired woman came out wearing a striped butcher's apron. It was Marion, who must have been cooking the Sunday lunch.

'You probably don't know who I am,' I said, having encountered Jeremy only that one time in South Molton, and never having seen her before.

'Yes, I do,' she replied.

'I don't expect you're very pleased to see me, but I must see Jeremy. Can I possibly speak to him?' I asked.

'I don't think he'll want to,' she replied curtly.

'Could you go and find out, please? I really need you to intercede. I just want to get this sorted out.' I was stammering terribly. 'I really can't go on like this. I'm starving. I've got no money. I can't go on.'

Marion gave a little sigh. 'Just hold on a moment.'

She went back inside and disappeared. Through the open door, I heard her say, 'It's your nut!'

When she returned, she said Jeremy wouldn't see me.

I begged her, 'Will you please, please make him speak to me?'

'I can't,' she said, shutting the door.

Shaking, I got into the car and started the engine, but I couldn't find the reverse gear. Every time I tried to move the car back, it inched further towards those immaculate doors. I thought I'd got it, and the car seemed to be going back, but then my foot was so tremulous it slipped off the brake and the car went straight into the beautiful wooden doors. They didn't break, but they were definitely bending inwards. I panicked, dragged the handbrake on and did the only thing I could think of. I ran back to the house and knocked at the door.

Marion came out, eyebrows raised.

'I can't reverse the car,' I blurted, shaking uncontrollably. 'Look at the state of me.' I continued, apologetically, 'I seem to be driving into your beautiful wooden doors. Could you please reverse the car for me?'

Marion got in and reversed the shooting brake neatly on to the road. I glanced back and noticed a very slight dent in the doors. 'I really didn't want any of this to happen,' I spluttered, as she handed over the car keys. 'Please, will you both remember that I tried?'

She looked at me and, in that moment, I felt she understood I was telling the truth and that I wasn't a bad person.

'Well, I'm very sorry,' she said, and returned to the house.

CHAPTER FOURTEEN

Nightmare on Exmoor

BY THE SUMMER of 1975, I had found a haven at the Market Inn in Barnstaple. The landlady, Edna Friendship, was a sprightly woman in her sixties, with jet-black hair and spectacles with big lenses. She owned a Great Dane so when I took Rinka out we joined up for dog walks and soon became friends. Edna didn't suffer fools gladly but she was very warmhearted and the Market Inn, staffed by Edna and her elderly barmaid, Alice, was typical of a pub in a country town. The clientele was mostly middle-aged or older, rather conventional and staid. They would sit for hours quietly putting away their pints. It wasn't really my kind of pub, but Edna always made me welcome, and when I was homeless I would sometimes stay there until closing time, enjoying the shelter and warmth until I had to return to the public lavatories to sleep. At the end of the summer, I stopped sleeping rough, first staying with friends in the storeroom of their café, then moving into a room above the Market Inn. Edna was generous and had become protective of me and I settled happily at the inn.

By then I had the support of a new GP, Dr Cracknell, who had been horrified by the amount of drugs Gleadle had prescribed for me and greatly reduced my dosages. I also had some appointments with a psychiatrist, Dr Flack, and through their joint efforts, Dr Ronald Gleadle was later struck off from practising as a doctor. I contacted a new solicitor, Mr Ferguson, and told him about my history with Jeremy. He had heard of other young men who had got into similar difficulties and agreed to help me, applying for Legal Aid. We went to see a barrister who was very sympathetic, and I got the impression that he had heard rumours about Jeremy as he seemed to believe my story. His final advice was for me to do nothing. He believed that if Jeremy Thorpe was threatened, the establishment would batten down the hatches and I would have a dreadful time trying to prove my case.

I was despondent for a while but, with new clarity from being on less medication, I felt more level-headed. I enjoyed helping out with the bar work when the pub was really busy and Alice the barmaid was overstretched. I'd pull pints and collect in the coasters, wipe the tables and lock the doors at closing time, grateful that I was inside them now. I had a comfortable bed with a view out onto the street, and every morning Edna and I would have toast and coffee before setting up the bar for service.

If I wanted to socialise, I headed to the lively Three Tuns a few minutes' walk away. This was the place where I could relax and be myself and I enjoyed being with the happy crowd there. They were all straight, but they knew I was gay, and they were very protective of me – although some of the people who drank in the Three Tuns were big fans of Jeremy and could be unpleasant. Among my tight-knit clique of friends was a man called Steve, who would always greet me with 'Look out – here comes Swish!' Then there was Michael, a young chap with a wonderful dry sense of humour, and Blues and Sonia, a rather bohemian couple, who often came to the pub with a pretty young girl from Northern Ireland called Hilary. Hilary was a hippie – what I used to call a weave-your-own-yoghurt kind of girl – who worked at the dry cleaner's in Barnstaple, where I sometimes took my clothes. Harry, a local businessman, was another good friend. He didn't come into the Three Tuns but would meet me out walking with Rinka and we'd have long chats. I felt grateful for the routine and the kindness of Edna, and felt at home in Barnstaple until little things started to happen that made me feel uneasy.

One day as I was stacking the glasses, a man telephoned saying he was a journalist but immediately I felt suspicious. There had been several journalists offering to publish my story, including Gordon Winter, to whom Jack and Stella had introduced me. Winter was based in South Africa and believed the story would be huge. I had met him when he was in England and spent hours telling him about me and Jeremy and the National Insurance cards, and giving him copies of my documents, but I wasn't convinced about breaking the story in South Africa. Instead, I was keener on the idea to write a book and thought Winter might help. Other journalists kept telling me how big the story would be, and most of the British papers were aware of it, but there were reservations. The *Daily Express* had been interested but had recently acquired a new editor, who wouldn't publish. The *Daily Mail*, who'd said I was the 'hottest thing since Watergate', also wouldn't publish. The press barons and newspaper editors at the different papers were probably going to the same clubs as Jeremy and wanted to protect him so nothing was published, although I could have done a deal with the *News of the World*. They promised to pay thousands but I said no. I didn't want anything to do with them because they always seemed to dig up dirt and publish untruths just to make a sensation.

As I listened to the man on the telephone asking to meet me at a hotel in Bristol, his voice sounded cultured and every now and then I could hear it break into a well-spoken accent. When I didn't meet him at the hotel, the man rang again. 'You are not cooperating,' he said, sounding irritated. When I asked him what he meant by this, he replied, 'It is not to my benefit to talk to you.'

I didn't understand what he meant and told him to come to the Market Inn if he wanted to see me. He never did, and although he claimed to be called Masterson, I later thought the voice might have belonged to David Holmes, Jeremy's associate.

There had been other odd calls. One evening at supper time, there was a telephone call for me from a stranger calling himself Ian Wright. 'I work for Pensiero Fashions in London. Can you get your arse up here?' Mr Wright said. 'We want you for two weeks' modelling at four hundred pounds per week.'

It had been years since I'd been on the books of a modelling agency. I looked much older now and was very gaunt after my weeks of living on rough cider. I said, 'There are about five hundred good-looking male models in London. Why on earth would you want me?'

'Oh, we do, we really do. Come up to London! There will be a room booked for you at the Royal Garden Hotel in Kensington.'

I needed to think about this and asked Mr Wright to ring back. He called again when I was out and left a number that I rang back but got through to a telephone box at an Underground station. Thinking the number might be wrong, I checked the London directory for Pensiero Fashions. No company of that name could be found. Feeling rather suspicious, I told Edna and Alice that if Mr Wright rang again, they should say I wasn't interested.

There was another caller whom Edna spoke to. She described him as having a 'rough' voice, and when he made a random request to buy a camera from me she hung up on him. I began to feel anxious, wondering who these people were and whether they were all connected. Then, a few weeks later, two police officers accosted me.

I was with Edna at a Roger Whittaker concert at Chequers, a new disco on the Quays in Barnstaple. I wasn't particularly keen, but I didn't want to upset Edna, so I went along. Chequers was crammed with locals and the place reeked of Estée Lauder's Tana Lawn perfume and Brut aftershave. Roger whistled and warbled his way through the songs, and everybody joined in the choruses with raucous abandon. In the interval, Edna sent me to the bar to buy drinks and I noticed Paul, my friend from the hotel I'd bathed in without paying when I was homeless. As I went over to say hello I saw him backing away from two burly chaps in dinner jackets. One of these men then turned to me, saying he was from the police, and I should go with him and his colleague.

235

'We need to see what's in your briefcase,' he said sternly.

'What business is it of yours?' I asked, afraid these might be more thugs, sent to beat me up.

'We can get you into Barnstaple police station because you haven't paid your hotel bill from the summer,' he said smugly.

Paul kept saying it didn't matter, but both men ignored him, grabbed me by the arms and hauled me out of Chequers so fast my feet didn't touch the ground. I tried to say that surely this was a civil matter and there was no need to be so rough, but they refused to let go.

When we arrived at the police station, instead of talking about my unpaid hotel bill, officers started asking me about the payment I had received from Dr Gleadle. They wanted to know whether I still had copies of the documents Dr Gleadle had taken that outlined Bessell's payments to me.

Then one said something that sent a chill down my spine. 'I'm working for the lord privy seal. We've got someone coming down from one of the ministries to interview you. We need your documents or there's somebody not a million miles from Cobbaton who won't be sleeping easy in his bed tonight. If you don't cooperate, I have the power to lock you away and you won't see the light of day for fourteen years.'

Cobbaton, of course, was where Jeremy lived. As it dawned on me that the establishment was obviously now implementing a major cover-up, I was bundled back into a police car and driven to the Market Inn so I could hand over the documents. My mind was racing. Some of Bessell's documents were with friends for safe-keeping but others were in my room. I wondered whether I could hide them, all the time panicking. I hadn't done anything wrong. I didn't know whether the policemen were corrupt, misled, or just conducting their business. I also wondered whether they treated everyone so roughly or if they were homophobic.

When we arrived at the Market Inn it was locked and I had no key so we waited. At 1 a.m. Edna returned, her expression ferocious at the sight of the policemen. 'We've been worried sick about Norman. I had no idea where he'd gone,' she said to them.

'No need to worry about him,' one of the detectives said, with a smile. 'We've got someone from the lord privy seal's office coming down tomorrow. Norman won't be crying in the cells. He'll stay the night with me.'

Edna blew up. 'If he stays anywhere, he'll stay here. And he'll come to the station tomorrow.'

The officer shook his head. 'Sorry, this has to be done tonight.'

I was told to go up to my room and get the briefcase. The officer was hot on my heels, though Edna tried to stop him to give me a chance to hide some of the documents. He insisted on accompanying me, grabbing the documents out of my hands as if he were a thief robbing me of a fistful of money.

Back at the station, I discovered that the suggestion of my spending a comfortable night at the detective's home was another fabrication as the officers became even more hostile. My briefcase was taken, I was searched roughly, and they removed my tie, shoes and a gold neck chain I had not taken off since Sue had given it to me several years before. I asked for my lawyer, Ferguson, but he didn't arrive that night. As a final insult, I was locked into a cell marked 'Females'.

Shortly after this, a man with tousled grey hair and large hands – a rather rough, workaday sort of chap – came to the cell with another officer. He immediately began bullying me. 'You've been a very naughty boy, saying these things about a decent man. You're lying, aren't you, you nasty little so-and-so?' He kept repeating, 'You're lying about Jeremy Thorpe, aren't you!'

At one point I gave a nervous laugh and tried to stand up for myself. 'You are so ridiculous. Of course, I most certainly am not lying!' I exclaimed.

Outraged that I had answered him back, the man exploded with anger, grabbed me and whacked my head against the wall, twice, then walked out, threatening he'd come back. To my huge relief, he didn't, but my head throbbed with pain for the rest of the night.

Edna and Hilary came to the police station to check on me but they were turned away, and when I woke at 8 a.m. I was told I was to be charged with obtaining a pecuniary advantage by deception as a result of booking a room at the Royal Fortescue without having any intention of paying.

Finally, at 1.50 p.m., twelve hours after I'd arrived at the station, Ferguson turned up. I was furious. 'What took you so long? Did you walk?' I asked.

Ferguson gave me an offhand apology and matter-of-factly instructed me to plead guilty, so I did. Forty minutes later, I went before a special court and was told to pay fines and compensation of fifty-eight pounds.

My briefcase was returned along with all the documents, once they had been copied, and before I left, one of the officers took me to one side to warn me that I didn't realise what danger I was in. 'I am only too aware of the danger,' I replied. 'And I wonder from which quarter there is the greatest threat.'

Back at the inn, I wrote to Ferguson to ask for clarification about what danger the police had been referring to. He replied stating he believed I was in very real danger of being badly hurt. He explained that detectives had told him they feared I would suffer severe injury, if I stayed in the locality and my views and intentions became publicly known. Ferguson ended his letter by advising me to leave the country. I didn't know what to make of this, assuming he was referring to the hidden powers of the establishment and possibly also the Liberal supporters who were very loyal and passionate in their support of Jeremy. I felt very frightened and started drinking a lot of gin and tonic. I asked my doctor for higher doses of my antidepressants and sleeping pills but, concerned that any more would have a negative impact, he kept me on the same dose. At night or whenever I was alone, the warning played out in my head on a loop and I started to fixate on the odd telephone calls, convinced they were connected. I thought about Jeremy and wondered whether he really had told the policemen to intervene as well as ordering the strangers to beat me up. I became jumpy, constantly looking over my shoulder when I went out. Rumours flew around the village and I'd hear Alice the barmaid muttering to Edna that I shouldn't be there, and that someone might come and murder Edna in her bed.

Not long after Ferguson had told me to leave the country, a stranger came into the Three Tuns. That night I was with Michael and Steve chatting at the bar. Just like in most small communities, everybody knew everybody else so when anyone from out of town came into the local pubs they immediately stood out from the crowd. We glanced at the stranger, who was wearing a dark-blue donkey jacket with a roll-neck jumper and smoking a strange pipe with a lot of silver on it. As we carried on chatting, I noticed the man kept edging towards me. Michael and the others teased me, saying he fancied me. I definitely didn't fancy him. He had a horrid little goatee beard, and the clouds of smoke from his pipe were so revolting I had to ask him to move away. He scowled at me and went to stand in the corner but kept looking at me. I felt very on edge, especially when someone remarked that the man had said he was an angler but seemed to know nothing about fishing.

Later, we walked home through the market and the man called, 'Hello!' to me from the public lavatories. Everybody laughed. 'Ooh, it's your boyfriend, Norman!'

A couple of days later, when I was walking Rinka, I noticed a yellow Mazda parked in the market. It was the only car, which was unusual. As I went past, a man called me over, saying he needed to speak to me, and I should get into the Mazda with him. Remembering Ferguson's warnings, I refused but the man persisted.

'You are in grave danger,' the man said. He had an estuarine accent, with a rather whining tone. 'There's a man who's going to come from Canada. He's being paid over four figures to kill you.'

Shocked, I let out a hysterical laugh and turned to go back to the pub but the man dodged in front of me. 'Please, you've got to come,' he said.

I looked around, hoping one of my friends might be near the market, but nobody was about.

'You don't remember me, do you?' the man said. 'I was in the pub the other night.'

As he said this, I recognised him as the man with the pipe who'd been staring at me. I didn't know what to do so I carried on walking away, my mind racing at this new, random idea of a man from Canada trying to kill me.

'Look, I promise you, you'll be quite safe,' the man said. 'I just want you to come for a drive. It'll be about twenty-six miles. There's someone who wants to see you. They're paying me to protect you.'

I was stunned, pausing. 'Who on earth would wish to do this?'

'It's a lady,' the man replied.

'The only lady who might want to talk to me would be Marion Thorpe.' I didn't believe it as I said it but the man nodded.

'She's at the Miners' Arms in Knowstone. It's not far to drive,' he said, his voice eager now I'd engaged.

'Phone the pub and ask her to come and meet us,' I said. 'If there's anything she wants to know, I'm only too happy to tell her.'

He shook his head, explaining that the lady could not be seen with us, so I told him we had reached a stalemate because I was not getting into his car.

The man was becoming flustered. 'I'm being paid to protect you. I want to know what I'm protecting.' He flung open the car door and pulled out his briefcase, opening it to show me the contents. 'Look – I have nothing in here to hurt you.'

Then he came right up to me, pushed his face close to mine and, with mad eyes, he said, 'Would you believe me if I told you that you were within a hair's breadth of being killed?'

I didn't know what to say. I didn't know what to believe but, shaken, I suggested we go to the Royal Fortescue where Paul worked because then he could keep an eye on us. I ran to collect my documents, Rinka striding next to me. When I got into the inn, Edna asked me why I was shaking.

'Look outside,' I told her. 'There is a yellow Mazda parked up. That man has just told me somebody is going to come from Canada to kill me. Can you get the registration?'

Edna put her Great Dane on the leash and went out, pretending she was taking him for a pee, and stood near the car, peering at it through her glasses, then returned, having noted the number. 'Are you sure you should be talking to this man?' she asked, as I raced upstairs.

I wasn't sure. I didn't like him, but the police were doing nothing to help me, and I thought he might hold the key to what was going on. I collected my documents from Mr Bessell and went outside. The man tried to get me into the car again, telling me he had telephoned the Miners' Arms and the lady was there and would be waiting in a layby. 'Come on!' he said, losing his cool, but I refused. The man seemed scared of Rinka and, already jittery, he walked awkwardly down the road to the hotel behind us.

Paul was serving at the bar, and as I ordered a double Scotch for me and a double bitter lemon for the man, who'd said his name was Peter Keane, I asked Paul to take a discreet look so he could identify him if necessary.

Keane was fidgety, shifting in his seat, complaining that

Paul kept staring at him. 'It's OK. He's a very nice chap,' I said, but Keane wanted to leave. There weren't too many quiet places to go in Barnstaple, but I suggested the Imperial Hotel. As we left, Paul took the precautionary measure of putting the glasses we had used into a plastic bag, which he subsequently handed over to the police.

Keane seemed calmer in the Imperial and we sat down and started to talk. I asked Keane what his job was and he told me he was a special investigator so I let him look through my documents. He made a few notes on the back of some pink paper, which I thought was an unusual choice. At one point, I went to the lavatory, and, foolishly, forgot to take my documents with me. When I returned, they were still there, as was Keane. I found this reassuring. It made me feel a little more confident that he was telling the truth about being a private investigator.

We then talked at great length about what had happened to me. 'There is one way out of all this, you know,' Keane said, once I'd finished. 'If you were to go to Michael Barnes, Jeremy Thorpe's solicitor, give him all the documents you have and sign a document stating that anything you have ever said to anybody is a lie, then a substantial sum of money will be given to you.'

'But I don't want the money. I want the truth to come out,' I said.

'You should be careful. It will not be you they get first but that which you love most in the world,' Keane said.

'Benjamin?' I asked, horrified.

Keane nodded. I panicked and was so upset I got up and left. Keane followed me, saying he would be in touch as soon as the man from Canada arrived, and telling me to reconsider what he'd said about Jeremy's solicitor.

That evening I telephoned Sue. Then I wrote to her, explaining the situation in detail and expressing the strongest desire to protect Benjamin from any harm, but my efforts backfired. A few weeks later in early October, my solicitor Ferguson was contacted by Sue's solicitors. Sue had shown my letter to them and was advised to have no more contact with me. This formal communication between solicitors about my own child made the truth even more devastating. I wrote letters and sent presents to Benjamin but never heard back and, not wanting to put him in danger, I didn't try to see him.

When I got back to the inn, Blues and Sonia noticed I was looking very strained. Thinking it might be good for me to have a change of scene, and needing someone to cat-sit for a fortnight, they asked me to stay at their cottage in Combe Martin, a small seaside resort nearby. I agreed and asked Hilary whether she wanted to come too, just as friends. I was wary because Hilary seemed to have developed a crush on me. I don't know why because she was aware that I was gay, but I'd be drinking with my chums and often I'd look round to see her staring at me with her huge, limpid eyes. Once when I was leaving the pub, she met me outside and gave me a little nosegay of rosemary, saying, 'Here's rosemary for remembrance!' and sometimes I'd be at the Market Inn and hear an 'Oh-oh!' from Edna, signalling Hilary's arrival. She would order a gin and tonic, squeezing the lemon, then eating it in a rather maddening way, while watching me over the edge of her glass.

She was a sweet girl, so quirky, and I liked her very much,

but I didn't want anything more than friendship with her, so when we set off for Combe Martin, I made it clear that our stay would be on a strictly platonic basis. We were a party of three, as Rinka came too. Janet and Chris were finding it too difficult to look after the Great Dane and had decided to give her to me. I was absolutely delighted Rinka was now mine. She had helped me through some very dark times, and the bond between us was very strong. For the first few days we went for long walks by the sea, and I borrowed a horse belonging to a friend and rode up into the hills. In the evenings, we visited a hotel and bar called the Pack o' Cards belonging to Peter Vernon-Evans, the son of the television cook Fanny Cradock.

Halfway through my stay in the cottage, Vernon-Evans rang me at the cottage to tell me a man named Peter Keane had called the Pack o' Cards from Porthcawl in Wales asking for me.

'What did you tell him?' I said, feeling the adrenalin pump through my body, wondering whether he had news about the man from Canada.

'I said you'd be down later on, and he'll ring you then,' Vernon-Evans replied.

I spoke briefly to Keane that day from the Pack o' Cards, arranging to meet him at 4 p.m. when he would then explain what he knew. I thought he would come to the cottage so I went there to wait but he didn't turn up. The next day, when I was in the Pack o' Cards, there was another call for me.

'Is that Norman? This is Andy.' The caller's voice was rushed as though he was in a hurry and I heard the sound of coins being put into the phone box at the other end.

'Andy who?' I asked. This was odd, as I didn't know anyone called Andy.

'Oh, sorry. I meant Peter!'

It was Keane. Puzzled, I asked why he hadn't turned up the previous day.

'Where were you? I was waiting at Delves Hotel,' he replied, which confused me more because we hadn't arranged that. Worried his money might run out and the call would be cut off, I asked for his number and he gave it to me, explaining he was in a phone box in Glasgow. 'I had to dash up here,' he said, still very flustered.

The pips went, and we were cut off so I rang the number back and, exasperated, I asked, 'What's this about? Is it important?'

'He's here. He's in Barnstaple!' Keane said.

I assumed this must be the man from Canada who was coming to kill me but I gave no outward reaction. It was all so surreal and confusing having a random person telling me that another stranger had come all the way from Canada to kill me. All I could do was take Keane seriously and follow instructions.

Keane told me to go to the Wellington pub in Minehead the next day. When I explained I couldn't get to Minehead, he began thinking aloud, muttering about catching a plane to Manchester. For someone who was supposed to be protecting me from a potential assassin, he seemed to be a long way off and completely disorganised but I was frightened. I didn't know how to deal with a death threat and this man was persistently telling me he was trying to help protect me so, finally, we agreed to meet the following day. I said out loud, so there was no mistake, 'Friday the twenty-fourth of October, at Delves Hotel in Combe Martin, at six p.m.'

He said yes and hung up.

I was nervous about this, but I was sure it was the only way to get to the bottom of Keane's claim that a hitman was on his way. Rumours about strange men being after me were going around town and, with my friends worried, I thought it was best to try to deal with it head on and trust Keane to sort everything out.

On Friday morning, I woke up feeling full of adrenalin, and when I saw Edna I told her I had a funny feeling that I might not see her again. She told me to be very careful. Hilary pleaded with me not to meet Keane but I had made up my mind.

'It's the only way I'll find out what's going on,' I told her. 'There's no point going to the police. They'll just turn up and make a big bumble of the whole thing. Don't worry. I'll be all right. I'll have Rinka with me. I'm frightened, but I don't think Peter Keane is a bad man,' I said, trying to re-assure myself as much as them.

That afternoon I met Harry for lunch and he raised the same concerns, continuing to question my logic as he gave me a lift to the Pack o' Cards. Once again I insisted it was the only way to find out what was going on but asked him to try to get the number of Keane's car.

Keane was in a callbox outside the hotel, and when I arrived, he took me over to a shabby dark-blue Ford Escort and told me he had to see a client in Porlock in relation to his private detective work.

'Come with me,' he said. 'But I don't want that in the car.' He pointed to Rinka, stepping back away from her.

'She goes everywhere with me,' I said, patting her head. 'I'll take her for a walk while you see your client. Either that, or you can see me here on your way back.'

Reluctantly, Keane agreed to have Rinka in the car. She climbed onto the back seat and I got in, moving Keane's briefcase and a book about scientology from the back seat onto my lap so that Rinka didn't slobber on them.

Dusk was falling as we drove along the coast and into Porlock, dark clouds gathering over the sea. I still wasn't entirely sure why we were going to Porlock or what was happening but all I could think about was the man from Canada. 'It seems so dreadful that a man would get on a plane knowing that he was embarking on a mission to shoot somebody,' I said.

'Well, you couldn't do it if you knew the person,' Keane replied.

'Why should that make any difference?' I said, surprised by his answer.

'If you got to know somebody, you just couldn't. I know a lot about you now and it would be impossible for me to kill you,' he said.

I could only reiterate that cold-blooded murder was a terrible thing. Keane said nothing and instead we had a short discussion on scientology versus spiritualism, after which I felt in great need of a cigarette. I didn't have a lighter, but I'd previously seen Keane get matches out of the briefcase to light his pipe, so I looked inside it. I found a matchbox that felt oddly heavy. I slipped it open and my fingers touched smooth metal objects. I didn't know what they were, but they weren't matches, and since I couldn't find any, I shut the briefcase and tried to forget about wanting a cigarette.

When we arrived in Porlock, Keane drove off to see his client, telling me he'd be about half an hour and to meet him at the Castle Hotel at 8 p.m. I went to the bar there, had a Scotch and spoke to the bar staff, who were very impressed by Rinka. I kept glancing at my watch and at 8.15 p.m., when Keane had not turned up, I began to worry that I'd have to walk thirty miles home in the pouring rain. Was all this just another ploy to undermine me?

I went out to look for a taxi and saw headlights flashing on the other side of the street. It was Keane.

'I thought you were going to come in!' I said, exasperated, already soaking wet from the rain that was falling hard.

'I couldn't, because I mustn't be seen with you,' he replied.

I ushered Rinka into the back seat, worrying she would shake the rain off her and drench Keane, who winced as she jumped in, but she lay down, as gentle as ever, looking out through the windscreen as Keane started the engine. I assumed Keane would start briefing me about the plan but he didn't say anything and just drove up the hill on to Exmoor. Whenever I asked for more details he told me he was feeling very tired. I still didn't know where we were going or why we had met in Porlock, but after about twenty minutes in the car, Keane's driving became suddenly erratic. He started swerving and I stopped worrying about the man from Canada and started worrying about Keane. He had driven from Scotland so I assumed he kept nodding off. The swerving grew worse, Keane narrowly missing oncoming traffic only to overcompensate and drive almost into the verge. Panicked, I asked if I could drive.

'Yes, in a minute,' Keane said.

Then he muttered, 'This'll be all right.'

He pulled across on to the hard shoulder at the Yenworthy Lodge turning. It was very dark, windy, and pouring with rain. I jumped out and walked round to the driver's side assuming Keane would shuffle over into the passenger seat but he got out. Rinka slipped out after him and started leaping around, thinking we were going for a walk.

'Sorry!' I shouted. The wind was howling, sucking up my words. 'I meant you to move over to the passenger seat, and then she would have stayed in the car.'

I grabbed Rinka by the collar to put her back in and heard Keane shout, 'No, this is it!'

During the next second, Rinka's legs splayed, and she crumpled to the ground. I had no idea what had happened. First she was there, then she was on the ground, and because it was dark, I couldn't see what was going on.

Kneeling down, I touched Rinka, and felt something sticky on my hands. It was blood. She was bleeding from her temple. I knew then that she was badly hurt. 'What have you done?' I screamed. 'You can't involve a dog. It's bad enough already, you can't bring an animal into all this.'

I shook Rinka. 'You haven't hurt her! You haven't killed her!' I screamed in complete shock but then Keane yelled, 'It's your turn now,' and I felt something hard press against my head and a click. But nothing happened. Keane moved away, and I saw him standing in the headlights, shaking something. Above the roar of the wind, I heard him shouting obscenities.

I was so traumatised it took a moment for me to understand it was a gun in his hands, and that the tiny click I had heard was him pulling the trigger. I ran away into the darkness, stumbling over the rough ground, but ahead of me, the lights of Cardiff glimmered on the other side of the Bristol Channel and I realised I must be a silhouette against the bright light, making me a perfect target. Not knowing what to do, I turned, thinking there was no way out. Maybe Rinka was still alive, and if I was going to die, I'd rather be with her so I ran back to her. In the headlights, I saw Keane levelling the gun at me but I didn't care. I just wanted to help my dog. He kept pulling the trigger but nothing happened. He shouted more obscenities and then he jumped into the car and drove away down the hill.

I bent over Rinka, my cries of despair ripped away by the wind. Unable to believe she was dead, I tried to resuscitate her, giving her the kiss of life. Some minutes later, I saw headlights approaching. Running to the road, I flagged the car down and a man got out.

'They have shot my dog and they tried to shoot me,' I shouted.

The driver turned out to be an AA patrol officer called Mr Lethaby on an evening out with his wife and two friends. All of them looked at me in horror. Weeping and shivering, I was covered with Rinka's blood, and at first Mr Lethaby thought it was me who had been shot. When he realised it was Rinka, we carried her to the roadside. She didn't move, but I still couldn't believe she was dead.

A vehicle came tanking up the hill in low gear. I couldn't see it properly, but I thought it must be Keane. 'It's him! He's coming back!' I yelled. 'Get back in the car and go!'

But they stayed where they were, grouped together in the

headlights. The driver of the approaching car spotted them and swerved onto the moor, bouncing over the rough ground, then sped away, back where he had come from.

Mr Lethaby went to call the Exmoor Ranger and the emergency services and it wasn't long before the police arrived. I was in deep shock and as I sat in the back of the stationary police car, I twisted Rinka's choke chain round my hand until it hurt. One of the women who had found me sat in the car too, and I asked her if Rinka was dead.

'I'm afraid so,' she replied.

Shaking with emotion, I shouted, 'It's all the fault of that bloody man Thorpe!'

I told everyone I was writing a book about Jeremy Thorpe's involvement in my life, and that he wanted to silence me. When they asked who the man with gun was, I told them he was a private investigator called Peter Keane. Then I burst into uncontrollable tears. An ambulance arrived to take me to hospital in Minehead, the paramedics saying there were police everywhere and that people had been stopped from leaving Porlock. I don't know what happened to Rinka's body, and was distraught that I had to leave her.

When I arrived in casualty a doctor was waiting for me. 'I'm Dr Patel. I just need to ask you some questions to assess whether you are concussed,' he said.

I looked up and saw a man in a white mackintosh watching me and became terrified that I was about to be put in a psychiatric hospital. Dr Patel quietly kept asking me what day it was but I just couldn't remember. I was in such a terrible pit of fear, gasping and shivering. I felt so alone. The nurses brought me some tea, and then the *Daily Express* popped into my head. I remembered that 'slobbery' had been the *Express* word of the day, which had made me laugh because of Rinka. Thoughts kept coming and 'target' popped into my head because that morning I had read that an IRA car bomb had gone off outside Sir Hugh Fraser's house in Campden Hill Square where Caroline Kennedy, daughter of the assassinated US president, was living. For her safety, she was now staying with Jane Ormsby-Gore's father, Lord Harlech. Aware that the man in the white mackintosh was still watching, I shared these random but specific thoughts with Dr Patel as clearly as possible and he reassured me that my memories were from that morning's newspaper. Confirming I wasn't injured or unstable, he told me I was in shock and asked if I wished to spend the night at the hospital, but I felt too vulnerable. I just wanted to go back to Combe Martin so he said he would request police protection for me.

The man in the white mackintosh accompanied me to Minehead police station. I was terrified of him but it turned out he was kind and thoughtful and was just there to arrange protection. The other police officers, however, were dismissive of my story.

Once the formalities were finished, the police drove me over the moor, which was full of other police cars. At the county boundary, I was handed over to Devon and Cornwall police officers, who drove me to Combe Martin. The cottage was in complete darkness and I suddenly became terrified that Keane might be hiding on the premises. The officers searched the surroundings of the house. Then I went in and called Hilary's name. There was no reply. As I went upstairs with the officers, I was sick with fear, thinking about Gwen's death. We opened the bedroom door and Hilary was lying flat on the bed. Rushing to her, I thought she had been shot, but there was no blood and no sign of disturbance. When I shook her, Hilary finally came to and sat up, looking very groggy. She had been so worried and upset when I hadn't returned that she'd drunk a whole bottle of wine and keeled over. When she saw I was all right, she became hysterical with relief.

The officers left, and I climbed into bed beside her. We wept as I told her what had happened to Rinka, holding each other close as we shared our grief. That night, seeking comfort and release, Hilary and I made love for the first and only time, and something wonderful came out of those horrific events. Our beautiful daughter Bryony was conceived.

CHAPTER FIFTEEN

The Newton Trial

IT WAS A month before 'Peter Keane' was arrested. To start with, nothing happened, and during that first week Hilary and I clung together as we recovered from the trauma. Everything seemed eerily quiet, and then a detective turned up to interview me, jumping straight in with the accusation, 'You did this yourself to publicise your book!'

It was hard to understand why anyone could think I would kill my beloved dog and I made this very clear. I was also asked to make a long statement to corroborate what I had already said to the police. To support this, I told Edna to go to the police station with the number of the yellow Mazda we had seen outside the Market Inn, a detail that would prove vital, but the shooting went unremarked on until a week later. Then the articles started coming out. First the *West Somerset Free Press* reported the story with the headline 'The Great Dane Mystery: Dog-in-a-Fog Case Baffles Police' followed by the *Sunday Express* with 'Exmoor Riddle of a Frightened Man and a Shot Dog'. People were starting to talk.

Within a few days, the police had traced the yellow Mazda to a hire firm in Blackpool and come up with the details of a man named Andrew Gino Newton, the real name of the man who had killed Rinka and tried to kill me. An out-of-work pilot, Newton had gone off on holiday with his girlfriend to the rather unlikely destination of Karachi in Pakistan, but on his return to Heathrow officers were waiting to arrest him.

Newton promptly fed the police a pack of outrageous lies. He claimed that I was blackmailing him over a nude photograph of him in a contact magazine. In the 1970s, these magazines were used by people who wanted to meet for sexual encounters and his story was that he'd arranged to meet a woman through the magazine, but when he turned up for the assignation I was there, demanding money from him in exchange for not revealing his naked image. I'd never even seen a contact magazine. When the police searched Newton's mother's house they found the gun and his notes about me on pink airline record papers. He was charged and committed to stand trial at Exeter Crown Court for possession of a firearm with intent to endanger life.

Blues and Sonia were due back from holiday but instead of returning to the Market Inn both Hilary and I, although not an item, moved into Gloucester Cottage in Combe Martin. Gloucester Cottage was empty and belonged to our friend Brian Cook, who was a journalist with the *North Devon Journal*. Brian was an absolute rock for me in the aftermath of my attempted murder, insisting that I needed a refuge from the press. 'Everyone will be after you,' he kept saying, worried I would be hounded even more in town. He believed unswervingly that I was telling the truth about Jeremy and understood, even better than I did at that time, the cold mendacity of those in high places, who would happily have seen me dead or ruined.

Journalists soon started turning up at Gloucester Cottage. Local press came, followed by two men who worked for the BBC, Barrie Penrose and Roger Courtiour, who were doing research for their book *The Pencourt File*, investigating supposed conspiracies against the government. The news travelled wider. Auberon Waugh, who wrote for *Private Eye* magazine, really disliked Jeremy, describing him as a public-school prefect who had never grown up, and seemed to be aware of the rumours that were going around. By December 1975, Waugh had published a short piece in *Private Eye* that mentioned the shooting and ended with the wry comment: 'My only hope is that sorrow over his friend's dog will not cause Mr Thorpe's premature retirement from public life.' Waugh later ran a series of satirical pieces about Jeremy in the magazine entitled 'The Tales of Jeremy Fishier'.

Hilary found the reporters very upsetting. When she realised she was pregnant, it all became too much for her and she went to stay with Blues and Sonia. Barrie Penrose then came to stay on and off so he could interview me. Barrie later admitted that at our first meeting he found me so nervous and emotional, with my eyes darting everywhere, he regarded me as something of a lunatic. But when he checked my story, he could find no proof that I was lying. We ended up getting on well, and he kept me up to date with everything that was going on and was very supportive.

Despite the interest from the press, I knew the establishment would close ranks and do everything to keep me quiet when Newton's trial came up, but then I had a stroke of luck. In February 1976, a month before Newton's trial, I received an erroneous double payment from Social Security. I had been receiving these payments since just before Benjamin was born when I had claimed health benefits for suffering from nervous anxiety. I realised I could use this mistake to my advantage. I deliberately kept the money and was subsequently charged with fraud, so, with the press already interested in me, I now had a platform to speak out.

Because the charge was related to benefits, which were related to my employment status, I knew I would have to explain why I didn't have my National Insurance cards and how Jeremy had refused to give them to me. At last my voice would be officially heard and the truth would have to be acknowledged.

I told my friend Mike Charleston, a reporter from the *Daily Express*, about my plan and he told several other journalists so my story slipped out. Mike gave me some advice for the court. 'You will get one chance to say something, and you will have to say it very quickly before they shut you down,' Mike said.

He was right. At court on 29 January, in front of a room packed with press and Michael Barnes, Jeremy's lawyer, who must have been tipped off, I stood up and said, 'I have been hounded because of my homosexual relationship with Jeremy Thorpe. It's all become so sick and I'm just tired of it.'

Then I was told to stop.

I wanted to explain how I just wanted my National Insurance cards back so I could move on with my life but I wasn't allowed to say any more. Instead, there was uproar in the court. The prosecution lawyer struggled to make himself heard as the reporters fell over each other in their rush to get out and telephone the copy through with the headline, 'Scott Tells All!'

Ferguson, my lawyer, was furious. He'd had no idea I was going to say that because, fearing he would somehow silence me, I hadn't told him the real reason for me allowing the case to go to court. Worried my statement would damage the proceedings, Ferguson told the court, 'He is young, excitable and anxious and needs assistance not punishment.'

Meanwhile Barnes, Jeremy's lawyer, sat there staring at me with a face like thunder. I was found guilty of fraud, put on probation, and ordered to pay back the money at a rate of two pounds per week. Well worth it, as far as I was concerned. The truth was officially out.

By then, Jeremy wasn't doing quite so well, the Liberals having lost more than two-thirds of their vote at the October '74 election. But he was still there. He was debating in the House of Commons, going about his usual business as a high-flying politician. While the story broke, which no doubt rattled him, he carried on as leader of the Liberals. The articles splashed across almost every newspaper must have come as an almighty shock to him, everyone in the Party, and Liberal supporters across the country.

After that, each day brought a deluge of reporters to the cottage, and while my friends stood by my side, the villagers turned against me. The area was a Liberal stronghold and there Jeremy Thorpe could do no wrong, so I automatically became the devil's spawn. Even the doctor could hardly bear to look at me. There was a pub opposite, and at closing time the locals would loiter in the street outside and point up at my windows. Homosexuality was still taboo and many people remained disgusted by it. Most people didn't talk about it so there was a feeling of shock in the community that I was openly admitting to being gay, speaking truths that many men had taken to the grave.

One Sunday, I was watching the news with Barrie Penrose, his colleague Roger Courtiour, and a couple of other journalists. It was rather a squash in the cottage's tiny living room. Suddenly, the coverage shifted to an outside broadcast from Combe Martin. We looked out of the window and saw the cameras in the street, and people coming out of the Methodist chapel next door. All the women were dressed up to the nines, topped off with smart Sunday hats decorated with artificial grapes and the like. Back on screen, we watched the interviewer ask one of them, 'What do you feel about this shooting?' and she, who had just come out of the chapel, said, 'I would have shot him myself. Jeremy Thorpe's a wonderful man.'

Many people felt like that about Jeremy, especially in his constituency. He was known for being charmingly inclusive, for engaging with everyone and for listening. He made people relax, which was a stroke of genius because it led people from all backgrounds to feel connected to him. But I had seen him take advantage of people's generosity and support. Once after I'd been out canvassing for the Liberals, I gave Jeremy some envelopes with money in them that old ladies in Braunton and Saunton had given me. It was intended for the Liberal Party but Jeremy whipped out the notes, and said, 'Here's ten for you and twenty for me!' I was deeply shocked at his dishonesty, yet no one had any inkling. He was seen as a gentleman, a role model and a national treasure. When I heard what the woman said I ran outside and confronted her. 'That's not Christian!' I said, looking her straight in the eye. The cameras missed me, so I didn't make a surprise appearance on the BBC news, but I had to say something. I was so hurt by her comment.

If any of the reporters knocked on the door, I would talk to them. Some offered me money, but I said, 'I don't want any money, I just want to get this out.'

I showed them Bessell's letters about the retainers and was very open about everything. At first this didn't have much effect, I assume because the press barons and editors were still afraid to rock the boat. Then, just before Newton's trial, the story of the payment for my dossier of documents broke, with the headline, 'I Paid £2500 To Norman Scott, Says The Godfather.'

David Holmes, who was godfather to Jeremy's son Rupert, had tried to pre-empt this being revealed at the trial by telling the Director of Public Prosecutions beforehand. To counter Holmes's confession, an article appeared in the *Sunday Times*, entitled 'The Lies of Norman Scott', which was not a surprise because Jeremy knew Harold Evans the editor. The article showed quotes from the letters that the Metropolitan Police took from me in 1962, presumably to try to make out Jeremy was innocent, so it looked like I was trying to exploit him.

Aware that they must have shared the letters with Harold Evans when they had no right to do so, I demanded their return from the Metropolitan Police. Without going to court or having to pay any fees, the police conceded immediately and gave them back. John Penrose, the most trusted journalist working for Dan Ferrari, the *Daily Mirror*'s news editor, had been assigned to me as a sort of minder. He soon became a good, protective friend, and went with me to collect them. I could hardly believe it. At last I had won a battle against the police. I had prevailed. I read through the Bunnies letter once more, and saw Jeremy's bold, black-inked words on the notepaper with the House of Commons letterhead and Jeremy's forceful character, right there on the paper, like a depth charge from the past. I thought that at last people would have to believe I was telling the truth about what he had done to me.

On 16 March 1976, five months after he shot my dog and tried to kill me, Newton went to trial. I arrived at Exeter Crown Court feeling desperately nervous at the thought of having to face the man who had tried to take my life. The press benches were packed and there was an atmosphere of excited anticipation.

Newton pleaded not guilty and continued to state adamantly that I was blackmailing him over a nude photograph. As he stood there lying, he kept looking at me, trying to make eye contact and intimidate me. His tone was sneering, rather whiny, with that horrible nasal twang.

I had been forbidden to mention Jeremy Thorpe's name by my barrister, Lewis Hawser, which I had to adhere to, but I had one moment of triumph. Newton had asked a girlfriend of his to be a witness and she told the court all about this 'Norman Scott', who had been going up to Blackpool every week to collect four pounds in blackmail money.

This was rubbish and also illogical. Barnstaple to Blackpool is a long and inconvenient train journey and the fare was about five times the alleged blackmail payment. When the judge asked, 'And is this gentleman in court?' the girl looked round, her eyes passing over me several times.

I got so angry I jumped up and said, 'Is it me?'

The press gallery rocked with laughter and the judge roared, 'SIT DOWN!'

The feeling of support was short-lived. When I was called to the witness stand and gave evidence, I described the events that had taken place on the road to Porlock. But, unable to refer to Jeremy, who, I knew, was behind the attempt on my life, I felt chilled by the silence in the court, wondering whether anyone believed me. I found it hard to speak up and got even more nervous when I started to stammer.

Newton's lawyer, Patrick Back, QC, went on to make horrible homophobic comments about me. 'Many homosexuals have a tremendous propensity for malice' and 'His false humility, his tears, his charade of fear – do you think that was real?' are just a couple of examples. These sentiments were being fed to the public by some of the newspapers at that time, along with photographs of me, modelling test shots purloined by journalists, where the eye area had been adulterated and darkened to make me look evil and satanic. This character assassination splashed across the papers and trickling down into village gossip was extremely difficult to deal with, though I did find one headline, 'QC Lashes Male Model', very funny. My friends kept telling me that the papers were just trying to cause drama, competing against each other to make their story as sensational as possible to sell more copies.

Remarkably, I did not have a nervous breakdown. With

the local doctor refusing to see me, my medication stayed at the prescribed dose and I accepted that, realising I needed to stay as clear-headed as possible to confront everything that came at me and embrace it. I hoped this attitude would help bring me closure and stop me becoming confused when questioned, either in court or by the press. The trial carried on and Newton did not mention Jeremy or blame anyone for hiring him, claiming no one else was involved.

Newton was found guilty of possessing a firearm with intent to harm and sentenced to two years in prison. In those moments, as people around me cheered and the press started shouting questions, my mind flashed back to that dark, windy night and to the weight of Rinka's body falling against me. I relived the shock, the confusion and the utter terror as I realised what Newton had been doing. People asked me whether I was happy at the verdict, assuming I would be pleased, but it was more complicated than that. I felt relief that Newton, despite the lesser charge, didn't get away with it completely, but all I kept thinking was how Jeremy had. Newton hadn't tried to kill me of his own accord. He had been hired.

As Newton was packed off to Exeter gaol, Barrie and I went to the Rougemont Hotel in Exeter for a drink. It was thronged with reporters. One of them – I think he was from *The Times* – stared at me with deep disapproval. I guessed he was wondering something along the lines of why he had to cover this awful homosexual story, and I was fed up with it. I was fed up with people's disgust and, as I had occasionally done as a child, I had one of my moments of brazen confidence and whispered to Barrie, 'Watch this.'

I went up the hotel's wide stairway as if I were going to my room, which of course I wasn't because I wasn't staying there. Then I came sashaying back down singing 'I'm the Queer in your copy! You make up things about me . . .' to the tune of the famous Nat King Cole hit 'You're The Cream In My Coffee'. Everybody fell about with laughter except the grumpy *Times* gentleman.

After Newton's trial, there were more headlines in the papers and I knew from Barrie and Roger that the tide was turning from Jeremy. They had been over to California to interview Mr Bessell, and told me he was going to explain everything to the press. This was the first major chink in Jeremy's armour. In May 1976 the *Daily Mail* published an article outlining an interview with Peter Bessell with the headline 'I Told Lies to Protect Thorpe'.

I imagined how Jeremy would have reacted as he read all the papers that morning, presumably in silence over break-fast as he had always done when I was with him at Marsham Court. When he saw the article, he must have been shocked rigid. Mr Bessell's admission was a deep betrayal. Add to this the depth of humiliation at seeing his own handwriting and highly private words published in the previous article, and it is hard to comprehend how he must have felt. It must have hurt Jeremy personally as much as it hurt him publicly, which was significant. The next day, on 10 May 1975, Jeremy resigned as leader of the Liberal Party. He was subsequently demoted to the role of party spokesman for foreign affairs. His ambition to become prime minister was over.

CHAPTER SIXTEEN

The Committal

NEWTON'S PRISON SENTENCE was for two years but he stayed in prison for just over a year. During that time, the stories in the press died down. I felt a mixture of emotions, knowing that justice had still not been delivered. Jeremy had not been accused, charged or tried for his involvement in Newton's attempt to kill me but I assumed that that would never happen. Even after the articles in the press, he was still a very popular man. People felt sorry for Jeremy and perhaps they weren't prepared to question his character because it would mean changing their ideals.

Life carried on. I moved into a rented cottage at Teigncombe Cleave on Dartmoor and I was given another dog, a sweet-natured black lurcher bitch called Chino. Peter Vernon-Evans, the landlord of the Pack o' Cards in Combe Martin, and his wife Pam had been driving on the motorway when they saw a car pull on to the hard shoulder and dump this beautiful creature. Chino was bewildered and terrified, so they picked her up and took her back to the pub with them. When Peter decided to sell up and move on, he gave Chino to me, as he knew I was very fond of her. She really was the sweetest dog, so loving and friendly to everyone. She woke up in the morning with her tail wagging, and when she lay down to sleep at night, that tail was still wagging.

Hilary, now heavily pregnant, lived with Blues and Sonia but we made plans for the future, deciding to move in together once the baby was born, just as friends. I would go round and have coffee with Hilary, noticing as the weeks passed how much bigger her bump was getting. I was so much reminded of Sue and Benjamin. I missed my little son so much, and, haunted by what had happened with my marriage, I was worried that the dramas I'd been through would affect Hilary and end up with her wanting nothing to do with me. I tried hard to stay cheerful and calm when I saw her, checking up on her regularly in the run-up to the birth.

That summer of 1976 was incredibly hot. One of my favourite ways to de-stress was to visit the Turn Teign pool, about a mile over the moor from the cottage. It was a remote, peaceful place where I could throw myself into the cool, peat-brown water and splash about trying to improve my non-existent swimming skills, then lie on the bank and sunbathe. Barry Penrose was horrified when I told him.

'Do you realise you could be found up there and drowned?' he said. 'The people who don't like you could hit you over the head and push you under. It would look like you'd slipped and knocked yourself out on a stone. The perfect crime.'

I looked back over the past attempts on my life, and took his words to heart.

Bryony was born on 18 June 1976. The first time I saw my daughter was after Hilary had returned from hospital to Blues and Sonia's cottage. I adored her as soon as I set eyes on her, determined to keep her in my life. A few months later, an amazing eight-bedroomed wooden house on Dartmoor came up, at a very reasonable rent. Kestorway, as it was called, had been a café for walkers and it had a dresser in the kitchen with all the prices for cups of tea, cakes and sandwiches handwritten on the wood. I kept all this. It added to the lovely atmosphere of the place. As soon as I had the house ready for Hilary and baby Bryony, they moved in, bringing Hilary's beloved Old English Sheepdog, Bumper. Hilary would sit with Bryony in the living room and come for walks with me when it was sunny and we would take it in turns to push the pram. For a while we were happy, watching our daughter grow, delighting together as she sat up for the first time, and took her first steps in the garden. But cracks in our friend-ship began to appear, causing strain on the set-up. Hilary and I were so different. She had no interest in horses and I was not interested in the esoteric sects she was fascinated by or her unusual diets. Hilary was a strict vegetarian but, worried that Bryony was not getting the right food for a small child, I'd sometimes give her chicken. She much preferred this to her mother's offerings but it caused a rift between me and Hilary. We began to avoid each other when we were both in the house.

I became increasingly involved with show horses, producing them for their owners, and also buying horses to school and sell on. There was a lovely bay thoroughbred mare called Blue Slipper who had done some dressage, and her half-brother Skye, by a stallion called True Code. They were best friends, and I took them both because I couldn't bear to separate them. I also had much showing success with a grey cob called Cromwell, who had been awarded Cob of the Year at the Horse of the Year Show while he was with the great showman Robert Oliver. I took him on when he returned to his owners in Chagford and we won just about everything for them.

The newspapers still printed articles, many of which were negative, so the horses provided solace and comfort. Barrie Penrose was constantly in touch, remaining keen to get the truth out, visiting Newton in prison to see if he could get information from him. People continued to gossip and point at me from the ringside at horse-show events, but I was doing what I loved, and I didn't care. My ability as a rider and a horseman was being recognised by the equestrian community, and I was becoming well respected. I began to get invitations to judge at some of the show classes. I was accomplishing what I had always wanted to, ever since I was a child camping out with Listowel, brushing his coat until it gleamed like sleek black silk.

When my mother heard about my lovely home at Kestorway, she said she would like to come and visit. I invited her to stay, and things were amicable on the surface but I felt very apart and distant from her. On the second day of her visit, I took her to lunch at the Three Crowns in Chagford. She charmed the regulars and the Irish landlady, a very good friend of mine. They got on like a house on fire but when she started saying, 'Oh, Norman always was a difficult child!' I found myself flinching and realised it was time for her to leave. Telling her I had to take a horse to a show the next day – a small white lie – I took her to the station. When I carried her suitcase over to the platform and put her on the train the relief was quite wonderful.

In April 1977, just over a year after Newton was convicted, he was released from prison. Later that year, in October, he went to an evening newspaper and offered to come clean about what had really happened. On 19 October, an article that would send shock waves through England was published with the headline 'I Was Hired to Kill Norman Scott,' detailing Newton's claims that he had been hired by a man called John Le Mesurier to kill me. The same man had given Newton five thousand pounds when he had been released from prison.

Newton's story unravelled the truth behind the mysterious and unsettling events leading up to the attempted shooting, and how Jeremy Thorpe and David Holmes, Jeremy's best man who was also former treasurer to the Liberals, had been behind everything. The man who had telephoned the Market Inn offering me a modelling job in London was Newton, who had been told by Holmes to greet me at the Royal Garden Hotel with a bunch of flowers, hiding a chisel he would then use to kill me. When I didn't go, Holmes telephoned me himself pretending to be a reporter, trying to get me to go for an interview in a hotel. Horrified, I learned that had I shown up at some of the other assignations I was invited to attend, I might have been drugged and chucked down a mine in Cornwall or thrown from a helicopter into the Everglades in Florida.

The next day, the press turned up in force, wanting to interview me, many from international newspapers. Behind the scenes police were investigating Newton's claims. Barrie Penrose travelled to America to speak with Peter Bessell, and more speculative articles appeared. The BBC approached me wanting to make a documentary about the cover-ups and the conspiracy to kill me, entitled *The Jeremy Thorpe Scandal*. The investigative journalist Tom Mangold, known for his work in uncovering the Profumo affair, led the project and visited several times to interview me.

Hilary hated the rumours that swirled around and the reporters camping out in their hordes, but I felt differently. For the first time, much of the press seemed to be on my side and I thought that maybe the truth would finally come out. I tried to make the best of the situation by being very open with the reporters. I made them tea and played football with some Japanese reporters, who were camping in tents just outside the door. Unfortunately, the stress exacerbated Hilary's and my differences and we began to argue. We were both very concerned about Bryony being photographed. She would be playing in the garden with reporters leaning over the fence and talking to her.

Maybe I should not have been so receptive to the press but when Dan Ferrari, news editor of the *Daily Mirror*, offered me an exclusive deal, I took it, thinking the money would help secure our life and that my words wouldn't be twisted. For a thousand pounds a day, around six thousand in today's money, I was to go and stay in London, live in a hotel, and give interviews only to the *Daily Mirror*. When I agreed, John Penrose, my friend and Ferrari's most trusted journalist, was put in charge of everything and I was booked into a room at the Howard Hotel in London.

John took me to a journalists' club on a boat on the Thames where we had a few drinks. He left but I stayed with some other journalists and soon realised I was becoming extremely drunk. This was odd, because I could hold my drink, and usually most people would be under the table while I was still going strong. I have often wondered whether my drinks were spiked that night. Whatever happened, the upshot was that I began nodding off and soon fell fast asleep in that floating bar. Sometime later, I woke up in my hotel room, lying on my bed, stark naked, with a photographer taking pictures of me. Though I felt extremely woozy, I had the presence of mind to stagger to my feet and knock him over. I took his camera, pulled out the film and threw it out of the hotel window. John was absolutely horrified. Both he and Anne Robinson (the redoubtable hostess of television show *The Weakest Link*), whom he later married, have remained good and loyal friends, and they still talk of that night and the appalling way that I was treated.

The *Daily Mirror* wanted me to stay on in the hotel and if I had done so, I would probably have made about sixty thousand pounds – well in excess of three hundred thousand by today's reckoning – but I decided to pack it in and go home after just two days. The money didn't matter, and suddenly all I wanted to do was to get back to Bryony, regretting I had left in the first place. When I arrived at Kestorway I couldn't find Hilary and Bryony. I panicked and ran round the house thinking they must be there, but when I realised Hilary's dog Bumper had gone, I knew they had left. I was devastated. I knew how worried Hilary had become but I couldn't understand how she could take our little girl away.

Kestorway was such a lovely place – heaven for a child to grow up in – but the stress of the stories breaking must have been too much to deal with. I didn't even know where Hilary was until mutual friends told me she had gone to Australia. Once they were set up, Hilary got back in touch and Bryony used to call me. I remember her little voice on Christmas Day all the way from Sydney. I missed her so much, and being without her added a huge weight to the allegations and speculation that continued to churn. Reporters carried on turning up wanting interviews, and all the while police investigations were still under way. Newton's claims eventually amounted to something that nobody thought would ever happen.

On 4 August 1978, Jeremy Thorpe was arrested and charged with incitement to murder. He was also charged with conspiracy to murder me, along with three other men: David Holmes, his best man and former deputy treasurer of the Liberal Party; George Deakin, a club owner and gambling-machine trader, who had allegedly been hired to kill me; and John Le Mesurier, a carpet dealer from Wales, who knew Deakin and Holmes. It was he who had allegedly connected Holmes with Deakin after Jeremy had instructed Holmes to kill me. Barrie Penrose rang me with the news of Jeremy's arrest. I couldn't believe it. I was probably as shocked as Jeremy was. When he was released on bail, Jeremy, surrounded by press, stated, 'I am totally innocent of this charge and will vigorously challenge it.'

In the 1970s all serious cases were dealt with by a higher court before a jury, but until 2013 committal procedures were still an option. These preliminary hearings determined the sufficiency of prosecution evidence and whether there was enough to warrant a trial. If the evidence was deemed too weak, the whole trial would be dismissed, which must have been why Sir David Napley, Jeremy's solicitor, requested a committal. The committal procedure meant that the prosecution would have to reveal their case and the defence was allowed to cross-examine the prosecution witnesses without revealing their defence. Because Newton had pulled a gun on me and shot Rinka on Exmoor, the committal hearing took place in the local magistrates' court, which happened to be in the seaside resort of Minehead, a town used to droves of summer tourists. In November 1978, hordes of press turned up instead, disrupting the sleepy town, and television gantries were set up outside the court's entrance.

The Crown prosecution lawyer was Mr Peter Taylor. He was in line for becoming lord chief justice, which he later achieved, and I had great faith in him and expected that, as I was a witness for the prosecution, he would contact me before the committal but he didn't contact me at all. The most peculiar thing was that I went to the court only on the days that I was summoned to give evidence, which meant that for the rest of the time I knew what was happening only from news reports. Even though the committal was about the attempted murder of me, I was, to all intents and purposes, just another member of the general public.

Inside the court for the whole duration of the committal there were many other people, including thirty-seven members of the press, Marion and Ursula Thorpe, nineteen other members of the public, the lawyers, the magistrates, and the four defendants. On the morning of 8 November 1978, the committal began. I was at home, watching the news. Everyone assumed the normal gagging orders would be put in place restricting the press to report only details relating to the charges, but Deakin's lawyer made a request for all restrictions to be lifted on the basis that his client had nothing to hide. With Deakin's request, the judge had no choice but to lift all restrictions for all four defendants. Within a matter of hours, the rest of the country's press descended on Minehead, crowding outside the court.

The evening-newspaper headlines read 'Murder Plot at the House' as I learned what Mr Taylor had said. Mr Taylor opened the proceedings for the prosecution with an eight-hour speech in which he unravelled the whole sorry story: how, over the years, Jeremy Thorpe had become adamant I needed to be silenced and had incited Holmes to kill me as far back as 1968. At Jeremy's request, Holmes gave money to Dr Gleadle to pay me in return for the letters, deliberately and urgently taking them the night before the February 1974 general election in case they fell into the wrong hands and ruined Jeremy's chances. Once Jeremy had secured his seat, he instructed Holmes to hire a hitman. Holmes struck a deal with Le Mesurier, who approached Deakin, offering him money to kill me. Although Deakin initially agreed, he then backed out and recruited Newton to fill his place. One of the biggest sensations of Mr Taylor's speech, which made his statement carry so much weight, was his announcement of Peter Bessell as a prosecution witness.

I had not heard from Bessell for more than four years, since he had gone to America. As he arrived in England, reporters described him as a Humphrey Bogart lookalike and photographs of him were printed in every paper. Although it was Mr Bessell's article in the newspaper that had prompted Jeremy's resignation, it must have been even harder for Jeremy when the two men sat in court. Mr Bessell spoke for eight hours while Jeremy sat in front of the press bench, looking at his former trusted friend and colleague as Peter Bessell's words were heard by him, the entire court and, within hours, the whole country.

'Jeremy confided in me that he was homosexual,' was the first blow, and the secret that Jeremy had tried so hard to keep was out. Mr Bessell then went on to explain how Jeremy showed him the letter I had written in 1965 to Ursula Thorpe and how Jeremy had confirmed the contents of the letter to be true. Together they had successfully tracked down my lost luggage, and Jeremy had taken the bundle of letters he had written to me from the luggage as well as my shirts because they linked me to him through the mark of the Marsham Court dry-cleaning label.

Much of Mr Bessell's account I knew at first hand – how he had come to find me in Ireland, accused me of blackmail and threatened me with extradition, listening to me as I explained the problems I faced because Jeremy had my National Insurance cards. He told of how he had set up the weekly retainer for me in the hope that I wouldn't feel desperate enough to expose the homosexual affair and that nothing would subsequently surface to damage Jeremy Thorpe or the Liberal Party.

I felt sick when I learned that a plot to kill me had been raised by Jeremy as early as 1965, but when I'd got married, Mr Bessell and David Holmes had talked him out of it. When

my marriage ended, Jeremy became worried that the homosexual relationship we'd had would surface in the divorce
proceedings so he, via Bessell, had funded my divorce lawyer
to make sure all traces of the affair were omitted. I had
already realised this was true, but it was still a shock to hear
it confirmed. I thought of Benjamin and wondered what Sue
would be making of all this coverage about me, wincing as
I imagined her talking about it with her mother.

Quickly Mr Bessell's testimony became more sinister as
he explained that when Jeremy discovered I had been
talking about the relationship and that there were copies
of the letters, he became desperate to silence me. '"We have
to get rid of him,"' Mr Bessell said were Jeremy's exact
words, then detailed several conversations between himself,
Holmes and Jeremy about disposing of my body: weighting
it and dropping it into a river, burying it on the moor or
under cement or down a disused tin mine in Cornwall.
Mr Bessell had originally thought it was a joke and had
become horrified when he realised Jeremy was becoming
increasingly fixated on the idea. When Mr Bessell asked if
he was serious, Jeremy justified it by saying, 'It's no worse
than killing a sick dog.'

This quote was splashed across the headlines the following
morning and the *Sun* had replaced their page-three model
with a photograph of me, albeit fully clothed.

Andrew Gino Newton followed Mr Bessell and quickly
became the subject of comic ridicule. He arrived to give
evidence in a car with blacked-out windows, wearing a balaclava. Relaying what he had said in his tell-all account, he
changed the claims he had made when defending himself

at his own trial. This time he admitted the blackmail story was a lie and how he had been hired to kill me.

Newton's manner was reported as jokey. He confessed to making up everything he had said to me, from pretending Marion Thorpe was funding my protection, to there being a man from Canada coming to kill me. But his version of events differed again from what he had said under oath at his own trial. Originally Newton had claimed that he had intended to shoot and deliberately miss, but when he pulled the trigger, the gun had jammed. This time he claimed he had pretended that the gun had jammed. Newton insisted he was only trying to frighten me, not kill me. When asked about shooting Rinka, he said he didn't like dogs and had been told there was no dog. The court had erupted into laughter and the judge had to call for order as he described Rinka's 'monstrous' size. This was horrible to read in the newspapers. The idea that my beloved dog, who had been killed in such horrible circumstances, was being mocked felt lower than anything else.

I was called to give evidence several days into the committal. A policeman, who was very polite and kind, collected me and drove me to Minehead. As we arrived at the court, so did Sir David Napley, Jeremy's counsel, in his gold Bentley. Also in the car were Jeremy and Marion. They parked up and looked around as if I was invisible. I felt such revulsion when I saw Jeremy. He was so much more cadaverous now, his skin pale as parchment and his eyes steely black. I wondered how I could ever have had anything to do with him. Any warmth I had once felt was completely gone. I was terribly nervous, but at the same time I keenly hoped that at last he would get his deserts.

Aware of the 'elders and betters' societal rule, I knew that I must respect the court and the process of justice, yet must tell the truth, which seemed like a contradiction because my truth was not what my elders and betters would want to hear. It was going to damn Jeremy, and the details of what I had to say would probably be abhorrent to everyone who listened.

That day, the proceedings were slow and I returned home without giving evidence. Next morning the officer collected me again. As we drove off, he said, 'I'm afraid I've got to tell you something. Your cats have been killed and laid out in a line by the back door. One of the officers will sort it out for you. I'm so sorry.'

Someone – a local Liberal supporter presumably – had poisoned them, no doubt to try to rattle me before I gave my evidence. They were sweet, affectionate cats that loved to drape themselves over my shoulders as I walked round the garden, and I was devastated. After this traumatic start to the day, I had to give my evidence. Napley, Jeremy's lawyer, began by saying, 'Mr Scott – before we go any further, last night, as you were leaving here, you had a red book in your hands, blatantly advertising *The Pencourt File*.'

He was referring to Barrie Penrose and Roger Courtiour's book, which detailed conspiracies against the government, but I hadn't had it with me.

'No,' I said.

Napley continued, 'Come, come. It was a red book!'

'Yes,' I replied. 'I have the same book here. It's a book of Anglo-Saxon poetry.'

I had wrong-footed him, but Napley continued to try to

279

intimidate me. At one point he said, 'Have you heard this phrase, "Hell knows no fury like a woman scorned"?'

I replied, 'But I'm not a woman.'

I think he was expecting me to burst into tears or wither away in the witness box but I didn't flinch and his expression was one of deep irritation mixed with shock. Once again, I had squashed him, and Napley's hands were now shaking. He changed tack and asked if I had ever seen Mr Thorpe with no clothes on.

I said, 'Well, obviously.'

'Did you notice any distinguishing marks?' Napley asked, leaning in.

'Yes. Jeremy has some nodules under his armpits and on his balls,' I replied.

At that point I saw Jeremy look at Marion and smile. He was taken off to be examined by a doctor, who couldn't find any nodules. Jeremy must have realised this would be the only way I could prove our intimacy and had had them removed. I very clearly remembered those nodules. It was a brilliant move on Jeremy's part to get rid of them.

I was asked a few more questions, then dismissed, the court hearing continuing as I went home. I wasn't hopeful, assuming that Jeremy's removal of the nodules would clear him and the whole thing was dead in the water. I'm sure Jeremy thought that too.

Back at Kestorway I waited with Barrie Penrose to hear the outcome of the committal. The telephone rang and a policeman told me the magistrate had decided that there was a case to answer. 'Mr Thorpe, Mr Holmes, Mr Deakin and Mr Le Mesurier are going to trial,' he said.

For a moment I couldn't believe what I had heard. Barrie and I stood there staring at each other, then cracked open a bottle of Champagne to celebrate, sitting down to watch the television news. I felt a bolt of elation followed by the dawning realisation of what this actually meant. I would have to go to the trial and give evidence at the Old Bailey, the most famous court in the world. When I realised this my first thought was who I would get to look after the horses.

CHAPTER SEVENTEEN

'The Trial of the Century'

COURT NUMBER ONE at the Old Bailey had been the stage for some of the most famous trials in history, from the Yorkshire Ripper to the Kray twins and now Jeremy Thorpe. As a member of Her Majesty's Privy Council, a former leader of the Liberal Party, and, until he had lost his seat in the general election five days before, a Member of Parliament, Jeremy Thorpe was the most senior politician to go on trial in modern history. The newspapers focused on this, hailing it as the 'trial of the century'.

Just like in the committal, I was only in court for the days I testified, which meant that for the first nine days of the trial and again after the four days in which I gave evidence, I knew what was happening only from news reports. However, the editors of the newspapers had 'cleared the front pages' to report on the trial. In many papers the coverage was given verbatim so readers could follow the trial in detail, and at the end of each day the press could be seen rushing from the court to write up their notes to print overnight.

Inside the court, for the whole duration of the trial, were sixty-nine members of the press, Marion and Ursula Thorpe, and the lawyers, judge and defendants. On the first day, the twelve members of the jury were sworn in, and the four defendants took to the stand to plead. Each one pleaded not guilty.

At the trial, Jeremy Thorpe was represented by George Carman, QC. Carman was known for a case in 1973 when he had defended the manager of Battersea Fun Fair, who was accused of manslaughter after a big dipper ride malfunction in 1972, which caused the deaths of five children. Carman's success with this case brought him to the attention of David Napley, Jeremy's solicitor, who instructed him to represent his client at the Old Bailey.

On the first day, the jury was asked to leave while the defence lawyers set about arguing how the case should be terminated due to unreliable evidence, despite the judge's ruling at the committal. This seems absurd now as many people believe that no jury would have been able to remain neutral before the trial because of the amount of press coverage from the committal. Perhaps the whole thing was doomed from the start. Mr Carman argued that no case should rest on the evidence of two liars and a perjurer, all of whom were profiting from the trial. Mr Carman was referring to me, Peter Bessell and Andrew Newton, but the judge dismissed the arguments, the jury returned, and the trial began.

In the run-up to the trial I had expected to hear from the prosecution counsel, Peter Taylor, but, as before the committal, he never contacted me. Mr Taylor opened the proceedings for the prosecution. 'In 1967, Mr Thorpe was elected leader of the Liberal Party but the higher he climbed on the political ladders, the greater was the threat to his ambition from Scott.'

For seven and a half hours Mr Taylor repeated what he had said in the committal with a focus on how Jeremy had incited David Holmes to murder. Needing money to pay the hitman, Jeremy went to Jack Hayward, a millionaire bene-factor who had funded Liberal campaigns in the past. Hayward was one of the other prosecution witnesses who would go on to testify that he had inadvertently and unwit-tingly funded the order of my murder by giving Jeremy thousands of pounds. Jeremy then transferred the money via the Channel Islands to his friend and son's godfather Nadir Dinshaw. Dinshaw was another prosecution witness, who at the time had no idea of the sinister plan linked to the money so passed the cash on to Holmes at Jeremy's request. Flush with a lump sum, Holmes struck a deal with Le Mesurier, who approached Deakin, offering him money to kill me. Although Deakin initially agreed, he then backed out and recruited Newton to fill his place after a mutual friend, David Miller, another prosecution witness, described Newton to Deakin as 'someone who would do anything for a laugh and a giggle'.

Parts of Jeremy's written statement were read out by Mr Taylor, where Jeremy denied he was homosexual as well as stating the Hayward funds had been kept as an 'iron reserve', when in fact the money had been passed on imme-diately to Holmes. The fact that Holmes had received it was confirmed as fact during the trial, but when Mr Taylor referred to this denial of the shocking misappropriation of Liberal Party funds, he showed no sense of outrage. Instead, his tone was very low key. The press consistently described him as overly polite and gentlemanly, making his case without passion or conviction. When he mentioned that fateful first night when Jeremy took me back to his mother's house and raped me, far from giving weight to the brutal incident Mr Taylor glossed over the point, saying, 'Homosexual relations took place.' He was allowed to give a broader character description of Jeremy so he could have detailed other homosexual affairs as further evidence, of which there were many proved through written correspondence, to show Jeremy was lying about his sexual orientation, but he didn't. At the end Mr Taylor reminded the jury that they 'must be sure before you can convict', as if to imply he himself wasn't sure.

Judge Cantley was the opposite of apologetic or gentlemanly, showing no friendly guise. He was described unanimously in the press as hostile and fierce. He referred to the defendants with what seemed like a brazen bias, describing Jeremy Thorpe as a 'national figure with a very distinguished public record', and Deakin, even though he had previously served time in prison, as having an 'unblemished reputation'.

Once Mr Taylor had opened the prosecution, the first witness, Peter Bessell, was called to the stand. He looked forlorn and physically weak in his navy pin-striped suit, his face tanned and wrinkled. Instead of being likened to an old Hollywood star like Bogart, as he had been in the past, he was described in the press as looking like a walnut. He gave evidence for four days. He spoke with a croaky voice and had a heavy cough due to suffering from the beginnings of emphysema, and the press made comments about whether the trial would kill him. Mr Carman, Jeremy's lawyer, had tried hard to have Mr Bessell's evidence excluded, but unfortunately for Carman, the judge allowed it and Mr Bessell was granted immunity so that he was free to speak the truth without legal repercussions if any of his evidence incriminated his business dealings. Mr Carman managed to turn this immunity into an advantage for the defence because, unlike Mr Taylor, he spoke with authority and conviction. He got Mr Bessell to confirm that he had fled to America from his creditors and accused him of embellishing, exaggerating and lying at every opportunity he got, managing to turn everything Mr Bessell said against him.

Mr Carman's manner was described as initially 'disarmingly gentle'. He got Mr Bessell to agree that Jeremy was a kind and loyal person who had funded and advised Mr Bessell in private business matters as well as, through Marion, providing a home for Mr Bessell's family when he fled to America. He painted a picture of Mr Bessell as a loyal character too, suggesting this loyalty was the reason why Mr Bessell had wanted to protect both the Liberal Party and Jeremy, his friend. Once Mr Bessell had agreed that he was also a loyal man, Mr Carman shot him down.

'Didn't you think Mr Thorpe must need a psychiatrist?' Mr Carman asked.

'Yes, sir,' Mr Bessell replied.

'What attempts did you make to acquaint the Liberal Party, Mrs Thorpe, the police and doctors with the fact that the leader of the Liberal Party was insane?' Mr Carman asked.

'None, sir,' Mr Bessell replied.

'Did you not feel it was your duty to tell the Party that its leader was a man intent on murder?' Mr Carman said, before carrying on to ask: 'Does that make you amoral?'

'Yes,' Mr Bessell said, clearly cornered.

With this Mr Carman had written off Mr Bessell as 'amoral, a hypocrite and a liar'.

The other defence lawyers went on to sneer at Mr Bessell, focusing on the idea that he was profiting from the court case because he had signed a book deal that would pay twice as much if there was a conviction. When Mr Carman asked the judge whether they should adjourn, the judge said there was enough time for 'one more whopper' and was reported in the press to have cheerfully mocked Mr Bessell throughout his testimony. At the end of Mr Bessell's questioning, Mr Taylor didn't help at all. He simply warned the jury to 'take care when considering evidence of an accomplice', and the jury must have been left with the overriding impression that Mr Bessell was a liar.

The trial continued for eight days and then it was my turn to testify. I stayed with Stella and Jack in London. The night before when I was watching the news with them Stella suddenly said, 'You do realise this is really big, Norman? Why are you being so calm?'

I had no idea why I appeared so calm. I think it was because it felt too surreal, like it wasn't happening. But when Stella said this, the enormity of what I was about to face really hit me. As I realised what a rough ride I was in for, a huge rush of panic hit me. To counter it, I jumped up and said, 'Let's go out and have some fun!'

Jack knew a club where a lot of young people liked to go, so we headed over there, danced like mad and got very drunk.

Probably not the best thing to do just before I was due in court, but it helped me forget. The clubbers were all staring, having recognised me from the news coverage. One young student came up and gave me a badge with a photograph of Jeremy on it and across his face the words 'It's a Bum Rap!' I was so touched by the support of a stranger, it really lifted my spirits. Very little of this support was ever commented on in the newspapers but it was there.

The next morning, as I arrived at the Old Bailey, the badge pinned inside my jacket, I was greeted by the Brixton Gays, who were out in full force. The crowd waved their placards and shouted, 'Hooray!' as I walked past them. I will never forget that, deeply appreciating their support. Everybody had heard my story, through the press, in warped versions of the truth. It seemed I was something of an enigma, being described as both 'weak' and 'soft' but also 'poisonous' and 'paranoid'. I was a 'fantasist' in one paper, a 'blackmailer' in another, 'deeply wronged' in some. The crowd of supporters outside the court helped remind me that my account had been clear enough in my own National Insurance tribunal and in the Minehead committal. This had led to the trial at the Old Bailey. Now I just had to speak the truth one final time.

A policeman ushered me into the courtroom and as I walked to the dock, my skin prickled with an acute awareness of every single pair of eyes burning into me. The room was much smaller than I had expected, its wooden panelling austere. There was an atmosphere of formal hostility and, glancing down into the sea of faces, I just froze. Everything became a blur. Someone, I think it was the policeman who had brought me in, noticed I was shaking and said quietly, 'If you look at somebody in the court and talk to them as if you're telling them the story, that's the best way of not feeling nervous.'

I took his advice, but as I scanned the faces in the well of the courtroom I found myself looking straight at my mother. She was sitting there like a little black bird in her old astrakhan coat, staring up at me. No smile, just a slight sarcastic lift of her lips. I don't believe she had come to support me. She was just there for the spectacle of it. I shivered at the thought of speaking about my sexual relationship with Jeremy in front of her. She would have read the sordid details in the papers, but I knew she would revel in my discomfort as I spoke about everything in public.

All the fear and shame of the past flooded through me and I felt as if I was the one standing trial. I could not help being aware, too, of Jeremy, sitting impassively in the raised dock with the other defendants. His face was even more parchment-pale and cadaverous than the last time I had seen him. He showed no emotion and did not look at me, though he occasionally glanced around the courtroom and once or twice scratched his head.

At first, I was allowed to give my evidence without any interruptions from questions. I found it very difficult to speak, and even though I was quite close to him in the witness box, the judge kept telling me to 'Speak up!' I tried but the more I pushed myself to be louder, the more terrified I became that I would stammer. Somehow I didn't. I bit the inside of my lip and kept going.

'When Jeremy turned me over and penetrated me it felt like he was trying to cut me in half,' I said, turning cold as I had to relive the horrific moment. The courtroom rocked with laughter. I felt deeply humiliated. Now I feel astounded and appalled that my description of being raped was openly mocked in court and then dismissed.

When I went on to explain about visiting Jeremy to try to get my National Insurance cards and how he pressurised me into having sex with him, the judge interrupted, saying he did not want to hear about these 'relations' again. I stood up for myself and rather lost it. 'Jeremy's use of me for sex is absolutely key. I don't want to talk about the relationship ever again, but I'm trying to make it clear,' I said. Looking back, it seems awful I had to justify myself like this.

I was relieved when the recess for lunch was announced, though no one told me where to go or what to do. I walked out of the main court into the lobby, and my mother was there, right in front of me. She looked as if she were about to say something, and I was just telling her, 'I don't think I should . . .' when Marion Thorpe shouted down from the gallery above, 'Stop that woman talking to that man! He's about to give evidence.'

They were all up there, about to go and eat a luxurious lunch. I didn't get to speak to my mother. I just walked out and went to a pub on my own.

That afternoon the cross-examination began. From the defence's point of view, my evidence was only really relevant to Jeremy's separate charge of incitement. This was because the main line of the defence as a whole was to claim that the defendants had conspired against me, but not to murder, only to frighten. So Deakin, Newton and Le Mesurier's defence questioned me briefly as I knew nothing of their clients' activities behind the scenes. My evidence was all about Jeremy, and the likelihood of his instigation of the conspiracy. When it was Mr Carman's turn, he needed to completely discredit my character or the motive for Jeremy wanting to kill me would ring true.

Mr Carman was a formidable barrister. Known for creating melodrama in court, when he died years later, Ian Hislop, editor of *Private Eye*, said that 'His name became a threat in itself,' explaining that he was the first barrister to understand that cases were about playing to the jury. Mr Carman went on to act for Mohamed al-Fayed, Elton John, Richard Branson, Imran Khan, Nicole Kidman and several tabloid newspapers.

When Mr Carman stood up to question me, the atmosphere in the court became heightened. I started shaking but, to begin with, Mr Carman adopted the same gentle approach he had used on Mr Bessell except his manner was even softer, unnervingly tender. His very first question was, 'Are you undergoing any medical treatment?' As though he was raising a genuine concern for my health.

'No,' I said. But despite this, Mr Carman fixated on my mental instability and my stint at Ashurst Clinic. All the time he spoke to me as though I were physically and mentally weak, repeating the same questions about whether I was delusional at the time. It became clear that he was out to prove me unreliable, unstable and a liar. He made much of the fact that while I was at the Ashurst Clinic I had shown people the love letters Jeremy had written to Van der Vater, addressing him with his real name 'Norman', and how I had pretended they were meant for me. I tried to explain that I had been on many drugs, but Mr Carman accused me of being unclear and the judge took the same approach in a scolding tone. 'You are not giving a proper answer. Listen and behave yourself,' the judge barked, treating me like a badly behaved child speaking out of line.

After talking at length about my delusional state of mind at the Ashurst Clinic, Mr Carman moved on to discussing little lies he accused me of telling, focusing on the fact that I had changed my name to Scott.

'I changed it because the modelling agency I worked for felt [Josiffe] sounded too foreign and was putting people off from booking me. I picked a name that sounded very English and was both easy to remember and pronounce and the bookings came flying in,' I explained.

'Scott is the family name of the Earl of Eldon, is it not? And you, at times, alluded to being part of that family?' Mr Carman said, his eyes smaller now, his stare steely.

'So what if I did? Why does it matter?' I said. I explained that there had been times when people had assumed I was part of that family and I hadn't always corrected them. People were obsessed with class and sometimes I didn't want to be judged for being of lower class. I didn't always admit I had gone to a secondary modern in Bexleyheath and said I went to public school instead. It was embarrassing but I didn't understand how it was a crime.

But the problem was that Mr Carman was able to make the point that if I lied about my name, or at least omitted the truth, it made me dishonest, which meant he could dismiss everything I said. Mr Carman continued to broadcast me as a liar, referring to the statement I had made to the police in 1962 when I'd been arrested for saying I wanted to kill Jeremy.

'Before your anal exam that night, you initially said there was no anal penetration the night you stayed with Mrs Thorpe and yet now you say there was,' Mr Carman said, his tone nasty.

I think he thought I would crumble but I had a perfectly reasonable explanation. 'Yes. Because in 1962 homosexuality was illegal and I didn't want to incriminate either of us,' I replied, feeling a rush of defiance. In that split second, I noticed Jeremy was fidgeting with the rings on his left hand. He looked up and, for the first time, I saw a flash of something in his eyes. What was he thinking? A memory came swiftly to my mind, of one night when I was with him and we were walking along the Mall. Selwyn Lloyd, chancellor of the exchequer at that time, had a house with a garden on one of the terraces above where we walked. Jeremy suddenly said, 'Let's go in here!' He shoved me over to some trees next to the garden and thrust his hand inside my trousers. 'This is my great friend Selly Lloyd's house,' he said, as he fondled me. The reckless, daredevil element of danger was what Jeremy craved. It added to the thrill of his sexual experiences. I didn't mention this incident but I knew I had to make this side of Jeremy's character clear so I shouted at Mr Carman, 'Jeremy Thorpe lives on a knife edge of danger.'

A gasp went through the court. Mr Carman seemed visibly shocked by my outburst but he tried to get it to backfire.

'What about you?' he asked, obviously hoping I would

succumb to the admission that I also liked to live on the edge. That wasn't true and never had been.

'I don't at all. I have certainly lived in danger of my life for many years because of your client, though,' I said, pointing at Jeremy.

Now Mr Carman attempted to corner me with this statement, too, by trying to get me to admit a hatred for Jeremy. I paused for a moment and then, with clarity and honesty, I said, 'I feel nothing, not vindictiveness or anything at all. Thorpe destroyed me but I didn't want to be destroyed and I do not wish to destroy him.'

This statement was the truth of it all. A monumental piece of information from my point of view, and saying it left me exhausted and emotional. But it didn't help Mr Carman's case, so he moved quickly on. As he spoke, the weight of what I'd just summed up – so many memories of years and years of twisted anguish flooding through me – made me feel bruised and stunned. When Mr Carman started questioning me about the sexual relations at Mrs Thorpe's house and my accusation that I had not consented to the sex, I felt tears mounting. 'There was nothing I could do because I was in their house. I was already crying and felt very woozy. I did not expect Jeremy to come into my room let alone turn me over and have sex with me. I did not realise what was happening until it was too late.'

I started to cry but Mr Carman snapped, 'Do not get excited.'

I shouted my reply, exasperated. 'I'm not excited. This is absurd. Do you think I enjoy describing these terrible things?'

I felt an enormous dread wash over me as I remembered my mother was there, listening to every word. That the whole country was aware of this wretched night at Stonewalls. Not only would most people be disgusted by it, but many thousands would side against me. Mr Carman looked smug and the judge, as though taking the opportunity to rub salt further into a wound, said drily, 'If only you spoke like this when you began, we would have heard you.'

He wasn't being nice. He was deliberately mocking me as though he was officially on Mr Carman's side. Mr Carman continued, bringing up the various letters, setting up the accusation of blackmail.

'No. It was never blackmail. I was afraid that, without the letters, I would have no proof that I was telling the truth about my homosexual relationship with Jeremy. Without proof I feared I would not be believed by doctors when I asked for medical help, diagnosed as mad and be either permanently or indefinitely committed to a mental asylum. I didn't want the letters for blackmail. I needed them to prove I wasn't insane.'

'Were you not being vindictive?' Mr Carman said, which was exasperating, but he was trying to set me up again, and went on to refer to me and Gwen going to Emlyn Hooson. 'You were trying to destroy Mr Thorpe,' Mr Carman stated.

'No, I was not. I was trying to sort out my National Insurance. National Insurance is my lifeblood. It has been throughout all this sordid time.' I paused, trying to collect my thoughts. 'I did not ever believe that this trial would happen. I thought the establishment would cover it up,' I added.

'You have an obsession,' Mr Carman said.

'Of course. So would you if people were trying to kill you,' I responded.

Mr Carman finished by making much of the fact that in 1961 Jeremy Thorpe was the most famous and distinguished person I had met, and that I was flattered by his attention and upset when he didn't want to have a sexual relationship with me.

By the end of the four days, I felt numb. Many times, I was scoffed at by the judge, especially when I broke down as I described what had happened to Rinka and how I had tried to resuscitate her, and his scorn at my description of what Jeremy had done to me sexually made me feel degraded. I thought of the twelve jurors who would undoubtedly be trying to work out whether it was all true, and I thought of Jeremy who knew, just as well as I did, that it was. This loop of thoughts was to go round and round my head throughout the twenty days that the trial continued, but for me, that was it. Finished.

Before I left the Old Bailey I went to the loo. I was just washing my hands when Newton came rushing in, about to give his evidence. We looked at each other and I felt the most awful repulsion and horror. All the trauma of that night on Exmoor came right back to me. We didn't speak, and when he left a few moments later, I went into one of the lavatory stalls and broke down.

The following day John Penrose drove me back to Devon. I was enormously grateful for his company and support, and we continued to follow the trial like everyone else – through the papers and the broadcast news.

Newton spoke in a strange slang and the press likened

him to a fictional character from gangster films like *Get Carter*. He told the court how, after talking to Miller (another prosecution witness) who had informed him of a possible hitman job, he had approached Deakin at the Showman's Dinner in Blackpool. 'I understand you want someone bumped off. I'm your man,' Newton had said, in his estuarine twang.

When the prosecution lawyer Mr Taylor asked him what he meant by this, Newton said, 'To take out a contract on a person unknown. To eliminate somebody.'

'Did the other guests at the dinner overhear?' Mr Taylor asked.

'No. If you proposition someone to murder you don't announce it on the Tannoy,' Newton said, going on to explain that he had then got very drunk and couldn't remember anything more but that he had met up with Deakin again. 'Deakin gave me photographs of the man and told me to go to Dunstable where the man lived. He said the fee was fifteen thousand pounds.'

I had never lived in Dunstable, but Newton went looking for me there, explaining that Deakin had got it mixed up with Barnstaple, so next day the papers ran reports mocking the pair's idiocy.

When Mr Taylor raised the subject of whether Newton had asked any questions about the job, he replied, 'Only the sort of questions you would expect a hitman to ask.'

After he had repeated his account of the events, the questions moved on to after Newton's arrest and he spoke of information that was entirely new to me. Of how David Holmes had rung Newton several times, reassuring him there were plenty of people to help with his defence. Fresh out of prison, Holmes took Newton for a drive. Accompanied by Le Mesurier, they drove Newton to a random cement factory in Wales where they told him there were people who were very keen that he stayed quiet. They gave him a wad of banknotes, totalling five thousand pounds, and Newton, taking it as a sinister threat and fearing they were at the cement factory to kill him, agreed to stay quiet and took the money. It sounded like a Mafia plot but, by then, nothing came as a surprise.

Mr Taylor played tapes of recorded telephone calls, where Newton was heard to say to Le Mesurier, 'A Thomas Becket was done – Thorpe ranting about getting rid of this man.'

'Yes,' Le Mesurier had replied.

'And someone obliged,' Newton said.

'Yes,' Le Mesurier confirmed.

In another recorded telephone conversation Newton talked to Holmes about almost being killed by a lorry and a car on two separate occasions, concluding they were deliberate attempts to silence him too, but Holmes said that it was nothing to do with him. When Newton mentioned Le Mesurier's name, Holmes snapped, 'Stop saying names because the whole thing terrifies me. I know who you're talking about.'

When Newton brought up the charge of murder, Holmes replied, 'Fine.' During this conversation Holmes did not dispute what Newton had just said. He did not correct Newton and say there was no plan to murder, only frighten. Unfortunately, Mr Taylor seemed to think it unnecessary to highlight the importance of this evidence for the jury.

Many smaller, less relevant points from Newton's testimony were relayed in the press for pure entertainment value. When Mr Williams, Deakin's lawyer, tried to get Newton to agree he was a buffoon, focusing on the fact Newton had turned up to the Minehead committal wearing a balaclava, Newton replied, 'One is entitled to wear what one likes. You wear that on your head,' referring to the barrister's white horsehair wig. And when Mr Matthew, Holmes's lawyer, asked: 'You find it difficult to remember fact from fiction?' Newton responded: 'I think you're falling into the realms of sorcery. I was lying to save my own skin in the same way as the defendants are,' while at the same time denying he had been hired to kill me, only frighten. The papers made the most of these farcical moments, describing Newton as a joker and drawing attention to his more absurd utterances, like the moment when he flew into a rant, telling Mr Matthew to stop prostituting himself.

Among these low blows and the sporadic bouts of laughter, Mr Taylor returned to re-examine Newton, but he continued to dodge questions and contradict himself. Although he had been granted immunity, meaning he could admit to being hired to kill me without suffering the consequences of conviction for attempted murder, he did not seem eager to tell the truth. Perhaps he was worried about a loophole. Maybe he had made a deal with the defence, as he had at his own trial. Maybe his life had been threatened, but the main problem with Newton was that he had lied so much that I'm not sure how anyone could have believed him. At one point he confessed that he had told so many lies about the events it was hard for him to remember what he had said. Despite this, Mr Taylor's attempts to convince the jury that the defendants were guilty were weak.

After Newton stepped down, many more witnesses took to the stand but their accounts were overshadowed in the press in favour of other elements of the trial. Detective Superintendent Challes spoke, explaining how Holmes had answered, 'No comment,' to a list of questions he had asked, but when Mr Taylor started to read the questions, the judge intervened, telling the court it was a charade and that answering 'No comment' did not mean guilty. Jack Hayward testified, saying he was horrified when he realised Jeremy had pressurised him for Liberal funds only to use the money to pay Newton to kill me. Jeremy's good friend Nadir Dinshaw took to the stand to say he had innocently passed Hayward's money to Holmes but then had become suspicious when Jeremy had asked him to pretend it was his own. When Dinshaw refused, Jeremy had threatened him, using his Pakistani nationality against him, and saying, 'It will be curtains for me and you will be asked to move on.'

A firearms expert from the Home Office forensic-science laboratory, who had tested the pistol Newton had used, confirmed the gun was prone to jamming. This was backed up by David Miller, who testified that on the night of Newton killing Rinka, Newton had fled to his house in Cardiff and passed the gun, which was jammed, to Miller. Miller had unjammed it. He also said he had dropped Newton off at the airport and had overheard Newton on the telephone to Deakin saying, 'Everything has gone wrong and I ended up shooting the dog.'

Once every witness had stood down, I hoped that there

was enough evidence to convict. I kept thinking that surely the firearms expert confirming the gun was prone to jamming, combined with Deakin saying it had, as well as Newton admitting he was a liar, made it clear that he had intended to kill me, and that, therefore, they were all lying. I was outraged that the judge was still declaring Jeremy a national treasure when he had racially threatened his friend. Every snippet of the trial went round and round my head.

On 7 June, after three weeks of prosecution evidence, it was the turn of the defence, which was really what the entire country had been waiting for. They had heard the prosecution case at the committal but this was the first time any of the defendants would give evidence. But on the day the defendants were expected to give evidence, the trial took an unexpected turn that shocked the nation. I watched the news at home and could not believe what I heard. With the exception of Deakin's lawyer, one by one the defence lawyers said, 'My lord, I call no evidence.' I sat there open-mouthed, flabbergasted. I simply couldn't understand the idea of them not defending themselves. Their silence in itself seemed like an admission of guilt. Slowly, I began to see how clever this was.

Only Deakin spoke. Mr Taylor, unlike the defence lawyers, was described as being very respectful when cross-examining. He openly admitted the case against Deakin was not strong, compared to those of the other defendants, and was mocked in the press for very politely accusing Deakin of being a crook. Then the defence lawyers took over, embracing Newton's account. They did not try to dispel the idea of the defendants conspiring, but instead claimed they were conspiring only to frighten, not kill me. Mr Carman read Jeremy's written statement, all of which was reported in the press. Jeremy branded me 'hysterical' and my allegations as 'pure moonshine'. He blamed me for his 'being unable to give proper focus on the affairs of the country'. However, he had changed his stance on how well we knew each other. In an earlier statement he had made to the press, he had said he hardly knew me at all. In his defence statement, presumably prompted by the 'Bunnies' letter being published, he said that we had had a 'close and affectionate friendship but no sexual relations'.

That Jeremy had lied about how well he knew me was not picked up, even though the deliberate omission was vital to the case, and the very minor lies I had told about going to a public school were exaggerated to label me an 'incorrigible liar'.

Because the three other defendants didn't take the stand, the trial was much shorter than the months it had been predicted to last and by 11 June the summing up began. Mr Matthew, for Holmes, ended that the verdict of guilt would be 'unsafe' because of the evidence being so unreliable. Mr Williams, for Deakin, said all evidence was uncorroborated. Mr Cowley, for Le Mesurier, argued that the whole alleged conspiracy to frighten me ended the night of Rinka's shooting. Finally, Mr Carman stated that the second charge on Jeremy Thorpe, of incitement, should be dismissed because Mr Bessell's evidence was unreliable.

But the most damaging closing statement, from the prosecution's point of view, came from the prosecution lawyer Mr Taylor. I could not believe his statement, which was repeated over and over again on the broadcast news and printed in all the papers. 'The tragedy of this case is that Mr Thorpe has been surrounded and his career blighted by the Scott affair. His story is a tragedy of Greek proportions.' He went on to explain how Jeremy's career had been damaged by one defect and summed up by saying, 'It would be inhuman if one did not feel sympathy for the defendants.'

Mr Taylor's words, along with his manner throughout the trial, made me feel that he thought Jeremy was the victim, not me. The evidence had shown Jeremy to be a liar, a manipulator, someone who threatened his most loyal friends and had managed to extract large sums of money under false pretences. It was as though Mr Taylor had forgotten that I was the one he should have been defending. I was the one who had had my teeth kicked out and my dog shot dead. Those things were facts even if no other evidence was believed.

The worst, however, was the judge, whose attitude was described by the press as 'cheerfully scathing'. He opened his summing up by reminding the jury that just because three of the four defendants had not given evidence it didn't mean their 'good character should be ignored'.

Again, his words were printed across the papers and later in many different written accounts, his lacerating character defamation of me there for all to see. 'You will remember Norman Scott well – a hysterical, warped personality. He is a fraud. He is a sponger. He is a whiner. He is a parasite. But, of course, he could be telling the truth. It is a question of belief. You have seen Scott for yourselves. He is a spineless neurotic character, addicted to hysteria.'

He went on to to dismiss Newton as a 'chump', who was 'capable of inventing a false story', and stated Mr Bessell was a 'liar', a 'humbug' and a 'scoundrel' before finally saying, 'If you are completely sure, you will convict, but if there is any reasonable doubt, you will acquit. I expect a unanimous verdict.'

The jury was out for fifty-two hours, staying in a secret location to deliberate. The four defendants were kept in Brixton prison, spending the two nights in cells with other prisoners. Except Jeremy. Complaining of a stomach upset, he spent both nights in the prison hospital, despite having apparently eaten smoked salmon delivered from outside the prison.

Down in Devon, I tried to busy myself, going for long rides and then to the pub, drinking with friends, trying to block it all out. Those hours, just like much of the trial, went by in a blur. I felt oddly detached. Perhaps I was preparing for what felt like an inevitable outcome. On 22 June, in the mid-afternoon, thirty-one days after the trial had begun, the verdict was delivered. I was with friends at the Bullers Arms in Chagford watching the news, waiting. The bulletin came just after half past two. The foreman for the jury delivered the unanimous verdict: not guilty, for Jeremy Thorpe and all the other defendants. All four had been acquitted.

I felt a terrible anger, followed by complete resignation. I sat in the pub as everyone else burst into highly charged discussions, but I stayed silent, totally numb. What could I do? After a moment, I just turned to my friends and said, 'Let's get another drink.'

A lot of friends came into the pub that evening to

commiserate. I think people in Chagford had realised by now that I was telling the truth. The rest of north Devon and the country seemed to be elated. Jeremy walked out of the Old Bailey with his wife and his mother to rapturous applause and cheers, grinning and flinging up both his arms in his signature gesture.

Tributes to Jeremy were printed in many newspapers, celebrating his innocence, the *Daily Star* calling him 'a statesman of courage and truth'. A punk rock band recorded a song entitled 'Jeremy Is Innocent' with a background riff of a dog barking and gunfire. Only *Private Eye* seemed to remain unconvinced, publishing a 'Special Acquittal Souvenir Issue' entitled 'Buggers can't be losers'. Auberon Waugh, who was then *Private Eye*'s editor and had been there throughout the trial, wrote up his notes in full, turning them into the book *The Last Word*, and several more books were written, although most were full of inaccuracies.

The following Sunday after the trial, in a little church in north Devon, a thanksgiving service was held for Jeremy Thorpe by the vicar, who was also the village chairman of the Liberals. Jeremy, Marion and Jeremy's son Rupert attended. During the service the vicar led prayers for Jeremy and declared him 'blessed' and a passage from the Bible was read out: 'Let us now praise famous men.'

CHAPTER EIGHTEEN

Home

IT WAS TIME to put the past behind me. I had failed to bring Jeremy to justice. There would be no chance for appeal because he had been acquitted but I had said my piece, spoken truth to power. The BBC put a stop to Tom Mangold's documentary *The Jeremy Thorpe Scandal*. It would have revealed in detail all the lies and cover-ups, but the BBC ordered all the copies to be destroyed.

I had to let it all go. There was an odd sense of elation in knowing it was over, and I was free to get on with my life. At the end of 1979 I moved from Kestorway because it was put up for sale. I was sad to go, but I found a flat in a farmhouse near Gidleigh on Dartmoor and my life returned to some sort of normality. I knew that people would always talk, and Jeremy would always have his supporters and I just had to move on.

Gradually I lowered the dose of my medication. I had managed to get through the trial without having a nervous breakdown and I felt stronger than I had done for years. Although I had been vilified in the press and ostracised by people in the community, my main issue had always been that I had been ignored and dismissed. To be tricked by a doctor and told I was a liar by the police had played with my sanity, making me doubt myself, and had fuelled a feeling of low self-worth and utter entrapment. For years, the police did not offer me protection and it took me a long time to recover emotionally from the officer in Barnstaple smacking my head against the wall when I explained what was happening to me.

Living on edge, knowing that people were trying to intimidate, silence and kill me was a burden of immeasurable proportion and only pills had offered any sort of solution. They had allowed me to escape into a mind that was foggy so I didn't jump out of my skin at my own shadow, or become too fixated on what my wretched reality was. But the trial put an end to that part of my life. Although the verdict meant that I had been officially dismissed, I felt liberated by being able to say my piece. I had not been silenced and, for me, that felt like progress. Surrounded by sneering lawyers, gossip-hungry press and in front of Jeremy, his family and my own mother, I had stood up for myself. I couldn't do any more. While the outcome didn't feel like justice, the trial gave me closure, and relief from knowing all the plans to silence me would stop because I had told the secrets. I wasn't trapped any more. I was free.

The village gossip died down but the newspapers continued to harass me, especially when the anniversaries of certain events like the attempted shooting and the Old Bailey trial came up. I hung a 'Private' notice on the gate, but the reporters would follow me when I was out riding, and Chino was hopeless at protecting my privacy. However intrusive the reporters were, she ran up to greet them, tail wagging with joy, and I'm sure she would quite happily have jumped into a car and gone home with any of them. Once she got into a car with some picnickers and they drove her all the way to Princetown, nine miles away, then dumped her. Luckily some people recognised her and I got her back.

I put my energy into my horses, Chino coming with me for every ride. My particular favourite was my bright bay ex-dressage mare, Blue Slipper. We won many prizes in the show ring, where the judges loved riding her so much that they didn't want to get off. By now I had become a well-respected judge throughout the West Country and beyond, known for my impartiality as I always considered the horses on their merits, not on the reputations of their owners. When I tried them out in ridden classes, to assess how they felt under saddle, the owners often commented that their horses went much better for me, maybe because of my careful and deliberately light hands and empathic approach.

In my private life, things took longer to heal. I had been so vilified in the press that deep down I still worried people would see me as evil. I found it hard to talk about the past and wanted to keep myself on an even keel so I had brief liaisons and fun, but it was many years before I found someone I could trust.

Conway remained in my life, albeit only through letters and telephone calls because he spent so much of his time in America, working at the New York Opera Centre. In 1982, he died in New York. Our mutual friend Shura Cohen, who was a wardrobe mistress for films (she applied the gold paint to actress Shirley Eaton in the Bond film *Goldfinger*), told me the sad news. She rang explaining that she had gone to visit Conway at his apartment in the Dakota building, which by then was famous because John Lennon had been murdered outside it in 1980. The day of Shura's visit the concierge told her he hadn't seen Conway so Shura returned a week later but Conway still had not made an appearance. Concerned, the concierge took Shura up to his apartment where they found Conway on the sofa, stone dead, with a TV dinner on his lap. He had had a heart attack around the time of Shura's previous visit. I was devastated. That image of him, sitting motionless in front of the flickering television, with no one to miss him, made me deeply sad.

My mother also died in the mid-1980s. I hadn't seen her since the Old Bailey trial, and I can't say that I felt any great grief at the loss. She was a wonderful mother in that she managed to bring up her six children in difficult circumstances, but I didn't get the care and the love that I needed from her. She left me with a legacy of anxiety and low self-esteem that has plagued me for much of my life. When my oldest brother Edward wrote to ask if I would contribute to her memorial headstone, I declined. I am still in touch with my brother Ralph, who is in his mid-eighties now and has Parkinson's. I am very fond of him, though we don't always see eye to eye, especially about my mother. All my other siblings have passed away now, except for my younger brother, John Josiffe, and I have not spoken to him for probably fifty years.

For five years I lived in the flat near Gidleigh, and as I reached my mid-forties, I had no idea that I was about to be uprooted once more, and in a momentous and life-changing way. In 1985 good friends bought an ancient, run-down

Devon farmhouse on the edge of Dartmoor. They knew the difficulties I had endured and offered it to me to live in for the rest of my life. The gratitude I have for their belief in me and their trust that I would take good care of the beautiful, unique building is beyond words.

The house is a Grade I listed traditional Devon longhouse, built from medieval granite blocks with seventeenth-century mullioned windows, surrounded by farm buildings. When I first moved in, the sitting-room walls were Germolene pink, and the floors were painted silver. The Claygate fireplace was silver too, and across the ceiling a fluorescent tube light was thrumming away with that horrid noise they make when they don't work properly. Upstairs the ceilings were coming down, and in one of the bedrooms a beam had fallen and the thatch was all over the floor.

The first time I saw the house I fell in love with it, despite its dilapidation. I had never moved into a house knowing I could settle down. Everything had always been rented and uncertain but the building's age made it feel innately secure, firmly rooted in time. There is still a wooden salt cupboard where families of the farm would have kept their Bible and their salt, which was worth more than money in past times.

I did much of the restoration work myself. Having just broken my leg after a riding accident when I first arrived, I took up the concrete surface that had been laid over the cobbled yard lying down. It was hard work but every day was a revelation as the beauty of the ancient, irregular stones was brought to light. Gradually the house transformed. I took out the Claygate fireplace and the four other fireplaces that lay beneath it to reveal the granite hearth that I now use. I reinstalled an eleventh-century lintel, which bears a fertility symbol: it had been taken out of the farmhouse many years before and dumped on the moor.

Structural work was done by a master craftsman, John, who spent so much time at the farm we became friends. Then I began decorating. Searching junk rooms and jumble sales, I picked up some wonderful antiques very cheaply. There's a dresser laden with eighteenth- and nineteenth-century blue-and-white china. The settle by the fireplace was made generations ago out of a log box and a coat cupboard, and the dining-room mantelpiece is an old form, rather like a school bench turned upside down. On the shelf by the dining table, I collected a miniature farmyard of toy ducks, sheep, cows and pigs moulded from lead. And in every room, the old clocks I love so much tick sweetly through the days. I am always on the lookout for copper pans, hot-water bottles and jelly moulds to add to the collection that sits on the windowsill. There is art here too. A vibrant horse's head sculpted by local artist Nina Cairns. My own head, by sculptor Hywel Pratley. And photographs. Test shots from my modelling days, and portraits of my prize-winning horses.

Horses and ponies graze in the farm's paddocks and look out for me over the stable doors. Some are prize-winners who now enjoy a happy retirement; others are my riding horses, many of them gifts from generous friends. One is the majestic eighteen-hand Cat Balou. Known as Loui, he is a beautiful bay, one of the sweetest-natured horses I have ever known. I ride Loui every day, either down at the school in Chagford for some training or up on Dartmoor for a bracing gallop. I am so lucky to have this glorious landscape to ride in. Sometimes I wake up to find the farmyard hidden within dense fog and the moor transforms, becoming ethereal. One morning recently, I rode up on to the high moor. There was no sound, only the soft thud of hoofbeats. As we dropped down into a valley hundreds of golden plovers were feeding, gently calling their mournful one-note cry. I reined in to watch this magical sight, but the birds had spotted us. They rose into the pale blue sky, turning as one into the morning sun, and I found myself looking at what seemed to be a shield of burnished gold. Moments like these instantly eclipse the dramas of my past, simultaneously granting me perspective and giving me pleasure.

As well as horses, there are several cats, poultry, ducks and tortoises. Ever since that awful day when I caught my mother with Phil and dropped my tortoise, I have had a great love of these creatures, and I always keep them at the farm. My girls Rigby and Peller have been with me for many years now. Before Rigby and Peller, there was Granny, who lived into her late seventies, and Torty, who had a drilled hole in his shell so he could be tethered on someone's lawn. Torty escaped one day and four years later I got a call from a pub miles away. 'Norman! Have you lost a tortoise again?' the publican asked. 'I've got one here with a hole in its shell.'

I hurried to the pub. There was Torty, his little feet worn down from pulling himself along on his epic journey. A survivor, just like me. I brought him back to the farm to live out his days in luxury.

Along with all the other animals, of course, there are dogs. Emma the whippet lived a long life, cared for by Stella and Jack when she wasn't with me, and died peacefully in her sleep. Chino passed away just before I moved to the farm and I buried her on the moor, planting a spindle tree over her. It's now a huge tree, almost forty years old, and I go every year to visit her resting place.

Now I keep Affenpinscher terriers, tiny black dogs, fearless and feisty, with the most exquisite faces, and I also have rescue dogs. After Chino there was Poppy, a Labrador-pointer cross. She was rescued through an organisation based in Cyprus, All About Freda, saved from having her throat cut, like so many others, after the hunting season. Now I have Pugsy and Max, from the same charity. Pugsy the pug was rescued from living in a rabbit hutch, punished when he barked by being sprayed with battery fluid. Max, a three-legged black-and-tan English terrier, had been living for two years in a disused aquarium in a vet's surgery with a sign on it, saying, 'Please re-home me', but nobody wanted a dog with a front leg missing. Max had belonged to some British people who owned a villa there, and they accidentally reversed over him in their car. They took the little dog to the vet and flew back to Britain, never to return. When I heard about Max, I said, 'Well, he's not staying there another year!' I just had to have him and give him a happy life after all he had endured.

These dogs have been through far greater adversities than I have and yet are never downcast. Their spirit and ability to embrace every day is infectious. Animals have given me companionship and unconditional love all my life, reminding me, even in the lowest of times, that things can get better and that there is always hope.

The saddest part of my life has been losing my son,

313

Benjamin. After one brief reunion, we have not been in touch. It's different with Bryony. Although it was hard being parted from her for many years, we never lost our connection. Hilary and Bryony stayed in Australia for a couple of years, then returned to England, settling in Devon. Hilary got married, and Bryony went to the Rudolph Steiner School, in Totnes, which is where I think she got her lovely romantic attitude to life. Hilary and I stayed in touch for the sake of our daughter, and when I first moved into the farm, Bryony came to stay. She was still a small child, and the house was chaotic with the restoration work, but she wasn't afraid. When she went to bed, I would say, 'I'm only at the end of the corridor if you get worried and I'll leave the door open.'

Whenever we spoke on the telephone she would ask, 'Are you still at the end of the corridor, Daddy?'

More than thirty years on she still says this when she calls me, and I reply, 'Still at the end of the corridor!'

Recently I was clearing out a drawer and right at the back I found an old piece of bamboo wood with a message written on it, 'I love my Daddy and I know he loves me.' She must have hidden it there on one of her childhood visits. Bryony lives not too far away now, and we have the most wonderful get-togethers when she brings my four grandchildren to visit. Just before the last Halloween we spent a hysterical afternoon together carving pumpkins, transforming them into ghosts and ghouls, our hands stained orange and our jaws aching from laughter. I just love it when the farmhouse resonates with the youth and energy of these wonderful young people.

Ben visited, too. Just once, when he was nineteen. I hadn't seen him since he was a small child and hadn't had any contact with him. I had sent letters and presents but never got any reply. When he came, Ben had just been through unimaginable trauma. Sue, who had been battling mental-health problems for years, had committed suicide. In the aftermath of her death Ben was sorting out her things and discovered unopened cards and presents I had sent to him. And after all the years apart he got in touch with me.

I showed him how to milk my Jersey cows and, despite the dreadful experience he had just endured, he enjoyed himself and we got on very well together. Bryony came over and met him then too, looking up at him in adoration, and I hoped that maybe we could mend our broken family. Very sadly, not long after Ben's visit, I was contacted by a reporter who said he was from *The Times*, and wanted to talk to me for a feature called 'A Day in the Life'. I had already been interviewed for this some time before, though the article had not been published, so I assumed they had just decided to pick it up again. A reporter and a photographer duly arrived, and I spoke to them briefly, mentioning Ben's visit. Then I had to exercise one of my horses so I gave them some French bread, cheese and a bottle of wine and told them to have lunch while I trotted round the block.

To my horror, I came home to see a bright white light shining out of the sitting-room window. They had found all my pictures of Bryony and laid them out on the sitting-room floor to take photos of. The reporter was a fraud. He was actually from the *News of the World* and a ghastly, sensational article was the result of his visit. Ben was terribly upset. He thought I had done the article to make money, exploiting the happy moments we had shared, although in fact I was paid nothing. After this, there has been no more communication between us, which has been a great sadness in my life. I still have the plastic cereal-packet toy he gave me when he was little, and whenever I see children at horse shows, beaming with pride over their rosettes, I think of him and what our relationship could have been.

There is a lot to make me melancholy if my thoughts return to the past. But I am so lucky in my present life to be surrounded by friends, Bryony and her children. I am so proud of them all. I have also now found happiness with a wonderful partner. He is the kindest person I know and has been by my side for twenty-six years. With no interest in the dark events of my past, he simply loves me for who I am. Though he doesn't ride, he helps me care for the horses and adores all the animals. He is an artist, and also a very talented gardener. We love to spend long summer evenings tending the walled garden together, and in winter, we enjoy companionable peace by the crackling fire. I no longer have the strong Catholic faith I grew up with but I do have a certain spirituality, a sense that something, call it what you will – karma, perhaps – is overlooking our lives. What goes around will come around.

After thirty-five years' restoring and beautifying the farm I was delighted when Pevsner, in the Devon edition of his *Buildings of England* series, described the village as 'the jewel of Dartmoor' with special mention of the farm. This felt not just like an inestimable privilege, but also proof that I have managed to retrieve my identity, make a life for myself, and a home. This is immeasurably precious when I think back to being turfed out by my mother at fifteen and put into a remand centre, being committed to psychiatric clinics, sleeping on the wretched camp bed at Marsham Court, bunking in single rooms and caravans, and those desperate months of sleeping in the public loos in Barnstaple's Rock Park.

I have, after so many tribulations, a good life. For Jeremy Thorpe, it was more difficult. After the trial, his career was over. He continued to work for the local Liberals and held some minor roles in public life including chairman of the political committee of the United Nations Association. In 1983, he was appointed secretary general of Amnesty International, but some of the members protested and in the end the offer was retracted. In 1985 the progression of his Parkinson's disease forced him to lead a more secluded life, with Marion as his nurse. He published an autobiography, *In My Own Time*, in which he continued to deny any sexual relationship with me.

In 2002 a documentary made by Yorkshire Television called *When Jeremy Thorpe Met Norman Scott* was aired. I was interviewed at some length by the filmmakers, and Peter Bessell and Andrew Newton also spoke to camera. Mr Bessell is quoted describing the conversations Jeremy had with him about getting rid of my body. Jack Hayward, the wealthy Liberal benefactor, also features, explaining that he was bitterly disillusioned when he learned his 'friend' Jeremy had conned thousands of pounds out of him to finance a murder. When I watched this documentary I saw clearly that it wasn't just me who had suffered travail and misery because of Jeremy Thorpe. He ruined so many lives. His charm and energy drew people under his spell, and it was then all too easy for him to manipulate them into colluding with his amoral activities. Peter Bessell and Jeremy lost their friend-ship, and David Holmes's reputation and career were ruined after the trial. Holmes, who had once lived in a luxurious apartment near the Ritz Hotel in London's Piccadilly, ended up managing a roller-disco in Camden Town and died in his fifties. He and Jeremy never spoke again. It's ironic that in 1962, when Harold Macmillan sacked seven members of his Cabinet, Jeremy misquoted the Bible to make this comment: 'Greater love hath no man than this, that he lay down his friends for his life.' That is exactly what Jeremy did.

The showing of the documentary was greeted with outrage in some quarters as by then Jeremy was too unwell with Parkinson's disease to respond. Steve Anderson, the controller of news and current affairs for ITV, robustly defended the programme, saying that though Mr Thorpe chose not to go into the witness box to give his side of the story, which was his right, this should not act as a gag on television's right to investigate a story of significant public interest.

Once the furore had died down, I thought that would be the last time the whole sorry affair came into the public eye. However, after Jeremy's death in 2014, Tom Mangold, the BBC documentary filmmaker, was out walking his dog in Chiswick Park when a man called Dennis Meighan approached him, saying he had been hired to shoot me. Meighan, a dealer in firearms, told Mangold that in the early 1970s he had met up with his friend Andrew Gino Newton and someone he believed to be David Holmes at the Ritz Café in Shepherd's Bush. Holmes had offered him £13,500 to shoot me and he had agreed. Meighan had never shot anyone before, but he had a gun, and travelled down to Devon to check things out. When he entered a pub and heard all the locals commenting on his London accent, he realised he had taken on more than he bargained for and handed over the job, and a gun, to Newton. In 1975, after Newton was arrested, Meighan went to the police and told them he had also been hired to kill me. The police gave him a prepared statement to sign, which was a total cover-up. All the references to Jeremy Thorpe had been removed, and Meighan was completely cleared. He was, therefore, not asked to give evidence at the Old Bailey trial.

Mangold set up an interview with Meighan, which was aired on Radio 4, and on 6 December 2014 the *Daily Mail* published an article with the headline 'I Was Offered £13k To Kill Jeremy Thorpe's Stable Boy Love'. Once again, most irritatingly, I was demoted to the role of humble stable boy. Nick Constable, who runs a press agency in Devon, arranged for the *Daily Mail* to come down and help me to find Newton and finally bring him to justice for attempted murder, not just for the lesser charge of possessing a firearm with intent to endanger life. More journalists became interested and the *Mirror* brought Meighan to the farm to talk to me. It was disturbing to have this rough-edged chap from west London sitting on my sofa, telling me how he had been going to murder me, but I focused on the possibility of justice being done.

In 2016, as a result of Meighan's revelations, Gwent Police instigated Operation Velum to investigate whether there were cover-ups made by the Metropolitan Police, Devon and Cornwall Police, and Somerset and Avon Police. They began conducting enquiries into Meighan and Newton, then came to interview me. On the day that the officers assigned to the case were due to arrive, I heard the dogs barking and went out to see who was there. I quite often get Jehovah's Witnesses calling at the farm. Usually, I don't know why, it's two men in suits and a woman. I always say, 'There's no point in you talking to me. I'm madly keen on men. You are anti that.' They thrust a copy of the *Watchtower* into my hands and depart post-haste.

That morning, it was about eleven o'clock and the dogs were barking their heads off. Through the gate came two men wearing suits, along with a woman, so I said, 'Look, I'm sorry, I'm going to give you my usual spiel. I'm Norman Scott. I am a homosexual. You've probably heard about me . . .'

'Mr Scott, we are from Gwent Police,' they said, rather confused.

It was an inauspicious start but I had high hopes of Gwent Police. They came back three or four times, and we had long talks. Then they took me to Exeter and filmed me for two days as I recounted my life story. Unfortunately, the upshot of this was that in 2017 they came back to say there was nothing they could do as Newton was presumed to have died a few years before. I simply couldn't believe this. Had they thought to check the death records at Somerset House? No, they hadn't, and when they did check, they couldn't find him. It transpired that Newton was alive and well, and now calling himself Hann Redwin, which is possibly an anagram for the alternative name 'Winner Hand'. A Google search could have revealed that the two men were the same: Mr Redwin had been in the news in 1994 when his female companion had a fatal fall while they were climbing in Switzerland, his real identity uncovered at the inquest of her death.

In 2004 'Mr Redwin' had joined a fetish group and was photographed at the Skin Two Rubber Ball in London wearing a silk top hat, a red hunting coat and a chunky leather thong. Because of his outfit, not because of who he was, this image was published in a few newspapers that covered the event. Even though he was wearing sunglasses, the gentleman in the photos was obviously Newton. Realising he was alive, Gwent Police interviewed him but took no action as they said he had not provided any further information. The investigation was closed, leaving me absolutely livid.

Journalists continued to fight for justice. When John Preston's book *A Very English Scandal* became the basis for the television drama of the same name, airing in 2018, my story came under the spotlight once more. Tom Mangold, who had wisely kept his copy of the *Panorama* film *The Jeremy Thorpe Scandal*, despite having been told in 1979 by the BBC to destroy it, updated the programme and it was finally aired. Tom and his colleagues at *Panorama* wanted to carry on the story, and highlight what seemed to be, if not another cover-up, at least the extreme incompetence of Gwent Police. In 2018 they approached the Labour peer, Peter Hain, who in turn spoke to Sajid Javid, who was home secretary at the time. He was to ask questions in the House, and to find out from Gwent Police why they had made such an inadequate investigation, but somehow it all just petered out. Javid moved roles to become chancellor of the exchequer in 2019 and Peter Hain thought nothing more could be done.

So many years after the Old Bailey trial, I am still some-times mocked and dismissed in the media. A highly respected political commentator remarked in one of his books, 'I am sorry Jeremy Thorpe did not try to have Scott murdered. I would have.' And after *A Very English Scandal* and the *Panorama* documentary were aired, I heard a talk show on the radio where the panel had great fun mocking my 'extraor-dinary voice' and expressing astonishment at the fact that I keep pugs. Fortunately, I have always had the ability to laugh at the absurdity of my life, which must surely have helped me to survive. It is all too easy to see things in black and white, and perhaps the wiser choice is just to 'be glad to be grey'.

I could wish that I had never met Jeremy. I would have been spared so much emotional trauma. I know what it's like to be living in hell and to want to end it all, as I have tried to do so many times. I believe that what ultimately saved me from being destroyed was my determination to stand up and tell the truth. When Ben Whishaw described me as an icon at the Golden Globe awards because of my courage and defiance, although immensely touched, I felt reluctant to take on that title. But those who are in power will always be tempted to think themselves above suspicion, and believe they will never be called to account for their wrongdoings. If my story gives courage and strength to people who may fall victim to this, I am deeply happy.

Jeremy Thorpe and I both had our dreams and ambitions – albeit in very different spheres. We both had the talent and drive to achieve these. If he had made different choices, I might have found employment with a reputable dressage trainer and ridden for Britain in the Olympics, and he might have become prime minister. 'For want of a horseshoe nail', as the old saying goes. And I never did get my National Insurance cards back.

One thing I am sure of is that my life at the farm will continue as it is for as long as I am able, and a big part of that will be Loui, whose proud bay head looks out for me over the stable door. Although I am in my eighties, we will compete at shows and, whatever life may throw at me in the coming years, Loui will bring me much joy. A horse at the heart of my life, as always, alongside the friends and family to whom I can never express enough gratitude and love.

ACKNOWLEDGEMENTS

F<small>IRSTLY</small>, I <small>WANT</small> to thank Tom Perrin, who has made the publication of this book so smooth and easy through challenging times. I must also thank Peter Westcott for insisting that I get to work on my autobiography again after so many years.

I am very grateful to Hugo Vickers for his earnest kindness and his strong belief that this book must be written. Thea Bennett brought lightness and fun to my writing process and helped me make sense of my sometimes erratic thoughts, and Hannah Bourne-Taylor's inspired editing skills were outstanding. Everyone at Hodder has been most helpful and efficient – special thanks to Rowena Webb, Steven Cooper and Zakirah Alam.

Huge thanks must go to Ben Whishaw. His portrayal of me in *A Very English Scandal* and his moving dedication to me at the Golden Globe awards in Hollywood mean more than I can ever express.

Without the support of my friends, I would never have found the courage to tell my story. Anne Robinson's stalwart and sincere friendship has sustained me through thick and thin, as has the support of Nick Constable, the most trustworthy journalist I have known. I must also thank Tom Mangold of *Panorama* for his tenacity and his determination to see the truth about the Jeremy Thorpe scandal in the public domain, and Steve Anderson of ITV for robustly defending the airing of the documentary *When Jeremy Thorpe Met Norman Scott.*

So many have supported me in this endeavour, both in person and on social media: Pammy Hutton of Talland Equestrian Centre, dressage rider Douglas Hibbert, and sculptor Hywel Pratley each in their own way have been exceptionally kind. Closer to home, I must thank my friends Jim and Sue Matthews for all they do, and also my other neighbours who have been so good to me over the years. You know who you are!

I am so grateful to my daughter Bryony for her incredible support, and for happy times spent with her and her family during the writing of this book.

Last but not least, my heartfelt thanks to Michael, who has been quietly there for me through the last 26 years. Without him none of this would have been possible.

PICTURE ACKNOWLEDGEMENTS

Page 6, middle right: © Alfred Markey/Mirrorpix/Getty Images

Page 6, bottom left: © John Walters/ANL/Shutterstock

Page 6, bottom right: © Wesley/Keystone/Getty Images

Page 7, top left: © Aubrey Hart/Evening Standard/Hulton Archive/Getty Images

Page 7, top right: © Central Press/Hulton Archive/Getty Images

Page 7, middle left: © Bill Rowntree/Mirrorpix/Getty Images

Page 7, middle right: © Photoshot/TopFoto

Page 7, bottom: © Daily Mirror/Mirrorpix

Page 8, top: © Author's collection

Page 8, middle: © Author's collection

Page 8, bottom: © Nia Catherine Turley, Nia Catherine Photography